Inventing For Dummies

Cheat Sheet

Pam's Golden Rules

- One inventor can change the world.
- He who has the technology wins.
- Getting a patent doesn't guarantee that you're going to make money — only about 7 percent of patented products ever do. A patent is only one piece of the total product pie.
- The successful inventors that I have worked with don't invent for the money, they invent because that is what they do.

Characteristics of Successful Inventors

To be a successful inventor, you must be:

- Able to tolerate failure
- Achievement-oriented
- Competitive
- Creative
- Demanding
- Goal-oriented
- Highly energetic
- Independent
- Innovative
- Inquisitive
- Open to feedback
- Persistent
- A risk-taker
- Self-confident
- Self-motivated

Sources for Innovative Ideas

- Demographic changes in society
- Imagination
- Luck
- Problem-solving
- Unsatisfied customers
- Vision

Going to Market

You have three choices on how to bring your product to market:

- You do everything — manufacture, market, and sell.
- You subcontract the manufacturing and concentrate on marketing and selling your invention.
- You license your intellectual property rights to a company that arranges the manufacturing, marketing, and selling aspects and pays you a royalty (a percentage on each unit sold).

A Product Lifecycle

Most inventions are in and out of the market within seven years. Years one through two and a half are the introductory years. You take your product through the idea and prototype stage while you check out the commercial market, apply for legal protection, and try to obtain funds. At year two and a half, the product enters into the market and sales start. They peak at about year five. During year six, you must cope with new competition and competitors and by year seven, the sales are on the downside. Remember, your patent life is for 14 or 20 years, depending on the type of patent. However, the market life is quite different. See Chapter 1.

Protecting Your Intellectual Property

Protect your idea with a patent, copyright, trademark, or trade secret. If your invention is really good, you are more than likely going to have to defend your rights. Get good legal counsel, as a product is only as good as it can be defended in a court of law. Use these tips:

- Document everything. Keep a journal and have it witnessed along the way.
- Conduct a patent search.
- Get sound legal advice from a professional.
- Use confidentiality, non-disclosure, and employment agreements with anyone and everyone with knowledge of your idea.

For Dummies: Bestselling Book Series for Beginners

Inventing For Dummies®

Planning Your Marketing Strategy

To paraphrase Thomas Edison, "I'm not going to invent anything unless it will sell." You can create the greatest invention in the world, but unless the world knows about it, what difference does it make? The way to make a difference is through creative marketing and advertising efforts.

Some marketing tips:

- ✔ Find out as much about the industry your product sells in as you can. Educate yourself about wholesalers and distributors, manufacturers, and competition.

- ✔ Use every resource you have for assistance, including the Internet, the Small Business Administration, the U.S. Patent and Trademark Office, local college and university business schools, and inventor organizations.

- ✔ Let the customer drive your product. Find out what customers like and—even more important—*don't* like about your invention and try to accommodate their preferences.

- ✔ Likewise, realize that the customer determines the price of your product. You charge what the customer will pay and work out your profit margins from that.

- ✔ Most importantly, once you have customers, pay attention to them.

Money Matters

Make certain you have adequate financial resources. You don't want to start developing your product and then be forced to quit halfway through. Funding sources can include:

- ✔ Anyone and everyone who tells you that your product is wonderful. Ask them to put their money where their mouth is. Don't deny them a wonderful investment opportunity.

- ✔ The Small Business Administration has a lot to offer.

- ✔ Investor and entrepreneurial networking meetings are really helpful. Follow up on any referrals; 85 percent of funding comes from referrals.

If you have to bring investors into your business, make sure to look for more than just money. You want an investor with business savvy, experience, and funding friends.

Licensing Tips

Only about 6 percent of all patents are licensed for a royalty, but it can be a profitable way to go if you can do it. Use these tips:

- ✔ Make contacts at trade shows and elsewhere who can help you get a foot in the door of the right companies and help you avoid the wrong ones.

- ✔ Take time to develop negotiating skills.

- ✔ Focus and concentrate on obtaining a win-win licensing agreement.

- ✔ Know when to sign on the dotted line and when to walk away.

- ✔ Leave room for further negotiations at the negotiating table by planning, listening, studying, and strategizing.

For Dummies: Bestselling Book Series for Beginners

Inventing
FOR
DUMMIES®

by Pamela Riddle Bird, PhD

Foreword by Dr. Forrest M. Bird

WILEY

Wiley Publishing, Inc.

Inventing For Dummies®

Published by
Wiley Publishing, Inc.
111 River St.
Hoboken, NJ 07030-5774
www.wiley.com

WILEY

About the Author

Pamela Riddle Bird, PhD, is a nationally recognized commercialization expert who's counseled thousands of inventors and entrepreneurs over two decades.

After directing one of the largest publicly funded innovation centers in the United States, Dr. Bird founded and serves as CEO of Innovative Product Technologies, Inc., a product- and technology-based market commercialization corporation. Dr. Bird works with independent inventors, serving as a liaison between inventors and inventor organizations, venture capital organizations and other investors, manufacturers, entrepreneurial networks, and research park facilities.

Dr. Bird is the author of more than 70 publications and has been quoted and featured in numerous newspapers throughout the country including *The New York Times, Barron's – The Dow Jones Business and Financial Weekly, Forbes Magazine,* and the *Miami Herald.* She's a featured speaker in a video titled *Inventing, Patenting and Profiting: How to Make a Fortune on a Small Budget by Inventing.* She has been a guest on various TV shows, including *Golden Lifestyles,* and she appeared in and served as a consultant to ABC's *20/20.* She's also taught classes on product commercialization and technology transfer at various universities throughout the nation.

Dr. Bird co-branded the first credit card in the nation with MBNA (one of the largest credit card companies in the world) to start the first credit card for innovators, patent attorneys, and patent agents. All proceeds Dr. Bird receives from this card are donated to the Inventors Educational Foundation. Dr. Bird founded this nonprofit foundation that assists innovators and entrepreneurs of all ages and walks of life with educational and commercialization needs.

Among her many memberships and organizational affiliations, Dr. Bird served under three governors as commissioner for the Governor's Commission on Women and an advisor for the Adult Community Education Board and also the Regional Coordination Council. She's been the recipient of various recognition awards, including the Outstanding Community Service award, and has received letters of appreciation for community involvement in labor employment issues, child abuse prevention, crime prevention, and education needs.

Dr. Bird is also a pilot who also enjoys horseback riding, snow skiing, hiking, fly fishing, and working with youth science fairs.

Dedication

This book is dedicated to the inventors who risk everything to be different, to be creative, and to change the world. You make a difference. It's also dedicated to the supporters and service providers to inventors — the people behind the scenes — including the families who sacrifice to allow the creators to move forward. It's also dedicated to those inventors in the National Inventors Hall of Fame who show all others the difference one person can make in improving mankind for all generations.

To my husband, Dr. Forrest M. Bird, inventor of the medical respirator, who's spent the major part of his life inventing so that others may live — including my own daughter. You stand in front of me to clear the way, beside me as my best friend and partner, and in back of me to protect me ahead. You are my great love and soul mate.

To my beloved mother, Julia Nicklyn Hudek. Mom made a large investment when she bore me — the last of eight children. She believed in me, encouraged me, and was always there whenever I needed her. And, to my children, Julie "Rachel" Riddle and Robert "Brandon" Riddle. Rachel and Brandon, you never cease to keep me laughing, amazed, and always proud. You are my pride and joy. You are my shining stars as I am your M.O.M. (Mother on a Mission).

To my father, Albin C. Hudek, Sr., as well as to my brothers and sisters, Albin C. Hudek, Robert J. Hudek, Ronald B. Hudek, Frank J. Hudek, Elaine L. Pingle, Kathleen A. Gerard, and the late Michael A. Hudek.

Acknowledgments

When a work of this magnitude is released, you can be assured that a number of individuals were heavily involved; therefore, I am indebted and thankful to many. First, I want to thank the innovators who make this book possible and who have changed the world.

I want to thank my husband for his willingness to write the foreword for me. Forrest is not only my husband; he is my best friend and soul mate. He's a man who's dedicated his life to saving other people's lives and is a man of honor who served in three wars and still continues his mission of inventing for mankind.

Undoubtedly, I will leave out some people who were important to the project, and for that I apologize. My official thanks must start with my official Dummifier *par excellence*, Ms. Kathleen Dobie. Kathleen is an incredible person and a delight to work with. She has insight and is an exceptional editor. I also want to thank my Project Editor, Ms. Chrissy Guthrie, for her drive, energy, and talents in making this book happen, and Copy Editor Jennifer Bingham for checking and verifying everything to make sure it's right. Ms. Kathy Cox, Acquisitions Editor, believed in me, my talents, drive, and work and was the champion for this project and instrumental in getting it off the ground.

I would like to especially thank Gerald G. Udell, PhD, a pioneer and supporter in the invention industry whom I have continually called upon for his knowledge and guidance. I would also like to thank Mr. Donald G. Kelly, my long time friend and business associate, for being an inventor's advocate and for the years of continuous support to the independent inventor community. In addition, I received much of the legal advice, not only for this book but over two decades of working with inventors, from the following intellectual property attorneys: Mr. James Beusse and Ms. Christine McLeod of Beusse, Brownlee, Wolter, Mora & Maire, PA in Orlando, FL; Mr. Robert Downey of Robert M. Downey, P.A. in Boca Raton, FL; Mr. William Hobby, III in Winter Park, FL; Mr. Robert Kain, Jr of Fleit, Kain, Gibbons, Gotman, Bongini & Bianco in Ft. Lauderdale, FL; Mr. John Kirk, Jr of Jenkens and Gilchrist PC in Houston, TX; Mr. Peter Loffler in Tallahassee, FL; Ms. Jennie Malloy and Mr. John Malloy of Malloy and Malloy, PA in Miami, FL; Mr. John Oltman of Oltman, Flynn and Kubler in Fort Lauderdale, FL; Mr. Thomas Saitta of Rogers Towers Bailey Jones and Gay, PA in Jacksonville, FL; Mr. David Saliwanchik and Mr. Jeffrey Lloyd of Saliwanchik, Lloyd and Saliwanchik in Gainesville, FL; Mr. Jesus Sanchelima in Miami, FL; and Mr. Brian Steinberger of Law Offices Of Brian S. Steinberger, PA in Cocoa, FL. I would also like to especially thank Mr. Craig Dahlin, CEO of MarketreaderPro.com for the many long hours he worked on establishing the computer linkages, follow-up, and phone calls from his associate and wife, "Moon Eagle," in order to calculate the statistics obtained from inventors used in this book. And then there are the indispensable ones behind the scenes: Mr. Eugene Andrews Grinstead IV, Ms. Kristine Homant, Lowell Salter, Mr. Ted Schaewecker, Ms. Joanne Hayes-Rines, Mr. Edward Miller, and Mr. Robert Loughler.

Finally, I am ever so grateful to the board members for my company: Dr. J. Robert Cade, MD, inventor of Gatorade; Mr. Lloyd Bell, physicist; Dr. Forrest M. Bird, inventor of the medical respirator; Mr. Philip D. Bart, holder of over 100 patents and marketer of the Cabbage Patch doll; Mr. Edward Shadd, development team member of the UPC Bar Code; Mr. John Weber, Founder and Former CEO, Monchik-Weber, Corporation; Mr. Harris Rosen, hotelier; Mr. Patrick Perry, attorney; the late Mr. Edward Lowe, inventor of Kitty Litter, and the late Dr. Jay Morton, scriptwriter for Superman. These innovators and entrepreneurs believed in me when I started my own business dedicated toward working with those who want to change the world. They've directed me through the thick and thin. They, too, believe in the undying spirit of the independent inventor.

Publisher's Acknowledgments

We're proud of this book; please send us your comments through our Dummies online registration form located at www.dummies.com/register/.

Some of the people who helped bring this book to market include the following:

Acquisitions, Editorial, and Media Development

Project Editor: Christina Guthrie

Acquisitions Editor: Kathy Cox

Copy Editor: Jennifer Bingham

Assistant Editor: Holly Gastineau-Grimes

Technical Editors: Gerald G. Udell, PhD and John J. Kirk, Jr.

Senior Permissions Editor: Carmen Krikorian

Editorial Manager: Christine Meloy Beck

Editorial Assistants: Melissa Bennett and Elizabeth Rea

Cover Photo: © Steve Bronstein/Getty Images/The Image Bank

Cartoons: Rich Tennant, www.the5thwave.com

Production

Project Coordinator: Maridee Ennis

Layout and Graphics: Andrea Dahl, Kelly Emkow, Denny Hager, Stephanie D. Jumper, Michael Kruzil

Proofreaders: TECHBOOKS Production Services

Indexer: TECHBOOKS Production Services

Publishing and Editorial for Consumer Dummies

Diane Graves Steele, Vice President and Publisher, Consumer Dummies

Joyce Pepple, Acquisitions Director, Consumer Dummies

Kristin A. Cocks, Product Development Director, Consumer Dummies

Michael Spring, Vice President and Publisher, Travel

Brice Gosnell, Associate Publisher, Travel

Kelly Regan, Editorial Director, Travel

Publishing for Technology Dummies

Andy Cummings, Vice President and Publisher, Dummies Technology/General User

Composition Services

Gerry Fahey, Vice President of Production Services

Debbie Stailey, Director of Composition Services

Contents at a Glance

Table of Contents

Part IV: Commercializing Your Invention *145*

Chapter 13: Developing a Business Plan 147

Chapter 14: Finding Funding 173

Foreword

· ·

*I*t was November 1995 when I first met Pamela Riddle. I'd been invited by the USPTO to lecture to inventors and would-be inventors at a special Educational Forum held at Walt Disney World in Orlando, Florida. This was my first lecture for the USPTO following my induction into the U.S. Inventors Hall of Fame.

I guess the reason why the Patent Office selected me as their keynote to that group of inventors was due to the fact that I was a loner in terms of invention. In other words, I conceived, developed, manufactured, educated, and marketed my Bird Respirator without financial obligation to others. Therefore, I understood most of the trials and tribulations facing my audience, because I'd traveled over the route before. The title of my lecture essentially was, "If I Can Do It, You Can, Too." After a ten-year period of patient introduction starting in 1958, the Bird Respirators were saving lives in both military and civil hospitals the world over.

Following my lecture was an all-business lady speaking on International Commercialization of New Technology. I figured the title alone would put her audience to sleep. Much to my surprise, within five minutes you could've heard a pin drop in the large auditorium. Ms. Riddle had her audience totally captivated; her lecture was informative and interesting, and I learned a number of interesting points. I met Ms. Riddle briefly after the meeting.

My next meeting with Ms. Riddle was at a similar inventors conference in Miami, which I was invited to speak at. This meeting was a combined venture between Ms. Riddle's company, various nonprofit invention groups, and the US Patent Office. I soon learned that Ms. Riddle was the organizer and director of the meeting. During the meeting, I was fortunate to be able to visit with Ms. Riddle during several luncheons and the formal banquet. I became fascinated with her ability to project her knowledge relative to inventing and the patenting process, and her marketing skills relative to inventions. She was a walking dictionary and resource in terms of innovation. If only I had been able to talk with such a knowledgeable individual following the development of my Medical Bird Respirator, it would have saved me considerable anguish.

During the next few years, our paths continued to cross more and more frequently. I increasingly became enamored with Ms. Riddle as a straight shooter — her frankness was overwhelming. You knew exactly where you stood with her at all times. As we learned each other's habits, it became evident that our personal interests were parallel. Our continued associations lead to our marriage on May 22, 1999.

As my wife, Pam continues to keep me amazed, and her projects continue to be challenging. Following her own innovative methodology, she copes with changing times. Her frankness with her clients is amazing. I've heard her on numerous occasions tell clients that she considers their newborn invention ugly and advises them not to bet the farm on its success. I've also talked with clients whom Pam had previously advised that their invention was not the best, only to have them go to a "commercial source" that advised them relative to what they wanted to hear: "Your invention is terrific!" They did indeed lose the family jewels before they realized that what Pam had originally told them was the truth.

It is wonderful being married to a challenging lady, whom you enjoy dating every day, with whom you can intelligently discuss the ever changing societies of the world and the ramifications thereof.

— Forrest M. Bird, M.D., PhD., ScD.

Introduction

● ●

Most people think of an inventor as a wild-eyed, gray-haired eccentric. Though this image may ring true in one or two cases, innovators come in all sizes and all ages — just look in the mirror.

When I initially started working with inventors, I thought that lack of funding was their primary difficulty. Now, after two decades of experience, I venture to say that the primary impediment inventors face is that they're sooooo blessed with creativity, they just can't get focused. Professional inventors don't come up with just one invention; they continually have new ideas and don't know which one to concentrate on. This book can't really help with your concentration problem, but it can help you focus on making the most of each idea you have.

About This Book

This book is designed to answer your questions about how to take an idea and turn in into a product. Put another way, this book can help you turn your dreams into reality. To do that, I put my 20-plus years of experience in helping inventors bring their ideas to fruition to work for you.

I tell you how to decide whether your idea is marketable and for how much. I fill you in on the steps you must take to bring your product to market. I point out potential funding sources and tell you how to get in touch with a vast array of folks who can help advance your project. I alert you to possible snags and help you avoid common pitfalls.

I offer this help in an easy-to-read, easy-to-access format. Each chapter in this book stands alone. Each chapter serves as one individual piece of the whole inventing-and-marketing pie. You can dip into any chapter or section that interests you, then skip on to the next topic, whatever and wherever it is. You may be interested in reading some chapters more than others; however, in the long run, you need the information in all of them.

Throughout the book, I explain concepts that may be new to you and give you information and advice in clear, straightforward language.

Conventions Used in This Book

When writing this book, I used a few conventions that you should be aware of:

- I use *italics* to highlight terms and concepts that I explain in case they're new to you. I also use italics for emphasis.

- The stories in gray boxes are known as *sidebars*. Sidebars contain information you may find interesting or useful, but which you don't need to understand the topic at hand. You can choose to read them or not.

- Web sites and e-mail addresses appear in `monofont` to help them stand out in the text.

Foolish Assumptions

I assume that you're reading this book because you have an idea and want to know what to do next. You want to find out whether your idea is marketable and how to get it to market and make a profit from it.

It doesn't matter whether you have a prototype or a patent yet. Maybe you have both and want to know what to do next. You want to move forward and do something with your idea. You not only want to see people buy it but you want to make money as well.

Rest assured that you've come to the right place.

How This Book Is Organized

Inventing For Dummies is organized into six parts. The chapters within each part cover specific topic areas in detail.

Part 1: Making Your Idea Yours

In this part, I show you how to how to protect your idea step by step. I give you the security of knowing what to discuss, with whom, and how to keep those conversations confidential.

These chapters also tell you everything you need to know about patents — how to do a patent search to find out if your idea is already out there, what a patent protects and doesn't protect, how to apply for a patent, and how to take care of your patent after you have it.

Part II: Securing Other Intellectual Property

Many innovations aren't patentable products. The chapters in this part tell you how to protect words, pictures, processes, and trade secrets with copyrights and registered trademarks.

Part III: Developing Your Idea

The next time you pick up a product that's new to you, take a step back and think about how that product got to the store. The inventor had to first visualize the idea, build a working model to see if the idea would work, test whether people would buy the product, figure out if it could be made for the price customers would pay, get it produced, and have it delivered to the retailer and end user.

The chapters in this part of the book take you through all the steps of this development process.

Part IV: Commercializing Your Invention

Very few people understand what it takes to bring a new product to market. After reading the chapters in this part, though, you can be one of those people.

The invention process is quite different from the commercialization phase. Most inventors have to license their intellectual property rights for a royalty or become entrepreneurs.

Becoming an entrepreneur requires a whole new knowledge base, skill set, and often a change in lifestyle. I help you understand the risks and rewards of starting a business to produce or sell your idea.

I also take you through the licensing process from contact to contract.

Part V: The Part of Tens

These short and sweet chapters list inventions that had an impact and inventors who continue to do so. I also list organizations that are of great help to inventors.

Part VI: Appendixes

Here, I provide forms and resources that you can use to protect your idea and find the help you need to make it a success.

Icons Used in This Book

The little pictures you sometimes see in the margins of the pages are called *icons*. They're there to draw your attention to the text they're next to. This book uses four different icons:

This icon directs your attention to information that can make your efforts easier or more effective. Pay attention.

Make note of the information next to this icon; the stuff is important and you'll need it.

This means watch out! Pay attention so that you don't make a mistake that can hurt you or your wallet. It marks things to avoid and common mistakes inventors make.

This icon highlights technical information. You can skip this information if you like, but just because it's technical doesn't mean you can't benefit from it.

Where to Go from Here

Look through the book and find which part, chapter, or section you're most interested in. That's the place to begin.

This book is written in such a way that you can turn to any section, in any chapter, in any order you like, and never feel that you've missed a lick. If you're the studious type, you may prefer to read about intellectual property issues in Part I or II. If you want to know all the development details, turn to Part III. If you're interested in the sales and marketing aspects, go to Part IV. Or, start at the end and read about and be inspired by ten individuals who changed the world.

It's written for you, it's your book, and by reading it, you're one step closer to making your dream into a reality and turning your idea into a marketable product or technology.

Now, you have the know-how in your hands. Take advantage of it and good luck!

Part I
Making Your
Idea Yours

The 5th Wave   By Rich Tennant

Dave used his time well while waiting for the USPTO
to approve his patent application.

In this part . . .

*I*f you're an inventor, and I just know you are, you need to know about patents. A patent lets other people know that you came up with a unique idea and that you — not to mention the Unites States Patent and Trademark Office — think it's special enough to protect with a patent. A patent gives you the legal right to protect your idea.

The chapters in this part tell you what a patent is, how to get one, and how to maintain and defend it.

Chapter 1

The Innovation Process

Maybe you can come up with an idea in the morning, make one phone call, receive a check by noon, and reach financial success, all in time to watch the sunset through your lovely rose-colored glasses. It's possible. (It's possible to win the lottery, too. It's possible to earn both an Olympic gold medal and an academy award.)

Being possible doesn't make it likely, however; just as getting a patent doesn't make your invention commercially viable. Try to accept right now that making money from your idea may well be a long, grueling, expensive, and perhaps unachievable task. Prepare to recognize little successes along the way as victories. Many people never see their idea converted into a real working model. Of these, few ever receive patents. Fewer yet ever see a return on their financial investment, much less their time. Only a *very* small percentage — about 7 percent — of patent holders ever make enough money to recoup even the cost of getting their patents. So, as you reach the milestones that you have set for yourself, be happy and proud of these victories.

In this chapter, I give you some practical advice on deciding what you want to do with your invention, how to protect it, and give you a few basic pointers on going to market. I also go over the product life cycle to give you a better idea of the process you need to go through.

Deciding Where to Go with Your Idea

You have an idea, now what? Where do you go? What steps do you take to bring your new idea to fruition?

Decide as early as possible what your true objective is. In other words, what do you want from your invention? Do you want to be famous? Is just getting a patent what you really care about? Are you all about the money? Are you all about the altruism and making the world a better place?

If you're an inventor with a commercialization bent, you're in good company. When Thomas Edison couldn't find a buyer for his first patented invention — an electric vote counter — he formulated a lifelong policy: Anything that won't sell, I don't want to invent!

Your goal plays a large part in how you proceed with your idea. If your true desire is to have your name on a patent and commercialization isn't important to you, your task is substantially different than if you're expecting to achieve financial independence through your invention.

Carefully consider where you are today and where you want to end up. It may be helpful to take a sheet of paper and list the steps involved in achieving your final objective. I suggest writing where you are today at the top, skipping several lines, and entering your final goal. Now enter the milestones that you consider to be of critical importance along the way. Some of the tasks you may list are

- Conducting a patent search (see Chapter 3)
- Submitting your idea for evaluation (see Chapter 11)
- Building a prototype (see Chapter 9)
- Researching the market (see Chapter 17)
- Filing a provisional patent application (see Chapter 4)
- Forming a company (see Chapter 15)
- Meeting with a potential licensee (see Chapter 20)
- Writing a business plan (see Chapter 13)

You don't have to fill in all the blanks if you aren't sure of all the steps; having a rough idea of some the steps is enough to get started (you may come up with additional ideas as you go through this book). But preparing even a preliminary list may make you realize that there is a lot more to the process than you had originally anticipated and that you may need some help along the way.

You should continually update the list and prioritize it as you go. If you have a target date for success, then you should include that as well, and then date the milestones that must be met accordingly.

One of your objectives, regardless of your overall goals, should be to make your idea yours. In order to do this, you have to patent your idea. If you're interested only in getting a patent, stick to the chapters in this part. The rest of this book, however, focuses on sharing my experience and expertise in bringing inventions to market. If you want to make money from your idea, and I hope that you do, every chapter and every section should be of interest to you.

Protecting Your Idea

Your idea — or at least your rights to your idea — can slip out of your grasp if you don't protect it well. Just bragging too specifically to the wrong person can be dangerous — people claim credit for ideas that aren't theirs all the time. So, though you may be proud of your idea (and you have every right and reason to be), be careful about how you talk about it and to whom. If you think about it, it isn't logical to share your brainstorm with the world without safeguarding it.

If you plan to market your invention, you probably will pursue getting some legal intellectual property protection — a patent, copyright, or other protection mentioned in later chapters in this part and in Part II. Taking some precautions from the very start can help bolster those claims and establish your ownership rights should the need arise.

Keeping good records

Keeping an inventor's diary, engineering notebook, or logbook is almost essential, not just to protect your rights, but to document your invention's history and progress.

Detailed documentation can be a valuable resource in many stages of your invention's life cycle. Potential investors interested in funding your project can use your logbook to make decisions about your product's potential and about your capabilities. Investors are often more interested in the person than in the product. A logbook that shows attention to detail and an organized, well-thought-out plan of action can mean money in the bank for you. If, for some reason, or no reason, the tax man audits you, your logbook can show and justify deductions you may have taken.

What if someone overhears an explanation of your invention and files a patent application before you do? Or an employee claims that she is the actual inventor or maybe a co-inventor? Or your lab may suffer a break-in, and whether the thief was hired by a competitor or is just an opportunist, you may lose your prototype and equipment. In cases like these, a well-kept invention log can help you prove your claim and pick up the pieces.

The notebook itself should be a bound book — one you can't take pages out of. Use permanent ink to make dated entries that detail the activity on a day-to-day basis. Get two witnesses to sign and date each entry. Keep your journal current and factual.

Record everything into the logbook, including

- The title of your invention
- The purpose of the invention — what you use it for
- A detailed description, including any unique features
- A sketch, drawing, or picture
- Various uses and applications for your product — these may even vary by industry
- The differences between your invention and similar products, if you know of any
- Advantages of your product compared to other products or close substitutes
- Names of the people with whom you speak with about your product, including consultants, prototype builders, packaging designers, and so on; names of people you know are aware of your product including employees, friends and family, and current or former colleagues
- Contact information of companies you talk to about licensing, production, pricing, and packaging

Document not only what you and any colleagues do to further your invention, but add in records of any correspondence, receipts and bills related to the project, and *letters of revelations,* which are any type of documentation or paperwork written to other companies about your product. For example, you may have correspondence about manufacturing cost estimates, potential licensing agreements, hiring an engineer or prototype builder, and so on. (The record of expenses comes in handy at tax time, also.) This type of information should be kept in a separate folder from your logbook. Figure 1-1 shows a sample logbook entry.

If your invention is very good, you almost certainly face having it copied. Or you may face a situation in which another inventor, working completely separately, comes up with a very similar item. Sooner or later you may end up in court defending your intellectual property rights. In the U.S., a patent is issued to the first inventor of a product, not the first person to apply for a patent on it. In many instances, those two are different people. Even after a patent is issued, it can be disputed by someone claiming to have invented it earlier, or by someone who just hopes to cash in. Often, your best defense is great documentation.

Inventor's Logbook

Title: Solar Dog House

Reference: Date of conception was on February 2004. Currently working with engineers regarding density of panels needed.

Description: A dog house that stays warm using solar panels. Currently working with professional prototyper, Jackson Murphy, regarding building of solar model for dogs under 30 lbs.

Picture or Drawing of Product showing solar panels on roof, windows, and energy-efficient siding.

Current Status: We tried a new double insulated window; however, this window made the dog house too hot. We are looking at alternative energy efficient materials for prototyping of dog house.

Testing: We tested the results of the heating panels. It is necessary to make further adjustments due to variation of sunrays during the winter months.

Results: Must keep working on product as it needs improvements with improved hardware usage. Will continue with CADCAM drawings.

Inventor/s: Date:

_____   _____

I have witnessed and understood the above-mentioned invention.

Witness Signature   Date

_____   _____

Witness Signature   Date

_____   _____

Figure 1-1:
A sample
logbook
entry.

Participating in the Disclosure Document Program

One of the services provided by the United States Patent and Trademark Office (USPTO) is the Disclosure Document Program. For a $10 fee you can forward a paper called a Disclosure Document to the USPTO as evidence of the date of conception for your invention. The document is in effect for two years, after which time your papers are destroyed unless you refer to them in your patent application, which must be filed within those two years.

Although there are no restrictions regarding the contents and claims of the Disclosure Document, the overall benefits depend upon what the document claims. You should write a clear and complete explanation of the manner and process of making and using your invention. The use of the invention should be described in detail, especially with inventions that are chemically related.

Cheering on inventors

Inventors are frequently made fun of, ridiculed, and criticized as crackpots. The general public thinks of them as wild and crazy eccentrics, best avoided. That is, until one of their inventions sells. The wild-eyed madman suddenly becomes a hero, the salt of the earth, the kind of person who makes this country great.

The truth is that inventors have changed and continue to change the way you live. The vehicle you drive, the medicines you take, the clothes you wear, the computer you use — the list of just everyday inventions you use without thinking about them could go on and on. Inventors contribute to society, often with no idea of how great an impact their creations will have on generations to come.

I asked an inventor in my office one day, "Why do you invent?" He replied, "Well, I never could be God, but I love to create." Down deep, we all like to help each other make life easier, and inventors do make a difference. Successful inventors share the same characteristics of any other successful individual. They have an extreme type of dedication in a particular field.

Although our base of technical knowledge has increased exponentially in modern times, revolutionary inventions don't have to be complicated. The paper clip and the safety pin are fairly simple pieces of engineering, but both continue to have a huge impact on everyday life.

Inventions, like inventors, come in all shapes, sizes, colors, and classes. You don't have to have an advanced engineering degree to be a successful inventor; in fact, a major study revealed that an inventor with a PhD is only a third more likely to bring an invention successfully to market than an inventor with a high school diploma.

The Disclosure Document needs to be just that — a document. Write on regular paper (you can use drafting paper) and don't include videotapes, prototypes, or a photo larger than 8½ by 11. Get the full specifications at `www.uspto.gov`.

The USPTO asks that you send two copies of your cover letter (not the whole disclosure document) so that they can send one back in the self-addressed, stamped envelope you include also.

A disclosure document is *not* a patent application. It merely establishes your invention's date of conception, which can certainly be a very important issue if the validity of your patent is ever challenged.

Spinning Through the Product Life Cycle

You've come up with a practical solution to a common problem and you want to make money from it. Where do you start? Well, first of all, don't quit your day job and take a credit-card vacation just yet. Your inventor's high may soon come crashing down amid the frustrations and setbacks of developing your idea and getting it to market. You must consider many things before running to a patent attorney to file a patent application.

There are specific steps you can take to discover whether you want to spend a lot of time and money on a new concept. In today's competitive market, you must not only have a great idea, but also know how to move the idea through the entire commercialization process.

Your very first step in the cycle is to think about how your idea will be used. Think about your idea in terms of marketability. Can you turn it into a saleable item? If so, will people buy it? Is there something already on the market that's very similar? What other competition is there? Remember, ideas are cheap and products are expensive.

Inventors often want to turn over their idea to someone else to make money for them. A good analogy for this desire is handing someone a newborn child and asking him to feed, clothe, potty train, educate, and otherwise care for the kid until the child is fully grown and through college. No one has more interest in, investment in, or ideas about your invention than you do. In order to maximize the potential profits, you have to be involved in bringing up your baby — er, your invention. Commercializing a product is like having a baby — easy to conceive and hard to deliver!

A product, like the aforementioned child, has a distinct life cycle, shown in the chart in Figure 1-2.

The life cycle of a product is basically seven years. The stages are as follows:

- ✔ **Evaluation and analysis stage:** The first two and a half years encompass the beginning stage of the life cycle. You receive no income because you're not selling anything yet. Your idea is in the evaluation and analysis stage, during which you test feasibility, viability, and reality. You conduct a patent search to make sure someone else doesn't already hold a patent on your idea. (Just because a product hasn't been marketed doesn't mean that there's no patent on it.) You make a prototype or otherwise refine your design. You do estimates of production costs, and do some market research to find out whether consumers are interested and how much they'd pay.

- ✔ **Introductory stage:** At approximately year 2½, your product enters the market. After introducing your invention, you continue to develop the markets for it and, hopefully, witness rapid growth and soaring profits. As a product's market presence grows, it has to be competitive in order to survive. Marketing is civilized warfare! Your product will go through all sorts of growing pains, much like a teenager moving to adulthood. You have to be as creative as you were during the invention stage in order to take and hold a place in the market.

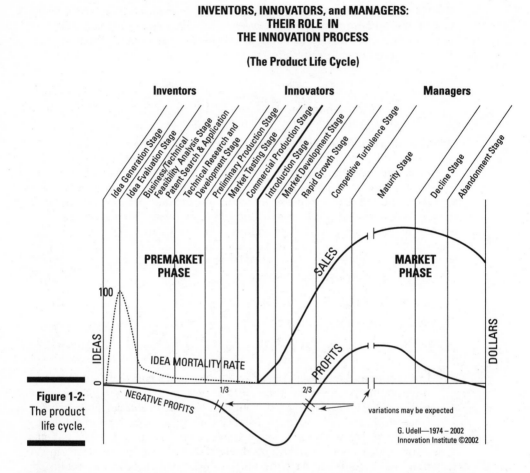

Figure 1-2:
The product
life cycle.

In the marketplace, your invention fights for the same dollar that can be spent on a family vacation, a mortgage, a new car, a child's education, and so on. Consumers only have so much money to spend and a variety of ways to spend their money. Your product is in direct competition with other products and services. How consumers choose to spend their money must be analyzed. Failure to do so and to understand consumer psychology can cause them to purchase similar products or close substitutes instead of your invention.

✔ **Development and Growth:** In Figure 1-2, note the point where managers take hold and their expertise takes over in order to move the product into the next stage, the Market Development and Growth Stage. Management teams come from various walks of life, with different fields of expertise and experiences. In fact, one of the most valuable things an investor brings to a company isn't necessarily funding, but the management expertise and experience to help push your product along.

Clearly, people with money to invest in your product don't have the funds because they're bad at business. No doubt they made mistakes, but that just means that they can advise you of errors to avoid. Try to build a solid and varied advisory team to help steer your invention down the most profitable path.

It isn't necessarily the best product that ultimately reaches the market. A product that has advantages in terms of knowledge, exposure, and information can succeed over similar products.

✔ **Maturity:** Your product eventually moves into a mature stage in which sales peak, capturing as much of the potential market share as possible. This generally happens during the fourth year of the product life cycle. Eventually, other new products with new technologies and improvements start competing in your market and your sales decline. This stage is one reason companies constantly develop new and improved products.

✔ **Abandonment:** Finally, at about the seventh year, a product reaches an abandonment stage, and it's no longer profitable to continue manufacturing, marketing and distributing it. Your patent is still in effect — a design patent is good for 14 years — but the patent isn't enough to make your invention profitable.

The merit of your product isn't the sole key to its success. So many factors can affect how your invention does in the marketplace. The most you can do is to cover all your bases as well as you can, which is what I help you do with this book.

Chapter 2

Patent Basics

●●

●●

*P*eople often assume that because a product is patented or has a patent pending, the product is better and that it actually works. Even though this isn't necessarily the case, a patented product or a product labeled patent pending definitely has a marketing advantage.

But what exactly is a patent, and what can it do for you and your invention? Who issues patents and how long do they last? If you're asking yourself these questions (and maybe others, too), you've come to the right place. In this chapter, I give you the lowdown on patents and why they're so crucial to making money off your invention. I also discuss how professionals such as patent attorneys and patent agents can help walk you through the patent process. Finally, I clue you in on foreign patents and how you can obtain a U.S. patent if you're from a different country.

Finding Out the Functions of a Patent

A U.S. *patent* is the grant of a property right to you, the inventor, issued by the United States Patent and Trademark Office (USPTO). In other words, a patent says that this invention belongs to you, and nobody else can make it, use it, or sell it as long as the patent is valid.

A patent *does*

- ✔ Give you the right to exclude others from making, using, offering for sale, or selling or importing your invention within the U.S. for a fixed period of time.
- ✔ Give you the right to sue others by filing a patent infringement lawsuit in federal court.

A patent *does not*

- ✔ Guarantee that your product or invention will make money.
- ✔ Give you the right to put the product on the market.
- ✔ Claim that the product is superior. It basically states that the product is "significantly different" from other products and ideas. A patent never says a product actually works — only that its intent is to work. (Very interesting — especially from an investment standpoint).

A patent issued in the U.S. is under the seal of the USPTO, and is signed by the Director of the USPTO. The patent contains a *grant,* which is an official paper to the patentee, and a technical drawing of your product, along with a legal description, the background of your product, and possibly, claims as to how your product is uniquely different from other products.

Generally, a new patent is issued for either 14 or 20 years depending on the type. It is issued from the date the patent application was filed in the U.S., and the patent is only good within the U.S., U.S. territories, and U.S. possessions. Under certain circumstances, you may be able to get an adjustment to the patent term because of delays or questions in the PTO. After your patent has expired, your invention is considered part of the *public domain,* which means anyone can make, use, or sell your invention without paying you a royalty.

A patent can't be renewed after its time has expired. During the legal life of a patent, you have ample time to introduce your product to the market and make money. The *legal life,* meaning patent life, is much different from the marketing or *product life* of your product. Most products have a consumer market life of only seven years. And market life can be even shorter in some industries, such as software, where products are outdated in six months.

After the patent has expired, your invention is essentially fair game. Anyone may make, offer for sale, or sell or import your invention without your permission, provided that items covered by other unexpired patent claims aren't sold along with it.

After you receive a patent, you have to enforce it — the USPTO doesn't. In Chapter 5, you can find out more about enforcing and maintaining your patent. Similar to the upkeep and maintenance on your car, a patent must be "maintained" as well to keep it going. A maintenance fee for utility patents is due at 3½ years, 7½ years, and 11½ years after the original grant. The maintenance fee must be paid at the stipulated times in order for the patent to remain valid.

Knowing What's Patentable

In order for an invention to be patentable, it must fall under the rules and guidelines of the USPTO. These rules and guidelines are available at www. uspto.gov. Any inventor who invents or discovers a new and useful *process* (defined by patent law as a process, act, or method, which primarily includes industrial or technical processes), *machine* (a new machine can be the product itself like a typewriter), *improvement* (an improvement upon an existing machine where the patent has expired — maybe a new keyboard designed with medical purposes in mind for people who are typing or doing data processing all day), *manufacture* (this refers to articles that are made and includes manufactured articles), or *composition of matter* (relates to chemical compositions, which includes mixtures of ingredients and new chemical compounds) may obtain a patent subject to the existing law.

Basically, just about anything made by man is patentable, as are the processes for making and compounding products.

You can't obtain a patent for a mere idea or suggestion. A full and detailed description of the actual item or process is required when you try to get a patent. Also, an invention can't be patented if the invention was known or used by others in this country or patented or described in a printed publication anywhere before the date of the claimed invention. (In plain English, this means someone else had done a newspaper article on the product before the date you stated was your date of conception. They beat you to it — you just didn't know it.) Finally, you can't obtain a patent if the invention was patented or described in a printed publication anywhere, or in public use or on sale in this country, more than one year prior to the application for a patent in the U.S.

You also must be the inventor in order to get the patent. You can own a patent without being the inventor, but you cannot be named on the patent as an inventor unless you're either the only inventor or a joint inventor.

Looking at the Types of Patents

Three different types of patents exist: utility, design, and plant. In this section, I give you the lowdown on each one.

You need to know and understand the type of patent you have not only from a legal standpoint, but also from a marketing and investment view as well. If you don't know, I can assure you a competitor will. In Chapter 14, you find out that one of the very first things a potential investor asks you is, "Do you have a patent?" and "What type is it?" in order to minimize risk on their potential investment.

Make yourself useful; get me a utility patent!

Anyone who invents or discovers any new or useful process or machine or a new and useful improvement on an existing product can apply for a *utility patent*.

The word *utility* generally means *usage*. For example, imagine owning the patent on the very first sitting apparatus known as a chair! Better yet, the first paper clip, baseball, or computer!

The present term of a utility patent begins when it's issued and ends 20 years after the filing date of the application and you must pay periodic maintenance fees on this type of patent (see Chapter 5).

Design patent

A *design patent* may be granted to anyone who invents a new, original, and ornamental design for a product. The design patent only protects the appearance of a product, but not its structural or functional features.

A design patent covers the unique, ornamental, or visible shape or design on a product. If you have a chair, purse, piano, computer screen, or pen that has a very unique shape, its design can be patented. However, the uniqueness of its shape must be aesthetic or ornamental. If its function is different, it qualifies for a utility patent.

If you're working with an attorney and the attorney states that your product qualifies for a patent, be sure to ask the attorney, "What type?" Many times, competitors can easily work around a design patent by changing the appearance of a product to make it "uniquely different." For example, look at a chair with a square back and change the square back to a more rounded back. This change can possibly qualify for a new "design" patent.

A word on public disclosures

Inventors tend to have a newspaper article written on their product or possibly advertise it for sale locally in a newspaper, craft market, and/or show it to their family and friends. Patent law states that your patent application must be filed in the U.S. and its territories within one year after you first publish details or commercialize your invention. If you describe your invention in a printed publication, use your invention publicly, or place it on sale, you must apply for a patent in the United States before one year or your right to get a patent will have been lost. In many foreign countries the rights may be lost if these acts occur at any time before the application is filed.

A good way to distinguish between a design and utility patent is to ask, "Will removing the novel features substantially change the function of my device?" Also ask yourself, "Is the novel feature in my product there for a functional or basic structural change, or is it strictly ornamental?" If it's ornamental in nature, a design patent is in order.

The design patent application must include a drawing of your product, along with the formal paperwork the USPTO requires and the filing fee (see Chapter 4 for more). It has a term of 14 years from the date it's granted, and there are no maintenance fees (see Chapter 5) for a design patent in order to keep it in force.

Planting the seeds of invention: The plant patent

Anyone who's invented or discovered or sexually reproduced any distinct and new variety of plant can apply for a *plant patent*. Here are some examples of patents issued on plants:

- ✔ Variegated trees that grow yellow apples, as well as green apples
- ✔ Citrus trees that grow oranges and grapefruits
- ✔ Hybrid roses that are cold and heat resistant or even bug resistant

A plant patent is good for 20 years and requires no maintenance fees.

Hiring a Patent Agent or Attorney

When you have an idea, you may want to seek an ethical patent attorney or agent for legal advice. You may be thinking, "Yikes! I don't want to spend money on an agent or attorney; I can't afford it." Well, I'm not going to lie: These professionals don't come cheap. However, their experience and expertise can be invaluable. Besides, you've heard the old saying that sometimes you have to spend money to make money.

In this section, I explain the difference between these two professionals and discuss how they both can assist you throughout the patent process. I also give you advice on choosing the best attorney or agent for your invention.

Patent agent versus patent attorney

A *patent agent* is a registered practitioner or representative who isn't an attorney but is authorized to act for or in place of an attorney before the USPTO. Basically, a patent agent is a skilled individual who's registered to practice before the office, and who isn't the inventor.

A patent agent is generally someone with an engineering, biology, scientific, or chemical background. This person in many cases has written her own patents and now writes patents for inventors. She must pass official exams administered by the USPTO in order to become a registered patent agent.

A *patent attorney* must be a member in good standing of the bar of any U.S. court or the highest court of any state who's registered to practice before the office. He or she likely has an undergraduate degree in engineering or one of the technical sciences.

When using the services of a patent attorney, expect to pay between $3,000 to $10,000 or more for your patent. The fees can rise even higher depending on the nature of the product and the time involved. Some attorneys charge a flat fee while others charge an hourly rate. Find out in advance who will pay for the filing fees, professional fees, postage, professional drawings, and copying fees.

Patent attorneys are *not* qualified to give a marketability opinion of your product, only a patentability opinion. These are two very different areas.

Knowing what they can do for you

A patent attorney or patent agent can assist you in capitalizing on your creation. These qualified individuals can conduct a patent search to further investigate the overall patentability of your product. They can also file a patent application for you using their legal expertise and can help defend you in a court of law to the degree of recognition that the courts are willing to enforce your patent rights.

In previous years, patents were the largest part of intellectual property (IP) law; so most attorneys who handled IP called themselves patent attorneys, even though they also handled trademarks, trade secrets (see Chapter 6), and copyrights (see Chapter 7), as well as unfair competition. Times have changed, though, and all forms of IP have become more important and more complex. As a result, more and more attorneys are referring to themselves as intellectual property attorneys rather than simply patent attorneys.

If you don't feel qualified to act on your own throughout the patent process, I recommend hiring an IP attorney or agent. See the section, "Choosing the right attorney or agent for the job" for tips on hiring the best attorney or agent for your situation.

Choosing the right attorney or agent for the job

A great way to find a patent attorney is through personal referral from another inventor, a friend, a local inventors' organization, or your attorney. You can also go to www.uspto.gov (the USPTO Web site) and www.uiausa.com (the United Inventors Association Web site) to find names of patent attorneys and agents.

After you find a candidate, you may want to review patents that he or she has written. Just go to the USPTO's Web site and enter the attorney or agent's name. When reviewing the patent, be sure to evaluate the attorney's writing by asking yourself the following questions:

✔ Is the writing clear and understandable?

✔ Is it concise? (The less that's written, the less to argue over later on.)

✔ Did he or she list advantages of the invention you're reviewing in detail?

These criteria are important; communication skills, both verbal and written, are essential for a patent attorney.

When selecting a patent attorney or agent, make sure the individual's background is in the same area as your invention. For example, if you have a mechanical product, your patent attorney or agent should have a mechanical engineering background. If your product is biology based, your patent attorney or agent should have a degree in biology.

After you find someone that meets your criteria, make a brief appointment to meet the attorney or agent personally or over the phone. Find out in advance the fees you will be paying.

It's a Small World: International Issues

Consider filing a foreign patent application. A U.S. patent gives you a potential monopoly in selling and distributing your product in the U.S.; if you think your new product has a broad enough market to be sold in large quantities abroad, you may want to create a monopoly there as well. Otherwise, anyone in another country will be able to make, use, and sell your invention in that country without paying you a cent. They simply can't bring the product into the U.S. without infringing on your U.S. patent.

If you're from another country and you want to obtain a U.S. patent, you must follow the same guidelines and rules that U.S. citizens do in applying for U.S. patents. Then you have the opportunity to commercialize your product in one of the largest consumer markets in the world — the U.S.!

 Today, we work in a global economy. Products are being manufactured and marketed throughout the world. You must be aware of intellectual property law not only in the U.S. but wherever you plan to sell your product. Find out about the etiquette and customs of those countries as well.

Applying for foreign patents

Because U.S. patent rights extend only throughout the territory of the U.S. and have no effect in a foreign country, an inventor who wants patent protection in other countries must apply for a patent in each of the other countries or in regional patent offices. Nearly every country has its own patent law. A person desiring a patent in a particular country must make an application for patent in that country, in accordance with their patent laws. However, some countries work together. These countries have adopted the *Patent Cooperation Treaty* (the PCT), which allows you, by filing in one country, to designate a number of countries as the ultimate countries in which patents are desired. This allows you to decide later which countries are important.

 Under U.S. law, if your invention was made in the U.S., you must obtain a license from the Director of the USPTO before applying for a patent in a foreign country. This license is required if the foreign application is to be filed before a U.S. application is filed or before the expiration of six months after the filing of an application in the United States.

Make sure you have a commercial market for your product in a country before spending a lot of time and money. Study your invention's overall marketability abroad before spending big bucks. Also, be very careful of the trademarks and words on the packaging you use when selling abroad. Vocabularies differ and various words have negative and derogatory meanings in foreign countries.

The laws of many countries differ from the patent laws of the U.S. In most foreign countries, publication of the invention before the filing date of the application in any country bars you from obtaining a patent. In most foreign countries, maintenance fees are required. And many foreign countries require that the patented invention be used in that country within a certain period, usually three years. If there is no use within this period, the patent may become void. Sometimes, use can be accomplished by paying a fee. In most countries, the patent may be subject to the grant of compulsory licensing to any person who may apply for a license if the patentee is not using the invention in that country.

In addition to knowing about the PCT, it is important for you to know about international patents and foreign filing under the *International Convention for the Protection of Industry Property*. This is a treaty that's adhered to by 140 countries, including the U.S., and is known as the *Paris Convention for the Protection of Industrial Property*. Under this treaty, each country guarantees that citizens of the other countries will receive the same rights in patent and trademark matters that it grants to its own citizens. The treaty also provides for the right of priority in the case of patents, trademarks, and industrial design (design patents). This right means that on the basis of a regular first application filed in one of the member countries, the applicant may, within a certain period of time, apply for protection in all the other member countries. These later applications will then be regarded as if they had been filed on the same day as the first application.

A number of patent attorneys specialize in obtaining patents in foreign countries. If you're seriously considering applying for a foreign patent, I recommend getting help from one of these individuals.

Foreign applicants for U.S. patents

The patent laws of the U.S. make no discrimination with respect to the citizenship of the inventor. Any inventor, regardless of citizenship, may apply for a patent on the same basis as a U.S. citizen. There are, however, a number of particular points of special interest to applicants located in foreign countries.

✔ In the U.S., you must be the inventor in order to obtain a patent. This is not so in most of the counties in the world. In other countries, it is whoever applies for a patent first — not necessarily the inventor.

✔ If your product was already patented in other countries, you can't obtain a U.S. patent and if you're filing patent applications abroad, you must file within 12 months after filing in the U.S. Only six months are allowed in the case of a design patent.

✔ Any U.S. patent application filed in a foreign country with reciprocating U.S. patent treaties has the same privileges as a patent application filed by a U.S. citizen. A copy of the foreign application certified by the patent office of the country in which it was filed is required to secure this right of priority in the patent application.

✔ You must make an oath or, alternatively, a declaration with every patent application that you're the inventor. If you're in a foreign country, your oath or affirmation may be before any diplomatic or consular officer for the U.S. or before any officer having an official seal who's authorized to administer oaths in your foreign country, whose authority shall be provided by a certificate of a diplomatic or consular officer of the U.S.

✔ If you take an oath before an officer in a foreign country to the U.S., all of the application papers (except the patent drawing) must be attached together and a ribbon passed one or more times through all the sheets of the application, and the ends of the ribbons brought together under the seal before the latter is affixed and impressed, or each sheet must be impressed with the official seal of the officer before whom the oath is taken. A declaration merely requires the use of a specific averment.

✔ If the legal representative of a deceased inventor files the application, the legal representative must make the oath or declaration. When a declaration is used, the ribboning procedure is not necessary, nor is it necessary to appear before an official in connection with the making of a declaration.

If you're a foreign inventor, a patent attorney or agent who is registered to practice before the USPTO should represent you.

Chapter 3

Conducting a Patent Search

. . . .

In This Chapter

▶ Deciding to do your own patent search

▶ Using a patent attorney

▶ Searching for patents

. . . .

*Y*our idea may be new to you, but you don't know whether it's truly new until you do a patent search. Millions of ideas have already been patented, although most never see the light of day as a product.

Until you conduct a patent search, you have no way of knowing whether you're infringing upon another's invention. And you don't want to wait until the United States Patent Office conducts its own search at the time you file your patent application to find out that your idea is not unique.

Although you're not required to conduct a patent search before submitting a patent application, I strongly recommend that you do so. In fact, even if you decide to hire an attorney to conduct a patent search for you, I suggest that you conduct one yourself, first. By doing so, you discover more about the intellectual property law process, similarities of other inventors' ideas, and possibly, new commercial applications. And doing so can prevent you from hocking the family jewels only to find that what you thought was a new, patentable idea was actually invented by the cave men.

In this chapter, I explain how to determine what's new about your idea, how a patent search can help improve your idea, how to prepare and start the search, and how to enlist the help of the pros. I also discuss how to use your search results.

Do I Really Need to Do a Patent Search?

You may say, "Well, I've looked everywhere. I've been to Wal-Mart, K-Mart, Target, Sears, and other places, and I haven't seen my product anywhere. It's not patented. I don't need to conduct a search."

Don't assume any such thing. Just because your product isn't on the store shelves doesn't mean that it isn't patented. Remember, only about 7 percent of patented products make money; therefore, 93 percent don't, so you won't find them anywhere but in a patent search. You don't want to work day and night to establish a small business around your product and then find out that someone else already holds a patent on it.

Large corporations conduct patent searches in their given areas of manufacturing to discover enticing potential improvements, applications, and alternatives that they can take advantage of in the manufacturing and marketing process. A wise investor usually wants to know whether you have a patent. If you don't, they usually ask if you have conducted a search. If you haven't, and are seeking investment money for prototype advancement (see Chapter 9), corporations generally run the other way. Do your homework!

Read the information on the United States Patent and Trademark Office's (USPTO) Web site, `www.uspto.gov`, regarding how to conduct a patent search; it will walk you through the step-by-step process.

Determining Whether Your Idea Is Really New

After you find a way to demonstrate to your own satisfaction that your idea works and does what you think it will do, you need to carefully decide what's really new about it, also termed the *overall novelty*. Until you identify what your overall novelty is, you can't conduct a search to find the ideas most like your own. The novelty is what a patent protects, so if your idea isn't really new, you won't be able to patent it. Suppose that you've invented a tire. Think about the specific features that you invented to make the tire novel or unique. Did you invent the tire or improvements on the tire? These features or new process of making a tire are what can be patented. Take a close look at all the similar patents to see if the features, functions, and novelty you thought of were really unique.

Prepare for an *ad*venture

Although some people refer to inventing as a venture, I find that the ups and downs involved make it more of an *ad*venture in understanding life and the realities of a business. Every successful inventor I've worked with went through the typical pain and misery associated with taking a significant amount of risk, spending long, hard hours dedicated to testing and improving their ideas, and enduring a shortage of available resources. Just get ready to put your boots on and come out of the corner fighting if you decide to go follow the typical pathway toward an *ad*venture.

Searching for Existing Patents

When conducting a patent search, you take in a significant amount of information by reviewing other inventors' patents. You see their drawings, legal descriptions, technical information, and possibly, their operational components. You may not have considered some of the ideas expressed in others' patents, and you can use those insights to improve the overall design of your product.

A patent search can enlighten you about additional commercial uses for your product. You may also find that the major breakthrough you think you have is only a small improvement on what was already available. Knowing this can help you better position your product when it comes on the market (see Chapters 17 and 18 for more on marketing your product).

Your patent search can also help you write your own patent application.

If your initial search looks favorable, hire a professional patent attorney or agent to conduct a more thorough search (see the section, "Getting Professional Help," later in this chapter for more). By conducting your own patent search, you can become more knowledgeable about your product and its competition. You can see if similar patents to your product exist.

Searching for patents via the Internet

You can conduct your own free patent search over the Internet, with help from Uncle Sam.

The USPTO has set up an Internet search process that enables you to fine-tune your search by combining words and phrases that are contained in the individual abstracts in a patent. The examples are very detailed in helping you conduct your search. The USPTO has made this Web site "user friendly" as it is fairly easy to use.

Searching by subject

You can search for U.S. patents at the USPTO Web site at www.uspto.gov/patft/index.html or the Delphion Intellectual Network site at www.delphion.com. The USPTO site provides most patents from 1790 through the present in image files. The Delphion site provides U.S. patents for 1974 through the present in image files.

Here are the basic steps for a patent search by subject:

1. **Search by keyword.** For example a baby buggy that's hand pushed. The keywords you use are "buggy" or "stroller" or "carriage."

2. **Locate a good patent.** A good patent is one that has features in it that are close to what you're trying to patent. That way, you know that you're in the correct area. When you're conducting a search, if there are no similar patents, determine whether you're really conducting the search in the correct area. It would be strange not to see similar patents appear.

   Look for similarities to your specific invention. Then, look for differences and distinctions that can be made between your invention and the patents you're examining.

3. **Look at the class/subclass number listing for that patent.**

   You can find it in the Index to the U.S. Patent Classification System at USPTO. Then use the class numbers to look up the classification of subjects related to your search terms in the *Manual of U.S. Patent Classification*. When you bring up the title and patent number, it will then show you the class and subclass where the patent is primarily referenced and cross-referenced. When reviewing this patent, it will contain the search list that the patent examiner who reviewed the patent went to when he did the actual patent search in order for the patent you're looking at to be issued in the first place.

4. **Do a search of that class/subclass listing to find more patents on the same topic.**

   Your search is only as good as your selection of the keywords in the first place. You must have included in the keywords the features of your invention that you think are important.

Using the USPTO Index

Another way to conduct a patent search is to search for common terms and phrases in order to find their class and subclass number in the Index to the U.S. Patent Classification System at USPTO. Then use the class numbers to look up the classification of subjects related to your search terms in the *Manual of U.S. Patent Classification*.

Searching by class/subclass listing

Finally, search by class/subclass listing by taking a close look at each of the patents located with the various classes and subclasses.

You may view and print the text of the patent for free at USPTO's Web site. To view the image of a patent on the USPTO's site, you must have compatible software; otherwise, you may have a difficult time viewing the image. The USPTO's Web site provides TIFF files (one page at a time for PCs). This requires TIFF software. Another option is using Delphion's Web site, www.delphion.com. Delphion provides a poorer quality image file, one page at a time, but doesn't require TIFF software. They provide patents in different formats, qualities, and date coverages. The Delphion site will provide you information on the abstract, background, claims, and other text. You have to be a paid subscriber in order to access anything on the Delphion site, however.

Searching for international patents

When searching for international patents, consider using the Delphion Web site, www.delphion.com. This site provides bibliographic searching of European, World (WIPO), and unexamined Japanese patents.

This site even allows you to view full pages of some patents. In the U.S., this ranges from 1971 to present and in Europe from 1979 to present. It also lists representative first pages of other countries; for example, patents issued in Japan from 1976 to present and from the World Organization from 1990 to present.

Many national patent offices now have Web patent databases. See the European Patent Office's extensive list at www.european-patent-office.org/online/index.htm.

Getting Professional Help

In this section, I discuss getting expert advice and how to go about it, as well as what to expect and look for in selecting your patent attorney (also known as an *intellectual property attorney*) or agent. Your patent is only as good as it can be defended in a court of law. If your product is really good, it will most likely be infringed upon, and it will only be a matter of time until you're in court defending it.

When selecting a patent attorney or agent, you should get references from local inventor organizations, other attorneys, and friends. One of the main things to look for in the selection is to make sure that the background of the attorney or agent is similar to that of your invention. A common mistake made by inventors is that they simply look in the Yellow Pages under "intellectual property attorneys" and get the name, not knowing about the specialization involved. (For more on hiring a patent attorney or agent, refer to Chapter 2.)

Patent searches are best conducted by patent attorneys or agents (see Chapter 2 for the lowdown on patent attorneys and agents) because they know the ins and outs of the system and can think of places to look that you may miss. Their search may find prior art similar to what you believe to be new about your project, or the search may show that your idea is an improvement on the invention of another. *Prior art* simply means products for sale, patents, published pending applications, or newspaper and other written information that's been made available to the public.

Questions to ask

As a novice inventor, you may not know the revealing questions to ask a patent attorney. Here are some questions to make sure the patent attorney can answer for you:

- ✔ **Is my product patentable?** You may not receive a direct answer as to whether or not your idea is patentable. You most likely will not get a "yes or no" answer but an opinion concerning the likelihood that you will get a patent. Then you will have to decide if the probability is great enough to justify the risk. There are no guarantees. You don't want to do all the work necessary to make money off your product if you don't have the possibility of obtaining a patent.

- ✔ **What is your area of expertise?** What did you get your degree in — mechanical, electrical, biology, chemistry, or maybe environmental engineering? Remember to select your patent attorney or agent by the type of product you have.

- ✔ **What is your experience?** How many patents has he or she filed? Has the attorney or agent been involved in any infringement cases? How long has he or she been practicing?

- ✔ **How do you do your billing?** Is it an hourly rate? If so, how much? Some attorneys and agents require a significant amount of money upfront, whereas others bill by the pay-as-you-go method.

- ✔ **How many patents are there similar to mine?** This question should be asked after the patent search is completed. Then, based on the results of the patent search, ask again whether your product is patentable.

  You may be surprised by the answer, especially if a large number of patents are similar to yours. If several patents are similar to yours, you may want to think twice before starting your venture. Those inventors have already taken a forward step. If you don't see any of the products from these patents for sale, is there really a market for your product?

- ✔ **What type of patent do I qualify for?** The various types are discussed in Chapter 2. They're different, so know what you're paying for.

Knowing the cost

If you hire a patent attorney, the cost of a search of U.S. patents only is generally between $300 and $800 dollars. If you conduct a patent search yourself, it's free for the asking. The patent attorney or agent is a trained professional, however, and well worth the investment. When conducting your own search, you may miss some prior-art references from the area you're searching. You may also miss foreign patent applications or recently issued patents that have not been placed in the specific search files.

Face it. Conducting a patent search with an attorney or agent is a cheap deal, in terms of money, in order to find out whether you're wasting time pursuing your idea.

Using Your Search Results

You may be wondering what should you do next if you locate similar patents. If you didn't find similar patents, you may wonder whether you did the search correctly because there are millions of patented products. If there are any exactly like yours, you should get a legal opinion as to whether or not you're infringing. If you are, stay home — don't spend the family jewels. If not, you may want to contact the inventors on similar patents and find out whether they've marketed their invention. And if not, why not? Was there a market for their product? What went wrong — were the manufacturing prices too high? If there is a market and the inventor is simply not capable of marketing the product, you may want to consider a joint venture with that inventor or even consider licensing his invention from him and paying him a royalty. (See Chapters 20 and 21 on licensing.) You have many options to consider.

In some cases, a product like yours may be on the market without a patent. Unpatented products can still be marketable, and millions of such products exist. However, if you choose to market your product without a patent and you use it publicly for more than a year without applying for a patent, you may lose the right to ever patent your product.

The last patent search I conducted was for a toilet design. Although I found more than 60 issued patents for toilets, I knew that you only see a limited number of toilet designs on the market. And those are controlled by a handful of plumbing-related manufacturing companies. My client decided to go no farther. When conducting your patent search, if you find many similar products, even though they are not necessarily the same, stop and think. Those inventors went through the same steps that you're now going through. Ask yourself, "Is my product uniquely different enough to be commercially viable?"

Chapter 4

Applying For and Receiving Your Patent

. . . .

. . . .

*N*ecessity may be the mother of invention, but patents are the guardians.

I'm sure you've noticed a patent number or the words *patent pending* on products in stores and in your home or office. In this chapter, I show you just how powerful these words are from a marketing standpoint and how you can get permission to display these words on your invention. I tell you about the various types of patents, the costs of getting a patent, and how to file a patent application.

I also tell you about hiring a representative, which is more important than you may think. Your patent needs to be defendable in a court of law. If your invention is really good, it is only a matter of time until you're in a court of law trying to defend your patent against infringers. Get ready and know that upfront.

Knowing Who Can Apply for a Patent

Three people have the right to apply for a patent on your invention:

1. You, the inventor

2. Your patent attorney

3. Your patent agent

The few exceptions to this rule serve extreme circumstances affecting the inventor:

- ✔ If the inventor is dead, the administrator or executor of the estate may apply for a patent.
- ✔ If the inventor is insane, a guardian may make the application.
- ✔ If the inventor refuses to apply for a patent or cannot be found, a person having a proprietary interest in the invention — a co-inventor or a spouse, for example — may apply on behalf of the inventor.

The United States Patent and Trademark Office (USPTO) patent examiner contacts the person who applies for the patent, no matter who the inventor is. If you hire a patent attorney or agent, part of what you hire them for is to act as your professional representative before the USPTO.

If a person who isn't the inventor or the inventor's representative applies for and is granted a patent, the patent is invalid. If someone falsely represents himself as the inventor when applying for a patent, that person is subject to criminal penalties.

Applying as co-inventors

Two or more people who work on an invention together are called *co-inventors* or *joint inventors* and must apply for a patent as such. Each joint inventor has an equal share in the patent.

Only people who actually contributed features of the invention are co-inventors, though. A couple of examples of people who aren't joint inventors and, therefore, cannot apply for a patent along with the inventor are

- ✔ **A financial contributor:** Someone who funds the research but doesn't do any of the actual work of invention cannot apply for a patent as a co-inventor.

    Listing the name of the financial supporter as a co-inventor is a nice gesture, but not a legal one. Even though the name of the actual inventor is on the patent also, if a noninventor is listed as a joint inventor, the patent isn't valid.

    The correct way to handle the case of a financial backer who wants interest in a patent is to establish a company and assign the patent rights to that company. You can sell shares of your company and get stockholders and each own a piece of the your company in return for funding. You can get free advice on starting your business and what type of business you want from your local Small Business Development Center. Locate the nearest center at `www.sba.gov`. You can also get a corporate attorney to assist you — they're the pros after all. (I discuss the various types of corporations you can start in Chapter 15.)

✔ **A spouse:** Couples frequently have both names on their cars, houses, and other personal property and may not think twice about listing both names on a patent application. But unless both people can legally prove that they're co-inventors, they should not be listed as patent owners. If it's shown that a listed co-inventor isn't, in fact, one of the inventors, a patent can be invalidated.

Choosing a representative

You may want to save money. But if you think that applying for a patent by yourself is one way to do it, think again. Although an experienced attorney or agent doesn't come cheap, hiring someone qualified doesn't cost nearly as much as losing the rights to your invention. Especially if you're counting on your invention to provide a source of income, you need to make sure that your patent is perfect.

You can probably figure out that a *patent lawyer* is a lawyer who specializes in patent law. A *patent agent* isn't a lawyer; an agent is an individual (many times an inventor like yourself) who has passed exams administered by the USPTO and is qualified to write patents for other inventors. A patent agent is helpful in the application process, but, in my opinion, you need a lawyer to represent you in court. A patent agent is generally a little less expensive than a patent attorney, and each can provide the required information; however, the patent attorney is expected to be the more knowledgeable individual. (Check out Chapter 2 for more on patent attorneys and agents.)

If your product is successful, chances are high that, at some point, you'll end up in some sort of litigation focused on it. It doesn't matter whether you initiate a lawsuit over patent infringement or a lawsuit is brought against you or your company over worker's compensation, a contract dispute, or a building code problem. No matter what the lawsuit focuses on, one of the very first items to be challenged is the validity of the patent. If your patent doesn't hold up under scrutiny, you may be out hundreds or thousands of dollars. Paying the price to have your patent done right from the start is the smart way to go.

You can assist your patent lawyer or agent with the application process by providing them with a clear and concise description of your invention. Try to be as broad as possible with many applications and selling advantages. You know your invention much better than the attorney or agent does.

Selecting an attorney

You may think that your telephone directory is the best place to start looking for a patent attorney. Not necessarily. Patent attorneys tend to specialize, just as physicians do, so look for a patent lawyer who knows law *and* something about the field of your invention. For example, if you have a mechanical product, look for a patent attorney with an undergraduate degree in engineering; if you invented a better light bulb, look for an electrical background.

Filing for Different Types of Patents

In Chapter 2, I explain the different types of patents you can apply for. In the following sections, I tell you how to apply for each type and fill you in on the process.

I've provided you the basic, need-to-know info here. For more detailed information, check out the USPTO Web site at www.uspto.gov or contact your patent attorney or agent.

Paying attention to the process

You have to fill out an application and pay an application fee if you want to get a patent. Many of the fees change around October 1 each year.

You file your application and send it to the USPTO in Washington, D.C. Be aware that all papers become the property of the USPTO.

If you want confirmation that the Patent Office received your application, attach a stamped, self-addressed postcard to the first page of the application that the Patent Office clerk can detach, stamp with the date received, and return to you. You get an official filing receipt when your application is filed, usually in about six weeks.

The office makes sure all the parts of the application are there and that the correct fee is paid and sends your application to the drafting department. Here, your drawings are reviewed for all the necessary formal requirements. If your patent drawings contain any errors, a drawing objection slip is put in your folder. (For more info on submitting drawings, see "Filing a utility patent" later in this chapter.)

Next, your file goes to an appropriate patent examiner who is trained in the field of your invention. The application waits in line until its turn comes for examination to begin. The examination phase generally takes a few months to a year.

You'll probably receive an *Office Action* from the patent examiner. This action usually does at least one of the following:

✔ Objects to one or more parts of your specifications

✔ Rejects some or all your claims due to unclear language or lack of description in the specification

✔ Rejects some of all your claims due to prior art

Prior art is an existing patent (foreign or US), a publication, a product, or a schematic of a product that shows that your invention isn't unique or physically different from any other patented invention. If it's already out there in physical form or print, your product isn't patentable. You can help avoid this problem by conducting a patent search. A search will reveal patents that have already been issued on the subject matter, as well as ones that have been applied for but not been issued yet (and are at least 18 months old). I discuss how to conduct a patent search in Chapter 3.

Upon receiving an Office Action memo, you should file an Amendment, which gives you the right to correct the objections. You can then make corrections, changes, additions, or deletions to your filing papers as long as you don't add new information. You may also amend the claims to change the scope of the invention that you're trying to patent.

You can also try to convince the patent examiner that the Office Action is in error. Keep in mind, though, that UPSTO examiners see inventions in their given field every single day, and I hate to say it, but you're a novice trying to patent possibly your first invention. Don't feel bad, though; about 95 percent of all patent applications are rejected the first time. The patent office informs you why they're turning your application down and what the problems are. Your patent attorney or agent can help you figure out what the errors are and how to fix them. The USPTO may cite an existing patent as the reason your application is rejected. Your attorney can help you by pointing out how your invention is truly unique.

After the examiner allows your patent application, you're given three months to pay an issuance fee (in addition to the application fee). Upon receipt of payment, your information, including the specification and claims, are sent to the U.S. Government Printing Office or an outside contractor. The information on your patent is printed verbatim.

Many things can affect the length of time the application is in the office. The whole process generally takes up to two years and sometimes longer, so you have to be patient.

Filing a utility patent

If you invent a new process or machine, you want to apply for a utility patent to protect your rights. One of the most important features of a utility patent is that it has claims. A *patent claim* is what defines your invention and establishes its legally enforceable components. The claims you make in your patent application specifically describe the unique features of your product and what makes it different from similar objects. The claims you make serve to determine whether your invention is patentable. Think of the claims as a fence around your yard — they define your property. You want your fence to be as broad, big, and sturdy as possible.

Along with the appropriate filing fee, your application must be typewritten (except as noted) in black ink on white 8½-by-11-inch paper (the standard letter size). The left margin should be 1 inch, and the top, right, and bottom margin at least ¾ inch. The application should contain the following elements in this specific order:

- ✔ **Utility patent application transmittal form or transmittal letter:** Basically, this form tells the Patent Office what type of application you're filing and what papers and enclosures your application includes. Make sure that your name, as the inventor, and the title of your invention are included.

- ✔ **Fee transmittal form and appropriate fee:** The fee transmittal form helps you calculate the filing fees and gives you a place to indicate whether you're paying the fee by check or by credit card. The number and type of claims that you apply for determine your actual filing fees. For a complete list of the most current filing fees, go to www.uspto.gov/go/fees.

- ✔ **Application data sheet:** This sheet contains the applicant's information, correspondence information, applicant and representative information, domestic priority information, foreign priority information, any provisional patent applications you may have filed, as well as patent assignment information if you're assigning your patent rights to another individual or company. If your invention was developed under a government contract, it should be stated on the application sheet.

- ✔ **Background of your invention:** This is a brief, one-sentence paragraph stating the general and specific areas in which your invention falls. For example, your sentence might read, "This invention relates to automobiles, specifically to an improved door hinge for the automobile." The field of your invention should be the technical, product, subject, or scientific area that it's relevant to, such as automobile. Do not state any of the specific details of your invention here.

- **Summary:** This part briefly describes a summary of your invention and its advantages. It can also paraphrase your main claim.

- **Main embodiment:** This info is a detailed description of your invention, how it works, alternative ways of working, and what it's used for.

- **Abstract:** A technical description of your invention that's in a summary form. It should be on a separate sheet of paper with the heading "ABSTRACT." Write a paragraph providing a concise summary of your invention. Keep it to 150 words and make it as brief, complete, clear and to the point as possible. This is generally the part of the application that's read first. You may want to view abstracts from other patents to give you an idea of what's needed.

- **Disclosure Document Statement:** Include this info if you've previously filed one with the USPTO and any other info you have and can prove the date of conception. See Chapter 1 for more info on this program.

- **Specification sheet and claims section:** The title of the invention should appear as the heading on the first page of the *specification sheet,* which is a written description of your invention. It must be in full, clear, concise, and exact terms and written so that any person who's knowledgeable about the field can understand it and practice the invention after the patent expires. The claims section must begin on a separate page with the heading: "I claim . . ." The claims are the legal description of your product that your patent protection is based on.

Claims are the foundation and nucleus of your patent and define the scope of your patent protection. They're absolutely one of the most important features of your application, because they're the primary features fought over in infringement cases. Whether a patent is granted is determined primarily by the patent claims section.

Any utility application claiming the benefit of a previously filed provisional or international patent application must contain a reference to this application in the first sentence of the application. It should identify this in the first sentence and reference a U.S. application, international application, or international filing date. It should cross-reference information to other related patent applications you may have filed dealing with this subject matter.

- **Drawings:** If drawings are necessary to understand the subject matter of your invention, you must include them with your application. The drawing must be on standard size white paper and must be in black ink. Leave a specified (about an inch) border around the sheet of the drawing. No printed matter may appear on the drawing except the figures you're talking about other than the reference numerals that refer to your product.

- **Oath or declaration:** This just says that you're who you say you are, that you have the right to file the application, as well as the name, city, the state or country of residence, country of citizenship, and mailing address of each inventor.

Filing a design patent

Because a design patent is all about the appearance of an object — the patent protects only the appearance of a product, not its structural or functional features — you need to provide extensive and detailed drawings with your application. The drawing defines the scope of the patent protection.

Designs are considered distinct if they have different shapes and appearances. For example, two vases may have the same function, but be of very different design. Each vase would have its own design patent application.

A design patent application should include the following:

- ✔ **Preamble:** This states the applicant's name, the *title* (something that identifies the design and gives a brief description of the invention), and its intended use. The drawing here is really your product's best description.

- ✔ **Description:** This is an optional explanation of what the drawings of the design show. For example, you may want to explain that the first drawing is a bird's-eye view, that the right side is shown, and that the left side is a mirror image of the right side.

- ✔ **Claim:** You make a single claim that covers the entire design.

- ✔ **Drawings or photographs:** By far the most important element of the application, you must include either a drawing or a black-and-white photograph of your design.

- ✔ **Oath or declaration:** Certifying that you have a right to file the application.

Notice that, unlike a utility patent application, you don't include the fee with a design patent application. If your design is granted a patent, the USPTO sends you a notice asking for the fee payment.

Filing for a plant patent

Plant patents are pretty rare. You have to discover or reproduce a distinctly new plant variety. If you do indeed find a new plant, you apply for a patent in very much the same way you apply for a utility patent (see "Filing a utility patent" earlier in this chapter).

Your application should include the following elements:

- ✔ **Description:** a complete detailed description of the plant and the characteristics that distinguish it from known plant varieties in scientific, botanical terms.

✔ **Origin:** Explain the plant's *predecessors* (its parent plants) and its *genesis* (how you got it to reproduce). If you discover a previously unknown plant, give a complete description of where you found it.

✔ **Botanical name:** State the genus and species of the plant in Latin.

✔ **Claim:** Because the patent is given for the whole plant, you need only one claim.

✔ **Two copies of a drawing:** Unlike a drawing for a utility patent, the drawing for a plant patent should be artistic. The drawing needs to show all the relevant features, and if color is one of those features, the drawings must be in color.

✔ **The oath or declaration:** in addition to stating that you have a right to file the application, a plant patent oath must state that you have asexually reproduced the new plant variety. If the plant is a newly found plant, the oath or declaration must also state that the plant was found in a cultivated area.

If the plant's color is a distinctive feature, use the color of a common color dictionary to identify it.

Something you *don't* have to provide is a seed or flower from your new plant. An examiner may want a specimen later, but don't submit any samples with your application.

Filing for a provisional patent

A provisional patent is a sort of pre-utility patent or "patent lite." A *provisional patent* application becomes abandoned one year after filing, costs just $80 or $160 to file, depending on size of the business filing, and doesn't require the detailed claims or oaths that regular patents do.

Originally designed to assist American inventors in competition with inventors around the world, the USPTO started offering provisional applications in 1995, in the wake of GATT Uruguay Round Trade Agreements. Because foreign patents are issued to the first person to apply for the patent and not to the first inventor (as is the requirement for a U.S. patent), a provisional applications gives American inventors parity with foreign inventors, by offering a way to register their invention in its early stages.

A provisional application is also a great marketing tool. It allows you to legally claim patent pending status without spending a lot of money. It gives you one year to test the market and determine whether your invention is worth the time and money it takes to file for a regular patent.

Face it: You don't know what the market really is for your product. You don't know whether it will sell. Large corporations spend millions of dollars to bring a single product to market, and most inventors have a budget of $20,000 or less and are fighting for the same store shelf space, television time, and catalogue space that large manufacturers want. During the one-year time span, you can investigate your product's commercial viability through a thorough evaluation and then review the market to look at some of the costs of commercialization.

A provisional application is good for 12 months from the date the application is filed, with no extensions or exceptions. So, if you decide to apply for a more permanent patent, do it before the year is up. If you file after that deadline, you lose the benefit of the filing date of the provisional to cut off prior art, and the validity of your patent may be challenged maybe because of your own commercial activity.

To be complete, a provisional application must include the filing fee, a written description of the invention, any necessary drawings, and a cover sheet that lists the following information:

- A statement that the application is for a provisional patent
- Inventor and correspondence addresses and any representative's name and address
- Title of the invention
- Any U.S. governmental agency that has a property interest in the application

You can use the cover sheet provided by the USPTO. It's on the Web site at www.uspto.gov.

Provisional applications aren't examined on their merits. You can claim that you have a patent pending, but you're not guaranteed an actual patent just because you file a provisional application. To qualify for a permanent patent, you have to prove your claims, detail your invention, and pay your fees.

You can't file a provisional application for design inventions.

Making the Most of a Pending Patent

The words *patent pending* on an item indicate that the inventor has applied for a patent, but it hasn't been issued yet. If you're such an inventor, the words *patent pending* on your product give you two definite advantages:

- From a marketing standpoint, you gain some consumer confidence.
- You ward off potential infringers.

Many inventors with patented products apply for additional provisional patents at a much lower cost, enabling them to label their products as patented with the patent numbers and having additional patent pending. These words alone frequently ward off potential competitors because they don't know what you have applied for a patent on. Think of a bicycle. A bicycle may be marked with the word *patent,* then list the various patent numbers, followed by the words *patent pending.* Now, what is the new improvement on the bike? Take a close look. Is it a screw, handgrip, the wheel, spokes, chain, or maybe the seat? You really don't know. Therefore, if you were a manufacturer who was considering copying this bike, do you think you would want to spend a significant amount of money on molds, warehousing, production, and other manufacturing costs when a patent can be issued any day. You don't know which item is patent pending, and you don't know what day that patent pending will turn into a patent.

A patent application in process is made public 18 months after the application date. Take advantage of those 18 months to market and test market!

On the other hand, no one has any legal recourse until a patent is issued. That means anyone can copy your product with no penalty during the patent pending stage. They don't have to pay you a royalty. This happens quite often, unfortunately. However, your chances of staving off copycats are better with a patent pending status than without.

Don't try to scare imitators away from your product by claiming that you have a patent or a patent pending if you don't. Misrepresenting your product is a criminal offense. Spend the money to actually apply, or you may have to pay criminal fines.

Getting Your Patent

After months (perhaps years) of waiting, you finally receive your patent. You breathe a huge sigh of relief and feel the urge to sit back and relax. Not so fast. Although getting a patent is a very big step, it is still only the first step in what can be a very long journey to making money from your invention. You should be prepared for the unhappy discovery that the end of the line for your idea may turn up well before you make money from it.

Even if you get your product produced, your patent isn't going to make any money until your product is sold. And even major corporations that do massive market studies hit clinkers all the time. Think of the Edsel. On the other hand, an idea so seemingly stupid that you'd think it was somebody's idea of a silly joke can make millions. Don't you wish you'd thought of the Pet Rock?

Face it; all a patent does is give you a right to prevent other people from making, using, or selling your patented product. You still have to produce it, market it, and sell it. Your patent doesn't help you accomplish any of those tasks. (However, the chapters in Part IV offer advice on all aspects of commercializing your invention.)

All this isn't to say that your patent isn't valuable. It is. You've taken the first step toward making money by protecting your property. You've also just gained a whole lot of credibility with retailers, wholesalers, and potential financial backers, who'd probably run the other way if you didn't have this piece of legal protection. Your patent's so valuable, in fact, that the moment your patent is granted, add the word *patented* or the patent number to your product. From a legal standpoint, if you don't indicate on the product that it's patented, you may not be able to recover damages from an infringer. (Of course, if someone is told that you have a patent and continues to infringe upon it, you have the legal right to recover damages.)

When a patent is issued, anyone interested, including your competitors, can look up the patent number and see an actual copy of your patent application, which, of course, includes your drawings or photographs and the claims you made as to your invention's unique qualities. Competitors may then try to work around your patent claims to produce a copycat product.

From this point on, be vigilant about protecting and maintaining your patent. It's your responsibility and no one else's to do so. The U.S. Patent Office issues the patents but it's the inventor's job to enforce them. (Chapter 5 is all about protecting and maintaining your patent, so check it out.)

Chapter 5

Maintaining and Defending Your Patent

*J*ust like your home, a patent is a real piece of property. You have to tend to its upkeep and protect it from squatters and violators. And just as the bank that holds your mortgage doesn't pay for your homeowners insurance, the U.S. Patent Office doesn't enforce your patent. You must enforce your own patent or else hire a representative, attorney, or agent who can.

In this chapter, I fill you in on how to keep your patent current *and* how to keep it yours by defending it if need be.

Keeping Current by Paying Your Fees

Don't think that the application and issuance fees for your patent are all you have to pay Uncle Sam. If you filed a utility patent application on or after December 12, 1980, you must pay maintenance fees in order to keep your patent valid.

These fees, which are levied only on utility patents, are due 3½, 7½, and 11½ years from the date the patent was granted. The U.S. Patent and Trademark Office (USPTO) accepts your money for a six-month period preceding each due date; if you miss the due date, you have a six-month grace period after your due date during which you can pay your maintenance fee along with a penalty. So, basically, you have a whole year to pay your fees — even the most absentminded inventor should be able to make that. If you do happen to miss the one-year window, you can pay a rather hefty penalty along with your maintenance fee to have the patent reinstated. The USPTO doesn't send you a bill stating it's due, so be sure to keep good records. Table 5-1 lists the various maintenance fees, along with possible penalty payments, giving both the standard amount due and the small entity amount due. (A *small entity* is an individual or a company with fewer than 500 employees. Chances are, you fall into this category.)

Table 5-1	Patent Maintenance Fees	
Maintenance and Penalty Fees	*Standard Amount Due*	*Small Entity Amount Due (If Applicable)*
3½ year maintenance fee	$910	$455
7½ year maintenance fee	$2,090	$1,045
11½ year maintenance fee	$3,220	$1,610
3½ year late payment penalty (within 6 months)	$130	$65
7½ year late payment penalty (within 6 months)	$130	$65
11½ year late payment penalty (within 6 months)	$130	$65
Penalty after expiration (unavoidable late payment)	$700	$700 (no small entity discount)
Penalty after expiration (unintentional late payment)	$1,640	$1,640 (no small entity discount)

The USPTO doesn't send you a bill when your maintenance fees are due. If you don't pay your maintenance fee on time, your patent may become public domain, making it up for grabs for anyone to use without paying you a royalty. However, even though the USPTO doesn't send you a bill before the maintenance fee is due, they do try to remind you of your obligation by sending you a late fee notice and to let you know that you can still pay the fee along with the penalty. So be sure to inform the USPTO of any address changes. You can do this through a form available on the Web site (www.uspto.gov). Another reason to keep your address current with the USPTO is that on several occasions, I've had companies contact me who were interested in licensing inventors' patents, only to find out that the inventor couldn't be located.

As you can see from Table 5-1, the fees go up on a sliding scale over time and can get quite expensive for the independent inventor. If your invention isn't making money, consider letting your patent lapse.

Valuing Your Patent

Patents, trademarks, copyrights, and so on are often referred to as *intellectual property*. And like any other property, intellectual property has intrinsic value. Certainly your patent is valuable to you, mainly because you hope that it will make your fortune. If you're paying maintenance fees (see the "Keeping Current by Paying Your Fees" section) and defending your patent in a courtroom, you want to be sure that the money you lay out is well spent.

Inventor Thomas Edison understood that his intellectual property represented his most valuable economic asset, and if managed properly, it could benefit both society and his own financial bottom line. Do everything you can to protect and manage your own intellectual property, and you may see the same results.

Taking a businesslike view

Businesses often compare the value of intellectual property to that of the goodwill a company builds up with its customers and suppliers throughout its operation. Setting a value to a patent is actually quite a bit easier than figuring out how much a customer's good opinion of a business is worth monetarily.

To evaluate a patent's worth, look at actual sales numbers if the product is on the market. If it's not on the market, estimate market share, make projections of the potential market share you plan to capture through growth, consider the competition, look at the overall industry, and translate that to a dollar amount. How defendable the patent is — how well the application and claims are written — also affects the value.

A patent can provide financial security even if you don't manufacture the product. The inventor holding the patent can *license* it and earn royalties. (Flip to Chapter 20 for more on licensing.)

Assigning your patent

If you work for a company whose business involves developing new products, you probably have an agreement with your employer to assign your patents to the company. An *assignment* is a legal document that the law recognizes as a transfer of ownership.

Assignments are pretty standard in such operations — after all, the company's paying you specifically to discover new products and/or processes. And keep in mind that the company assumes the risk by paying you whether or not you develop a patentable product, as well as paying overhead costs.

As the inventor, your name goes on the patent, but you give your patent rights to the company. Sometimes these inventor-employer agreements involve sharing the patent. For example, you assign the company 80 percent of the rights to your invention and retain a 20 percent interest. These arrangements are more common in situations with a financial backer who wants a share of the patent rights in return for his or her money. (Chapter 10 has more about assigning rights.)

Record the assignment of your patent to another party with the USPTO as soon after you reach the agreement as possible. If the person or company you assign your patent to transfers the patent to a third party and that second assignment is registered with the USPTO before the original assignment, the second assignment is the one the USPTO recognizes.

You can assign your patent to someone else before you apply for the patent itself and send the patent application and the assignment to the USPTO at the same time. However, I recommend waiting until you have the patent application serial number so that you can include the correct application patent number on the assignment form.

Licensing your patent

Most inventors don't have all the skills they need to undertake their own production, marketing, sales, and distribution. Instead, they try to license their patents to companies who have the resources to make inventions profitable. In a *licensing agreement,* you give permission to someone else (a company or an individual) to manufacture, market, or distribute your product in return for a set amount of money or for a *royalty* — a percentage of the proceeds. (Chapter 20 explores licensing in more depth.)

Defending Your Patent Against Infringement

If you're successful at marketing your patented product, it's only a matter of time before you end up in court defending it. You may not want to hear that, but frankly, defending your patent is sometimes unavoidable. Intellectual property litigation is becoming more and more common, especially among high-tech products and companies.

Infringement of a patent in the U.S. is the unauthorized production, use, or sale of a patented invention. Infringement can also occur when a product made by a process patented in the United States is imported into this country from abroad. Patent infringement is a federal offense, so if you sue someone, you must file in federal court.

Generally, you first ask for an *injunction* — a court order to stop the infringement. You may also sue for the cost of damages due to the infringement. Under U.S. patent law, if you win an infringement suit against a willful infringer, you can collect up to triple damages.

Probably the first thing the defendant is going to do is question the validity of your patent. The judge decides this question based upon certain factual inquiries. This is where the money you spent on a good patent attorney pays off. It also pays to hire a good trial lawyer when you have to go to court.

Patent infringement is determined primarily by the language of the claims section of your patent. Make the claims for your invention as clear and thorough and far reaching as possible. You want the claims section of your patent application to describe your product thoroughly, so if someone begins selling a similar product, that product or potential deviation is described in the claims section. If the defendant's product doesn't include each and every part recited in the claim, there's no infringement.

The defendant may also claim that her product is uniquely different or that your patent should have never been issued in the first place. You may think that if the USPTO granted you a patent in the first place, you're in the clear. Unfortunately, that isn't always the case. A couple situations in which a granted patent may not be valid are:

- ✔ **The patent application was filed more than one year after public disclosure of the work on the patent.** For example, if you, as the inventor, and your invention are featured in a newspaper article in March 2003, but you don't file your patent application until April 2004, you may be legally stripped of your patent rights.

- ✔ **The patent holder turns out not to be the first inventor.** More often than you think, two or more people come up with the same patentable idea at nearly the same time. One inventor may file for and be granted a patent, but the USPTO later finds proof that an inventor who filed later actually came up with the patentable item first. First come, first served doesn't work with the USPTO; you have to be the first inventor.

International patent law is different. In other countries, whoever applies for the patent first is issued the patent and gets to keep it.

Believe it or not, the U.S. government can use your patented invention without your permission. Uncle Sam can use any patented product. You, as the inventor, are entitled to compensation, but you can't stop the use.

Insuring Your Patent

Defending your patent in court is costly. The average cost of patent litigation through trial ranges from $500,000 to $2,500,000 or even higher if a high-profile company is involved. A patent litigator usually charges $250 to $500 per hour. If you're defending your patent on foreign soil, you have to add in additional costs for travel and interpreters.

Then you have the hidden costs of litigation: If you're in the courtroom, you're not attending to business, so your business is open to a variety of problems. You and your family come under unaccustomed stress. You may also be in the center of a large or small media storm, which brings a whole new level of stress to you, your business, and your family.

In a patent infringement case, an independent inventor or smaller start-up company stands a great risk of being overwhelmed by a bigger, wealthier company. Fortunately, patent insurance can help level the playing field — or the scales of justice as the case may be. If you're a smaller inventor going up against one of the big boys and you don't have patent insurance, you're stuck looking for a lawyer to represent you on a contingency basis, which means the lawyer gets paid only if you win. That's not a likely scenario.

I explore the two types of patent insurance — offensive and defensive — in this section.

Offensive patent insurance

Offensive patent insurance, also called *patent enforcement insurance,* protects you, the patent holder, against any losses you may suffer as a result of someone infringing upon your patent.

Offensive insurance is like putting your patent behind a chain-link fence guarded by a big pit bull, an armed guard, *and* an alarm system.

Like health insurance, offensive patent insurance often has a copay, though instead of $25, it's more like 25 percent of the cost of the defense. Premiums are generally around $5,000 per year, and for that you get legal expertise should you need it, up to a $500,000 cap. Protecting your patent is pricey no matter which way you go. But if you're making (or expect to make) a bundle with your invention, you're quite likely to attract an infringer or two, and having experienced patent attorneys at your beck and call is a great comfort should that happen.

Before issuing a policy to you, the insurance company is going to seek out a professional legal opinion from an independent patent attorney regarding the overall validity of your patent. The company wants to make sure that you have a good, strong, enforceable patent with valid patent claims. The issuing insurance company looks at your company's competitors, the market for your product, and current patent cases and products in that market. They also investigate any previous attempts that you have made to keep infringers away and whether you've been aggressive in doing so. They want to make sure you've done everything you can to enforce your patent and keep it valid.

For example, if a company tried to infringe on your patent, the insurance company wants to make sure that you didn't simply sit on the sidelines, but had your attorney send them a cease-and-desist letter.

The major advantages of patent enforcement insurance include the following:

- ✔ Gives you the strongest tool to protect your patent and go after infringers
- ✔ Reassures potential investors in your company
- ✔ Staves off the threat of crushing legal expenses fighting future infringement lawsuits

The major disadvantages of patent enforcement insurance are:

- ✔ Premiums represent money you can spend marketing your product
- ✔ Premiums are generally not based on actual legal expenses but on the number of patents covered
- ✔ Policies don't cover your liability for damages

Don't let insurance coverage give you a false sense of security and lead you to litigate just because you can. Going to court may bring you negative publicity, and don't forget that you can lose!

Defensive patent insurance

Infringement defense insurance protects you in the event that you're accused of infringing on someone else's patent. This type of policy is relatively new — policies first started being written around 1995.

Your search for existing patents may have been as thorough and diligent as possible. However, patent applications are kept under wraps for 18 months after they're filed, so if your search was during these 18 months, you may unwittingly have applied for a patent on someone else's invention. (After the 18 months, or after the patent is issued, the application becomes public.)

If you're a smallish fish in a market with much bigger sharks, infringement defense insurance can protect you should one of those sharks go after you and accuse you of patent infringement. Without liability insurance, legal fees may bankrupt you and the shark wins by forcing you out of the pond.

Defensive patent infringement policies usually cover both damages and defense costs, within limits. You may be able to get a less expensive policy that covers only the legal costs but not the damages involved. Premiums typically run around 2 to 5 percent of the insured amount (for instance $20,000 to $50,000 per $1 million in coverage) and copayments typically range from 15 to 25 percent.

As with a life insurance policy, your company undergoes a complete checkup before you're granted a policy. The insurer investigates patents for products similar to yours and has your product checked by an independent party before granting you a policy. The company checks out how you've handled patent matters in the past to see if you're aggressive in protecting your intellectual property rights or simply sit on the sideline. The insurer also reviews your overall business practice to see if you're strong in the market and are willing to seek outside legal and patent assistance, as well as other consultants in the new product development arena, before they make a commitment.

The best policy for you in this case is to fully investigate the market to make sure you're not infringing on someone else's patent before you spend a lot of time and money in bringing your product to market.

Part II
Securing Other Intellectual Property

The 5th Wave   By Rich Tennant

Bob Muhar Re-Invents Himself

Trademark Nickname: "Shady-M"

Copyrighted Logo

Slogan: "I'm Bob Muhar, Ready When You Are."

In this part . . .

This part gives you the lowdown on protecting your intellectual property — the fruit of your creation.

If you need to know the difference between a trademark and a trade secret, Chapter 6 is the place to go. Copyrights to protect the written word are covered in Chapter 7, and Chapter 8 reveals how to protect yourself by keeping things confidential.

Chapter 6

Trademarks and Trade Secrets

*I*n this chapter, I talk about giving a trademark or service mark to your product or company, how to apply for one, how much it costs, and what's involved in the application process. I also discuss how to get consumers to be more aware of your company and product versus your competitor's. Finally, I talk about how to keep secrets that can give your company an advantage.

What Is a Trademark?

A *trademark* is typically a word, phrase, symbol, or design — or a combination of words, phrases, symbols, or designs — that identifies and distinguishes your goods from those of others. A trademark gives you the right to keep others from using your identification. If you own a trademark, it is considered your *intellectual property*. It gives you legal right to own your company or product's name, as well as design, symbol, or combo of words. If you use a trademark owned by anyone else, you can be sued.

Trademarks and trade logos

A trade logo or symbol is simply the picture or mark that consumers recognize as associated with a brand name. For example, McDonald's name is trademarked, and the company's trade logo is the yellow golden arches. Nike is trademarked, and its logo is the "swoosh."

Trademarks may also consist of colors, smells, and sounds. For example, next time you turn on your computer, listen for Microsoft's trademarked sound during your boot-up. Or next time you see an Intel commercial on TV, listen for its trademarked chime at the end of the commercial. A trademarked smell is the distinctive scent of a specific perfume such as Giorgio, Polo, or Shalimar. Everyone knows the distinctive color of McDonald's golden arches. Owens Corning owns the trademark on the color pink for home insulation.

A trademark or brand name helps others to identify your company or product. People purchase products based on the name or trademark of a product. For example: Coke, Motorola, Ford, McDonalds, Rolex, Starbucks, Evian, and Levi's. A successful brand or trademark planted in the consumer's mind states that no other product is quite like yours.

A *service mark* is the same as a trademark, except that it identifies and distinguishes the source of a service rather than a product. For example, Kindercare childcare provides a service; therefore, it owns a service mark instead of a trademark.

Throughout this chapter and this book, the terms *trademark* and *mark* refer to both trademarks and service marks.

Federal versus State Trademarks

In the U.S., you have to choose whether you want to obtain a state trademark or a federal one. You can obtain a federal trademark if you've used your mark in interstate commerce. *Interstate commerce* is generally defined as conducting business between two or more states. However, you don't have to physically conduct business in two or more states. For example, if you advertise in a trade journal that's distributed outside your state or if you have a company Web site, you probably satisfy the interstate requirement for federal trademark registration.

Generally, an individual state trademark is cheaper than a federal trademark; however, as you may expect, a state trademark is only good in one state and isn't recognized in most cases at a federal or national level. For example, if you start a daycare center in Florida and obtain a service mark there, that service mark is only good in Florida. Assume that another individual, who lives in Idaho and is assuming room for growth and potential franchising, applies for a federal trademark for the same name. The Idaho applicant didn't know anything about the individual owning a state trademark in Florida. When the Idaho applicant is going through the trademark process, the trademark notice is published in the *Gazette* (for more on this publication see the "Drawing your mark" section later in the chapter). If the individual in Florida didn't review and notice the trademark being applied for and file a petition, the Idaho individual would be issued a federal trademark. In most cases, a federal trademark will supercede a state trademark.

Go ahead and assume that your product or service is going to expand. Spend a few extra dollars and obtain a federal trademark or service mark that's good nationwide.

Owning a federal trademark rather than a state one gives you several advantages:

✔ It gives a constructive notice to the public of your claim of ownership of the mark as well as a legal presumption of your ownership of the mark.

✔ It allows you the exclusive right to use the mark nationwide on or in connection with the goods or services listed in the registration and also gives you the permission to bring an action concerning the mark in federal court.

✔ It gives you the right to use the U.S. registration as a basis to obtain trademarks in foreign countries.

✔ It also gives you the right to file the U.S. registration with the U.S. Customs Service to prevent importation of infringing foreign goods.

A tale of two (burger) kings

Innovators frequently ask, "Do I have to register my trademark?" You can establish rights in a mark based on legitimate use of the mark. Consider, for example, the Burger King mark. Obviously, Burger King Corporation has registered their mark on the Principal Register of the U.S. Trademark Office and has exclusive rights to use and franchise their mark. Interestingly, a fast food restaurant in Florida also operates under the Burger King mark. This restaurant was established before Burger King Corporation but didn't register their mark on the Principal Register, because they operated exclusively in Florida. As a result, they were allowed to continue use of the Burger King trademark even though Burger King Corporation obtained federal registration of the Burger King mark and didn't franchise the mark to the solely owned restaurant.

You may also register a mark even if you haven't begun to use it in interstate commerce. Such a registration requires an *intent-to-use* trademark application (discussed in the "Filing an Intent-to-Use Application" section later in this chapter), which also requires you to prove use of your mark within a statutory deadline. Speak with a trademark attorney to find out more about intent-to-use registrations.

Using the Trademark and Service Mark Symbols

When you claim rights to a mark, you may use the ™ *(trademark)* or ˢᴹ *(service mark)* designation to alert the public to your claim, regardless of whether you've filed an application with the United State Patent and Trademark Office (USPTO). However, you may use the federal registration symbol ® (meaning registered) only after the USPTO actually registers a mark and not while an application is pending. When your mark is still pending, never use the ®, because it's against the law. You can either use ™ or ˢᴹ to put others on notice that you're in the process of applying for a trade or service mark.

Also, you may use the registration symbol with the mark only on or in connection with the goods and/or services listed in the federal trademark registration. This list states each individual category in which you can register your trademark or service mark. You can obtain your trademark in several classes but must pay a fee for each additional class.

Understanding the Basics for Filing a Federal Trademark Application

If you file a trademark application, it must include the following elements:

- ✔ The name of the applicant
- ✔ A name and address for correspondence
- ✔ A clear drawing of the mark
- ✔ A listing of the goods or services
- ✔ The filing fee for at least one class of goods or services

Your application must also include a sworn statement, usually in the form of a declaration, that the mark is in use in commerce, listing the date of first use of the mark anywhere and the date of first use of the mark in commerce. A properly worded declaration is included in the USPTO standard application form. You or your authorized representative must sign the statement. The application should include a specimen showing use of the mark in commerce.

If your application doesn't meet these requirements, the USPTO will return the application papers and refund any fees submitted.

In this section, I discuss the ins and outs of applying for a federal trademark.

Having a basis for your application

Before you can get very far in the application process, you must have a *basis for filing*. Most applicants base their application on their current use of the mark in commerce, or their intent to use their mark in commerce in the future. (For more on intent-to-use applications, see the section, "Filing an Intent-to-Use Application" later in this chapter.)

Although not as common, you may also base your application on international agreements. Under certain international agreements, you may file in the U.S. based on a foreign application or on a registration in your country of origin (if you qualify).

Many times, in the course of talking with your intellectual property attorney and applying for a trademark or service mark, you'll hear the phrase "to use your mark in trade or commerce." For the purpose of obtaining federal registration, *commerce* means all commerce that the U.S. Congress may lawfully regulate; for example, interstate commerce or commerce between the U.S. and another country. *Use in commerce* must be a bona fide use of the mark in the ordinary course of trade and not use simply made to reserve rights in the mark. Generally, acceptable uses are as follows:

- **For goods:** The mark must appear on the goods, the container for the goods, or displays associated with the goods at the point of sale, and the goods must be sold or transported in commerce.

- **For services:** The mark must be used or displayed in the sale or advertising of the services, and the services must be rendered in commerce.

If your application is based upon use in commerce, you must already be using the mark in commerce or in connection with all the goods and/or services listed. If it's based upon an intent-to-use and/or a foreign application or registration, you must have a bona fide intention to use the mark in commerce on or in connection with all the listed goods and/or services.

Filing electronically

There are specific formats for filing trademark applications. For example, you must provide a scanned JPG image in a specific format designated the by USPTO. Using the Trademark Electronic Application System (TEAS) available at www.uspto.gov/teas/index.html, you can file your application directly over the Internet. Features of electronic filing include:

- ✔ **Online help:** Hyperlinks provide help sections for each of the application fields.

- ✔ **Validation function:** This helps you avoid the possible omission of important information.

- ✔ **Immediate reply:** The USPTO immediately issues an initial filing receipt via e-mail, which contains the assigned application, serial number, and a summary of the submission. TEAS information is available 24 hours a day, seven days a week (except 11 p.m. Saturday to 6 a.m. Sunday), so receipt of a filing date is possible up until midnight EST.

If you don't have Internet access, you can access TEAS at any Patent and Trademark Depository Library (PTDL) throughout the U.S. Many public libraries also provide Internet access. The quickest way to locate your nearest PTDL is to look on the USPTO's Web site.

If you transmit your application over the Internet, the filing date is the date the transmission reaches the USPTO server. At the time of filing, an e-mail summary including a serial number is sent to you. You won't receive a paper filing receipt. If through a later review, the USPTO determines that your application didn't include the required necessary information, it will cancel the serial number and filing date, return the application, and refund the filing fee. Because trademarks are awarded to the first person to apply for one, you need to be sure to follow through with your paperwork whether it's electronic or through the mail.

Filing via snail mail

Although the USPTO prefers that you file your trademark or service mark application electronically using TEAS (because filing electronically is easier, more efficient, and quicker), you may either mail or hand deliver a paper application to the USPTO.

To obtain a printed form, you can call the USPTO's automated telephone line, at 703-308-9000 or 800-786-9199. The mailing address to file a new application via mail is: Commissioner for Trademarks, 2900 Crystal Drive, Arlington, VA 22202-3514.

Note: You may *not* fax your application to the USPTO.

If you file a paper application and it meets the minimum filing requirements, the USPTO will assign a serial number and send a filing receipt. You should review this receipt for accuracy, and notify the USPTO of any errors immediately, following the directions on the receipt.

Owning the trademark

The application must be filed in the name of the owner of the mark. The owner of the mark is the person or entity controlling the nature and quality of the goods identified by the mark and/or the services rendered in connection with the mark. The owner of a trademark may be an individual, corporation, partnership, or other type of legal entity.

You don't have to be a U.S. citizen to be the trademark owner.

Providing correspondence info for the USPTO

The USPTO must have a name and address for correspondence concerning the application. That contact information may be your own or your legal representative's.

You should always keep your mailing address up-to-date with the USPTO. If your address changes at any time during the application process, you must notify them in writing. At the top of the request, list your name or the applicant's name, mark, and the application serial number. Mail the change of address to: Commissioner for Trademarks, 2900 Crystal Drive, Arlington, VA 22202-3513.

Legal counsel, again?

You, as the inventor or small-business person, have the right to file your own trademark or service mark application. However, if you prepare and submit your own application, you must comply with all requirements of the trademark statute and rules that are listed on the USPTO's Web site. If you choose to appoint an attorney to represent your interests before the USPTO, the USPTO will correspond with your attorney only instead of you. The USPTO cannot help you select an attorney.

Drawing your mark

Every application must include a clear drawing of the mark you want to register. After receiving your drawing, the USPTO files the mark in the USPTO search records and prints the mark in the *Official Gazette* and on the registration certificate. The *Official Gazette* is the USPTO's office booklet in which they publish patents, trademarks, or service marks. This document is published weekly and is also available on the USPTO's Web site. The *Gazette* is officially required to publish all trademarks after they're approved. This way, anyone looking through it can see whether they have one that's similar and can oppose the mark being issued.

TEAS generates a proper drawing for you, based upon the information you enter and image you scan in. If you're preparing the drawing page yourself (rather than hiring a graphic artist to prepare it for you), use matte, white, 8½-x-11-inch paper and include the following elements at the top of the page:

- ✔ Applicant's name
- ✔ Correspondence address
- ✔ Listing of goods and/or services
- ✔ Dates of use (if already using the mark in commerce); if not already in use, you must use the wording "Intent to Use"

The representation of the mark must then appear below the heading, in the middle of the page, in the proper format for either a typed drawing or a stylized or special form drawing. After you file, you can't make a material change to your mark. In other words, you can't change how the mark looks. After you submit your papers, it's done.

A typed drawing

To apply to register a mark comprised of words, letters, and/or numbers, with no particular stylization or design element included in the mark, you should select *the typed drawing format;* something that can be typed out on a typewriter or computer keyboard. "Big Mac" and "Velcro" are examples of trademarks that don't utilize any special drawing or design.

For this format, the mark must be typed in all capital letters, as in the following example:

NOTE: Actual size would be 8½ x 11 inches (21.6 x 27.9 centimeters)

Applicant's Name: Upstate Medical Group

Correspondence Address: 200 Maple Street, Nowhereville, FL 696969

Goods and Services: Medical supplies, namely online magazine in the field of business management

Date of First Use: January 15, 1995

Date of First Use in Commerce: May 15, 1995

The Mark: "BIRD'S MEDICAL RESPIRATORY MANAGER"

A "Stylized or special form" drawing

Stylized drawing

If the particular style of lettering is important or the mark includes a design or logo, you must select the stylized or special form drawing format. The drawing page should show a black-and-white image of the mark, no larger than 4 x 4 inches.

Don't submit a drawing with color or gray shading, even if the mark is used in color; instead, specify any color designations in a description of the mark within the body of the application. For example: "The mark consists of a bird with a blue body and red wings."

Be sure to include this description within the body of the application and not on the drawing page. Also, don't submit a drawing that combines typed matter and special format.

See Figure 6-1 for an example of a stylized drawing.

Listing goods and services

You must list the specific goods and/or services for which you're seeking registration, regardless of the basis for the application (see "Having a basis for your application" earlier in this chapter). When specifying the goods and/or services, use clear, concise terms — common commercial names and language that the general public easily understands. For example, if you have a software product, place it in the category where software applies. If you have a new coffeepot, place it in the category for small appliances.

Figure 6-1:
This stylized
drawing
should be
familiar!

If you don't list any recognizable goods or services, the USPTO will return your application and refund your fee. You must check a specific category from the *International Schedule of Classes of Goods and Services* available at `www.uspto.gov/web/offices/tac/doc/basic/international.htm`. If you leave the space blank for what category your trademark or service mark is to be registered in, your application is sent back to you.

Keep in mind that the terms in the classification listing of goods and services in the *International Schedule of Classes of Goods and Services* are generally too broad and shouldn't be used alone as an identification; they're more of a starting point. Also, an international class number alone is never an acceptable listing. For a listing of acceptable wording for goods and services, see the USPTO's *Acceptable Identification of Goods and Services Manual*, at `www.uspto.gov/web/offices/tac/doc/gsmanual`.

Including a specimen

A *specimen* is an actual example of how you're using the mark in commerce on or in connection with the identified goods and/or services. This isn't the same as the drawing of the mark, which merely represents what you're claiming as the mark. The USPTO wants a real sample of what you are applying for a trademark or service mark on. For example, you can send in a copy of your letterhead, envelopes, bills, manuals, brochures with your trademark displayed. It's not necessary to send your product.

Knowing what the USPTO will accept

The proper specimen for a mark used on goods shows the mark on the actual goods or the packaging for the goods. You may submit a tag or label for the goods, a container for the goods, a display associated with the goods, or a photograph of the goods that shows use of the mark on the goods. Don't submit the actual product.

Invoices, announcements, order forms, bills of lading, leaflets, brochures, publicity releases, letterhead, and business cards generally are *not* acceptable specimens for goods.

Filing your specimen electronically or by mail

If you want to file the specimen electronically, you must attach an image of your specimen in GIF or JPEG format. In order to show the context in which the mark is used, the image should include as much of the label or advertisement as possible.

When you file a paper application, the specimen submitted with the application must be flat and no larger than 8½ x 11 inches. If you submit a larger specimen, the USPTO will create a facsimile of the specimen, insert it in the *application file wrapper* (a record of all correspondence between you and the USPTO), and destroy the original submission. However, specimens consisting of videotapes, audiotapes, CDs, or computer diskettes are acceptable for marks, such as sound marks, that cannot be transmitted any other way.

Paying to play — filing fees

As of January 1, 2004, the fee for filing a trademark application is $335 per class of goods/services. Additionally, the fee for amending an existing application to add an additional class or classes of goods/services will be $335 per class, for classes added on or after January 1, 2004.

Fee increases, when necessary, usually take effect on October 1 of any given year. Please call 1-800-PT0-9199 for up-to-date fee information.

Here are some points concerning fees to keep in mind:

✓ **Filing fees for applications must be paid in U.S. currency.**

The USPTO accepts payment by credit card, check, money order, or through an existing USPTO deposit account.

Personal, business, and certified checks are accepted and should be made payable to "Director of the USPTO."

✓ **A form for authorizing charges to a credit card can be accessed through all TEAS forms.**

If you're filing on paper, you can download the form for authorizing credit card charges from the USPTO Web site at www.uspto.gov/web/forms/2038.pdf.

For a complete listing of all trademark processing and service fees, go to www.uspto.gov/web/offices/ac/qs/ope/fee2003oct01.htm.

Note: After the application meets the minimum filing requirements and is given a filing date, the application filing fee cannot be refunded.

Filing an Intent-to-Use Application

If you haven't yet used your trademark, but plan to do so in the future, you may file an *intent-to-use application* based upon a good faith or bona fide intention to use the mark in commerce.

Building a brand with a trademark

The essence of branding is to build a name in the minds of potential consumers. The power of your trademark in branding a name lies in the ability to influence potential consumers in their purchasing toward your product. If a brand name is listed on a package, it is interesting and informative; however, if it sticks in the consumer's mind, generally a larger percentage of the market share will be gained.

A new brand name must generate positive publicity or it won't survive in the market. If you want to be successful in influencing the minds of potential consumers with your invention, build a brand that no one else has in the minds of consumers.

How about a few examples? Look at the word "overnight." In the mind of consumers, Federal Express was successful by being the first overnight air delivery service. They created the word "overnight" in the minds of their potential consumers. When you think of having a package delivered overnight — whom do you think of? Most likely FedEx. If we need a facial tissue, we automatically think of the trademark "Kleenex."

Kleenex is by far the leading brand of tissue. Even if a person looks across the room and sees a box of Scott facial tissues, they may ask, "May I have a Kleenex?" What happens if you need something copied? Do you ever say, "I need to go to the Minolta or Hewlett Packard machine?" You most likely say, "I am going to the Xerox machine." This is the power of trademark and brand recognition. It is implanted in the minds of consumers.

There is a danger, however. If the mark becomes too well known and commonly used to the point that it becomes the name of the product, it has become generic, and you have lost your mark because, once generic, anyone can use it to name the product. Examples include aspirin, nylon, and escalator. Did you know that they used to be registered trademarks? Your trademark rights can be maintained only through proper use (as an adjective) and rigid enforcement when someone uses your mark incorrectly or as an infringement. Consult your attorney for assistance.

An intent-to-use application must include a sworn statement, usually in the form of a declaration, that you have a bona fide intention to use the mark in commerce. You can find a properly worded declaration in the USPTO standard application form. The applicant or a person authorized to sign on behalf of the applicant must sign the statement.

If you file based on intent to use, you must begin actual use of the mark in commerce before the USPTO will register the mark. That is, after filing an application based on intent to use, you must later file another form, *Allegation of Use*, to establish that you've begun using the mark.

Trade Secrets — Shhhhhhhh!

A *trade secret* is basically information that you want to protect and keep secret to give yourself an advantage over your competitors. Whether this information is a design, process, formula, composition, or technique, if it gives your company an advantage over another company, it can be considered a trade secret.

Often your trade secrets embody patentable information. You must decide whether you want to obtain the patent and have time-limited protection or to take the steps, as mentioned later, to keep it for an unlimited time as a trade secret. Much depends upon the ease with which your competitors can determine the secret. For example, if the secret is in a mechanical device that you sell and can be easily disassembled to reveal the secret, you should probably opt to get the patent. If determining the secret from the product is difficult, then the trade secret route may be the best to follow. There are no hard and fast rules about trade secret protection. It depends upon your imagination and willingness to be diligent in setting up the protection and enforcing your rights.

Looking at examples of trade secrets

Some of the common trade secrets are recipes and processes, such as the formulas for food, soft drinks, cosmetics, and chemicals. One common process that is a trade secret is the process for making Coca-Cola. The name Coca-Cola is a registered federal trademark. Coca-Cola isn't patented. If it were, we would all be able to find out the formula because a patent is public information. The process of making cola was at one time patented; however, that patent expired years ago. Now, several different brands of cola soft drinks are on the market. However, the formula for Coca-Cola is a trade secret. If you look on the back of a Coke can, the ingredients are listed. The listing of these ingredients is required by the Food and Drug Administration; but we don't know how much of what ingredient to put into making this product, nor the method of combining the ingredients in order to obtain a specific taste.

One of my favorite examples of a trade secret is KFC's secret recipe for their chicken. Such a recipe isn't shared with customers because it is a valuable asset for the company. If KFC printed their secret recipe on every box of chicken, they would most likely forfeit their trade secret rights to the general public and it would be fair game for others to make their chicken.

Trade secrets don't always include complete recipes. Some trade secrets may simply include names. For example, a friend of mine went to a chocolate store one day to buy some goodies. When he entered the store, he noticed that the chocolates weren't listed by names. Rather, they were listed by numbers. When he asked the clerk why this was the case, she told him that if the names of the chocolates were disclosed to their customers, their customers would find the recipes on the Internet and make the chocolates at home rather than buy them at the store.

Business methods and techniques can be considered as trade secrets. This may include customer mailing lists, pricing and distribution techniques, and warehousing turnover, which allow a business a competitive edge.

Pondering the pros and cons of trade secrets

A trade secret has several positives, including:

- ✔ **A trade secret doesn't have the same time duration or constraints as a patent, which expires after a certain amount of time.** A trade secret can remain perpetually protected, as long as it remains a secret.

- ✔ **The cost of a trade secret is minimal.** You don't have to go through the cost of patenting.

- ✔ **A trade secret is an immediate form of legal protection.** You don't have to wait in line at the USPTO to find out if you or your company is issued one! Declaring a product a trade secret is an internal process, something you take care of with your attorney. Employees exposed to the info or method need to have written agreements as mentioned.

- ✔ **Also, when compared to a patent, a trade secret is hard to work around, because people don't know what your secret is anyway.**

However, trade secrets do have some disadvantages.

- ✔ **Competitors conduct as much reverse engineering as they can, in order to obtain a leading edge.** No matter how hard a company may try to keep a trade secret, it can be very difficult. With the use of very sophisticated tools that are now available, including scanners, spectrophotometers, and microscopes, many things can be copied no matter how sophisticated they are.

- ✔ **Someone else who legitimately derives your trade secret can patent a trade secret.** For example, suppose you invented a formula for a new hand lotion and kept it a secret. Then, by mere coincidence, another person you've never seen, met with, or spoken to about your product develops the exact same thing and then patents it. This person now has the right to sue you for patent infringement. (In certain instances you may be able to take advantage of the "prior user defense.")

Protecting your trade secret

Precautions should be made to keep and enforce your trade secrets. If a company is sloppy in keeping its trade secrets, potential court cases may be dismissed. Throughout the years, the courts have developed a series of tests for determining whether the owners of a trade secret have taken necessary precautions in maintaining their trade secret.

Swearing employees to secrecy

Most precautions that you can take to protect trade secrets are common sense things such as having employees sign agreements that they won't disclose trade secrets outside of the business. If your secret needs to be disclosed to third parties, for whatever reason, have them sign an agreement not to disclose the secret to anyone else. These agreements vary widely depending upon the nature of the secrets and their value to the enterprise. Where the secret is in a facility such as a manufacturing plant, put a fence around it to restrict access. Have visitors sign in and be escorted when on the premises.

When an employee is hired, have him sign an *employability contract,* the terms of which include keeping all pertinent business information confidential. If the employee breaks this agreement and discusses confidential information (thus potentially giving or leading to a competitor having an advantage), you have *a breach of contract,* which means that the employee didn't do what he agreed to do in the contract. Large corporations pay millions of dollars to enforce trade secret protection within their companies, as well as within their industry, in order to keep their competitive business advantage. See Chapter 10.

Preventing former employees from spilling the beans

When an employee quits, conduct an exit interview to remind her of her obligation to keep your secrets confidential. At the exit interview, get all your information back and get the keys and badges that you issued to her during employment. Have the departing employee sign a statement that the obligations have been explained and that she understands them. The employee should also acknowledge in writing that she has no company property in her possession.

If a competitor is hiring the employee, write the competitor a letter and tell him that this new hire is under an obligation not to disclose your secrets. Tell the competitor that your ex-employee shouldn't be placed in a position where she must use *your* protected information in the conduct of work for the new employer. By doing this, you place the new employer on notice concerning the prohibitions against the new employee, and you pave the way to enforcing these obligations through a court injunction should the employee be placed in a position that harms you.

To help your employees know what documents include the trade secrets, mark them with a legend that says "CONFIDENTIAL." But you must use some thought and discernment in identifying your trade secrets. Don't mark everything confidential. Courts have said that if everything is marked confidential, then nothing is confidential and you will lose any case you bring on the subject.

Chapter 7

Stopping Copycats with a Copyright

. . . .

In This Chapter

▶ Defining the copyright

▶ Should you copyright your work?

▶ Going over the basics

▶ Getting registered

▶ Transferring copyrights

. . . .

After putting in all the hard work on designing your product, having it packaged, and getting ready to sell it, you need to find out how to legally protect and own the artwork, its instructions, brochures, and maybe the video that goes along with it.

In this chapter, I explain exactly what a copyright is, how you can obtain one, it's advantages, where you'll need one, how to apply, and how long the copyright will protect you.

Obtaining a meaningful copyright is a serious undertaking, which can affect you and your heirs for years to come.

What Is a Copyright?

A *copyright* is a form of protection provided by the laws of the U.S. to the authors of "original works of authorship." These original works include literary composition, drama, musical arrangement, artistic creation, and certain other intellectual works. This protection is available to both published and unpublished works.

The *Copyright Act* established by Congress generally gives the owner of the copyright the exclusive right to do and to authorize others to do the following:

- ✔ To reproduce the work on paper copies or upon phonographic records.
- ✔ To prepare derivative arrangements based upon the work.
- ✔ To distribute copies or phonographic records of the work to the public by sale or other transfer of ownership, or by rental, lease, or lending
- ✔ To perform the work publicly, in the case of literary, musical, dramatic, and choreographic works, pantomimes, and motion pictures and other audiovisual works
- ✔ To display the copyrighted work publicly, in the case of literary, musical, dramatic, and choreographic works, pantomimes, and pictorial, graphic, or sculptural works, including the individual images of a motion picture or other audiovisual work; and in the case of sound recordings, to perform the work publicly by means of a digital audio transmission

In addition, certain authors of works of visual art have the rights of attribution and integrity of the 1976 Copyright Act. For further information, request Circular 40, *Copyright Registration for Works of the Visual Arts*. Contact information is listed in the section "Contacting the Copyright Office," later in this chapter.

Who Can Claim Copyright?

The copyright relating to the work of authorship immediately becomes the property of the author who created the work. Therefore, only the author or those deriving their rights through the author can rightfully claim copyright. (The authors of a joint work are co-owners of the copyright, unless they have an agreement to the contrary.)

Minors may claim copyright, but state laws sometimes regulate the business dealings involving copyrights owned by minors. For information on relevant state laws, consult an attorney.

In the case of works made for hire, the employer and not the employee is considered to be the author. Section 101 of the copyright law defines a "work made for hire" as:

- ✔ A work prepared by an employee within the scope of his or her employment; or
- ✔ A work specially ordered or commissioned for use as

- A contribution to a collective work

- A part of a motion picture or other audiovisual work

- A translation of a supplementary work

- A compilation

- An instructional text

- A test or answer material for a test

- An atlas if the parties expressly agree in a written instrument signed by them, that the work shall be considered a work made for hire

See Chapter 10 on hiring helpers to assist you while keeping control of your copyright.

Mere ownership of a book, manuscript, painting, or any other copy or phonographic record doesn't give the possessor the copyright. The law provides that the transfer of ownership of any material or object that embodies a protected work doesn't of itself convey any rights in the copyright. For example, if you buy a CD with music on it, you own the CD, but you don't own the rights to copy what's on the disc and sell it to others. The artist owns the rights to the music.

Copyright Protection

By now, you may be thinking, "I have a product. It's patented. Why do I need a copyright?" If you're going to bring your product to market and get it packaged, you most likely will want the packaging copyrighted. You may also want a video explaining your product or written literature on the back of the box, or simply your promotional material that you give to suppliers, wholesalers, and distributors. The author or artist owns all these "works" until they're transferred to you. When your product starts making money, the owners of the "work" can (and most often do) sue you for copyright infringement unless you've done your homework. Make sure that you understand who owns what and get the proper forms signed.

In this section, I talk about what a copyright protects and what it doesn't. I also talk about who's the legal owner of the copyright, how to secure yours, and how to keep it. If you're not the owner, I tell you how to get it transferred into your name so that you can use it.

What works are protected? You took the words out of my mouth

Copyright protects "original works of authorship" that are fixed in a tangible form of expression. The fixation need not be directly perceptible so long as it may be communicated with the aid of a machine or device. Copyrightable works include the following categories:

- Literary works
- Musical works, including any accompanying words
- Dramatic works, including any accompanying music
- Pantomimes and choreographic works
- Pictorial, graphic, and sculptural works
- Motion pictures and other audiovisual works
- Sound recordings
- Architectural works

These categories should be viewed broadly. For example, computer programs and most "compilations" may be registered as "literary works"; maps and architectural plans may be registered as "pictorial, graphic, and sculptural works."

What's not protected by copyright

Several categories of material are generally not eligible for federal copyright protection. These include, among others:

- Works that haven't been fixed in a tangible form of expression (for example, choreographic works that haven't been notated or recorded, or improvisational speeches or performances that haven't been written or recorded)
- Titles, names, short phrases, and slogans
- Familiar symbols or designs
- Mere variations of typographic ornamentation, lettering, or coloring
- Mere listings of ingredients or contents, ideas, procedures, methods, systems, processes, concepts, principles, discoveries, or devices, as distinguished from a description, explanation, or illustration
- Works consisting entirely of information that's common property and containing no original authorship (for example: standard calendars, height and weight charts, tape measures and rulers, and lists or tables taken from public documents or other common sources)

Securing copyright protection

The way in which copyright protection is secured is frequently misunderstood. No publication or registration or other action in the Copyright Office is required to secure copyright. There are, however, certain definite advantages to registration. (See the section "Registering Your Copyright" later in this chapter for more information.)

Say that you're an artist. Most artists draw, paint, or design several thousand pictures and art forms during their lifetime. It costs money to register each piece of art, and the artist, like an inventor, doesn't know whether each individual piece of artwork is going to sell. Copyright law basically gives the artist the legal right of ownership on his artwork without actually registering each specific piece. One can automatically place the copyright symbol, ©, on his work of art, as well as his name and the date. This is considered a "poor man's copyright," but it works.

Because you'll be using a copyright to protect the packaging of your product, as well as any written literature regarding your product, I suggest that you spend the extra money and register your "works" with the Copyright Office. The cost is minimal, so simply consider the formal registration as part of finishing up.

Copyright security is automatic!

Copyright is secured automatically when the work is created, and by definition, a work is *created* when fixed in a copy or phonographic record for the first time. *Copies* are material objects from which a work can be read or visually perceived, either directly or with the aid of a machine or device, such as books, manuscripts, sheet music, film, videotape, or microfilm. *Phonographic records* are material objects embodying fixations of sounds (excluding, by statutory definition, motion picture soundtracks), such as cassette tapes, CDs, or LPs. Thus, for example, a song (the work) can be fixed in sheet music (copies), in CDs or cassette tapes (phonographic records), or both.

If a work is prepared over a period of time, the part of the work that is fixed on a particular date constitutes the created work as of that date.

The importance of publication

Publication is no longer the key to obtaining federal copyright, as it was under the Copyright Act of 1909. However, publication remains important to copyright owners from a legal, as well as marketing, standpoint. Getting your work to publication informs others that you're the original author of the material.

The 1976 Copyright Act defines publication as follows:

> "Publication" is the distribution of copies or phonographic records of a work offered to the public by sale or other transfer of ownership, or by

rental, lease, or lending. The offering to distribute copies or phono-graphic records to a group of persons for purposes of further distribu-tion, public performance, or public display constitutes publication.

A public performance or display of a work doesn't of itself constitute publication.

Notice of copyright

The use of the copyright notice is the responsibility of the copyright owner and doesn't require advance permission from, or registration with, the Copyright Office.

The 1976 Copyright Act attempted to decrease the strict consequences of failure to include notice under prior law. It contained provisions that set out specific corrective steps to cure omissions or certain errors in notice. Under these provisions, an applicant had five years after publication to cure omis-sion of notice or certain errors. Although these provisions are technically still in the law, their impact has been limited by the amendment, making notice optional for all works published on and after March 1, 1989. For further infor-mation, request Circular 3, *Copyright Notice*. Contact information is listed in the section "Contacting the Copyright Office," later in this chapter.

In this section, I explain how to format your notice on various types of works.

Notice of copyright on visually perceptible copies

The notice for visually perceptible copies should contain the following three elements:

- ✔ One of the following:

  The symbol ©

  The letter C in a circle

  The word "Copyright"

  The abbreviation "Copr."

- ✔ The year of first publication of the work. In the case of compilations or derivative works incorporating previously published material, the year date of first publication of the compilation or derivative work is suffi-cient. The year date may be omitted where a pictorial, graphic, or sculp-tural work, with accompanying textual matter, if any, is reproduced in or on greeting cards, postcards, stationery, jewelry, dolls, toys, or any useful article

- ✔ The name of the owner of copyright in the work or an abbreviation by which the name can be recognized, or a generally known alternative des-ignation of the owner.

  Example: © 2004 Jane Doe

Notice of copyright on recordings

The © notice is used only on *visually perceptible copies* (ones that we can see). Certain kinds of works — for example, musical, drama, and literary works — may be fixed in an audio recording. Because audio recordings such as audiotapes and phonograph disks are phonographic records and not copies, the © notice isn't used to indicate protection of the underlying musical, drama, or literary work that is recorded. *Sound recordings* are defined in the law as "works that result from the fixation of a series of musical, spoken, or other sounds, but not including the sounds accompanying a motion picture or other audiovisual work." Common examples include recordings of music, drama, or lectures. A sound recording is not the same as a phonographic record. A *phonographic record* is the physical object in which works of authorship are embodied. Items that fall under the category *phonographic record* include cassette tapes, CDs, LPs, 45s, as well as other formats. The notice for phonographic records embodying a sound recording should contain the following three elements:

1. The symbol (the letter P in a circle).

2. The year of first publication of the sound recording.

3. The name of the owner of the copyright in the sound recording or an abbreviation by which the name can be recognized or a generally known alternative designation of the owner. If the producer of the sound recording is named on the phonographic record label or container and if no other name appears in conjunction with the notice, the producer's name shall be considered a part of the notice.

Example: 2004 X.Y.Z. Records, Inc.

Notice of copyright on unpublished works

The author or copyright owner may wish to place a copyright notice on any unpublished copies or phonographic records that leave his or her control.

Example: Unpublished work © 2002 Jane Doe

International copyright protection?

No international copyright automatically protects an author's writings throughout the entire world. Protection against unauthorized use in a particular country depends, basically, upon the national laws of that country. However, most countries do offer protection to foreign works under certain conditions, and these conditions have been greatly simplified by international copyright treaties and conventions. For further information and a list of countries that maintain copyright relations with the U.S., request Circular 38a, *International Copyright Relations of the United States*. Contact information is listed in the section "Contacting the Copyright Office," later in this chapter.

How long does copyright protection last?

Nothing lasts forever, but a copyright gives you protection for a long time. In order to move forward, I need to take a few steps backward to let you know how copyright law has changed, what stays the same, and the changes that affect you.

Works originally created on or after January 1, 1978

A work that is *created* (fixed in tangible form for the first time) on or after January 1, 1978, is automatically protected from the moment of its creation and is ordinarily given a term enduring for the author's life plus an additional 70 years after the author's death. In the case of "a joint work prepared by two or more authors who did not work for hire," the term lasts for 70 years after the last surviving author's death.

For works made for hire, and for anonymous and pseudonymous works (unless the author's identity is revealed in Copyright Office records), the duration of copyright is 95 years from publication or 120 years from creation, whichever is shorter.

Works originally created before January 1, 1978, but not published or registered by that date

These works have been automatically brought under the statute and are now given federal copyright protection. The duration of copyright in these works is generally calculated in the same way as for works created on or after January 1, 1978: The life-plus-70 or 95/120-year terms applies to them as well. The law provides that in no case does the term of copyright for works in this category expire before December 31, 2002, and for works published on or before December 31, 2002, the term of copyright will not expire before December 31, 2047.

Works originally created and published or registered before January 1, 1978

Under the law in effect before 1978, copyright was secured on the date a work was published with a copyright notice, or on the date of registration if the work was registered in unpublished form. In either case, the copyright endured for a first term of 28 years from the date it was secured. During the last (28th) year of the first term, the copyright was eligible for renewal. The Copyright Act of 1976 extended the renewal term from 28 to 47 years for copyrights that were subsisting on January 1, 1978, or for pre-1978 copyrights restored under the Uruguay Round Agreements Act (URAA), making these works eligible for a total term of protection of 75 years. Public Law 105-298, enacted on October 27, 1998, further extended the renewal term of copyrights still subsisting on that date by an additional 20 years, providing for a renewal term of 67 years and a total term of protection of 95 years.

Public Law 102-307, enacted on June 26, 1992, amended the 1976 Copyright Act to provide for automatic renewal of the term of copyrights secured between January 1, 1964, and December 31, 1977. Although the renewal term is automatically provided, the Copyright Office doesn't issue a renewal certificate for these works unless a renewal application and fee are received and registered in the Copyright Office.

Public Law 102-307 makes renewal registration optional. Thus, filing for renewal registration is no longer required in order to extend the original 28-year copyright term to the full 95 years. However, some benefits accrue from making a renewal registration during the 28th year of the original term.

Registering Your Copyright

In general, copyright registration is a legal formality intended to make a public record of the basic facts of a particular copyright. However, registration is *not* a condition of copyright protection.

The copyright law, though, does provide several inducements or advantages to encourage copyright owners to register their copyrights. Among these advantages are the following:

✔ **Registration establishes a public record of the copyright claim.** This informs all that you're the author and owner (unless you assign your rights to someone else). It also gives you the right to sue potential infringers and helps ward off the copycats who want to profit from your work.

✔ **Before an infringement suit may be filed in court, registration is necessary for works of U.S. origin.** If made before or within five years of publication, registration establishes prima facie evidence in court of the validity of the copyright and of the facts stated in the certificate. If registration is made within three months after publication of the work or prior to an infringement of the work, statutory damages and attorney's fees are available to the copyright owner in court actions. Otherwise, only an award of actual damages and profits is available to the copyright owner.

✔ **Registration allows the owner of the copyright to record the registration with the U.S. Customs Service for protection against the importation of infringing copies.**

For additional information, request Publication No. 563 *How to Protect Your Intellectual Property Right,* from: U.S. Customs Service, P.O. Box 7404, Washington, DC 20044; Web site www.customs.gov.

Registration may be made at any time within the life of the copyright. Before 1978, when a work had been registered in unpublished form, it was necessary to make another registration when the work was published, but this is no longer the case. However, the copyright owner may register the published edition if desired.

Knowing who may file an application

The following people may file an application for copyright registration:

- ✔ **The author:** The author is the person who actually created the work or, if the work was made for hire, the employer or other person for whom the work was prepared.

- ✔ **The copyright claimant:** The copyright claimant is defined in Copyright Office regulations as either the author of the work, or a person or organization that has obtained ownership of all the rights under the copyright initially belonging to the author. This category includes a person or organization that has obtained by contract the right to claim legal title to the copyright in an application for copyright registration.

- ✔ **The owner of exclusive rights:** Under the law, any of the exclusive rights that make up a copyright and any subdivision of them can be transferred and owned separately, even though the transfer may be limited in time or place of effect. The term *copyright owner* with respect to any one of the exclusive rights contained in a copyright refers to the owner of that particular right. Any owner of an exclusive right may apply for registration of a claim in the work.

- ✔ **The duly authorized agent of the author, another copyright claimant, or the owner of exclusive right(s):** Any person authorized to act on behalf of the author, other copyright claimant, or owner of exclusive rights may apply for registration. No requirement states that applications must be prepared or filed by an attorney.

Applying for an original registration

To register a work, you need the following three elements:

- ✔ **A properly completed application form.** This form is available on the Library of Congress's Web site at `www.copyright.gov`.

- ✔ **A nonrefundable filing fee of $30 for each application.**

  Note: Copyright Office fees are subject to change. For current fees, please check the Copyright Office Web site at `www.copyright.gov`, write the Copyright Office, or call 202-707-3000.

✔ **A nonreturnable deposit of the work being registered.**

The deposit requirements vary in particular situations. The general requirements follow. Also note the information under "Considering special deposit requirements." If the work was first published in the U.S. on or after January 1, 1978, include two complete copies or phonographic records of the best edition.

If the work was first published in the U.S. before January 1, 1978, two complete copies or phonographic records of the work as first published are required. If the work was first published outside the U.S., one complete copy or phonographic record of the work as first published is required. If sending multiple works, all applications, deposits, and fees should be sent in the same package. If possible, applications should be attached to the appropriate deposit. Whenever possible, number each package (for example, 1 of 3, 2 of 4) to facilitate processing.

Send these elements in the same envelope or package to:

Library of Congress, Copyright Office, 101 Independence Avenue, S.E., Washington, DC 20559-6000

Applications and fees received without appropriate copies, phonographic records, or identifying material will not be processed and are ordinarily returned, as are unpublished deposits without applications or fees.

Renewing your registration

To renew your copyright registration, send the following to the Copyright Office:

✔ A properly completed application *Form RE* and, if necessary, *Form RE Addendum.*

✔ A nonrefundable filing fee of $60 without Addendum; $90 with Addendum. Each Addendum form must be accompanied by a deposit, representing the work being reviewed.

Complete the application form by typing or using a black ink pen. You may photocopy blank application forms. However, photocopied forms submitted to the Copyright Office must be clear, legible, on a good grade of 8½-x-11-inch white paper, and suitable for automatic feeding through a photocopier. The forms should be printed, preferably in black ink, head-to-head so that when you turn the sheet over, the top of page 2 is directly behind the top of page 1. Forms not meeting these requirements may be returned, resulting in delayed registration.

All those crazy numbers

A Library of Congress Control Number is different from a copyright registration number. The Cataloguing in Publication (CIP) Division of the Library of Congress is responsible for assigning LOC Control Numbers and is operationally separate from the Copyright Office. A book may be registered in or deposited with the Copyright Office but not necessarily catalogued and added to the Library's collections. For information about obtaining an LC Control Number, see the following homepage: pcn.loc.gov/pcn. For information on International Standard Book Numbering (ISBN), write to:

ISBN, R. R. Bowker, 630 Central Ave., New Providence, NJ 07974; phone 877-310-7333; Web site www.isbn.org.

For information on International Standard Serial Numbering (ISSN), write to:

Library of Congress, National Serials Data Program, Serial Record Division, Washington, DC 20540-4160; phone 202-707-6452; Web site www.loc.gov/issn.

Registering unpublished collections

Under the following conditions, a work may be registered in unpublished form as a collection, with one application form and one fee:

- ✔ The elements of the collection are assembled in an orderly form.
- ✔ The combined elements bear a single title identifying the collection as a whole.
- ✔ The copyright claimant in all the elements and in the collection as a whole is the same.
- ✔ All the elements are by the same author, or, if they are by different authors, at least one of the authors has contributed copyrightable authorship to each element.

An unpublished collection isn't indexed under the individual titles of the contents but under the title of the collection.

Considering special deposit requirements

Special deposit requirements exist for many types of works. The following are prominent examples of exceptions to the general deposit requirements:

✔ If the work is a motion picture, the deposit requirement is one complete copy of the unpublished or published motion picture and a separate written description of its contents, such as a continuity, press book, or synopsis.

✔ If the work is a literary, dramatic, or musical work published only in a phonographic record, the deposit requirement is one complete phonographic record.

✔ If the work is an unpublished or published computer program, the deposit requirement is one visually perceptible copy in source code of the first 25 and last 25 pages of the program. For a program of fewer than 50 pages, the deposit is a copy of the entire program. For more information on computer program registration, including deposits for revised programs and provisions for trade secrets, request Circular 61, *Copyright Registration for Computer Programs*. Contact information is listed in the section "Contacting the Copyright Office," later in this chapter.

✔ If the work is in a CD-ROM format, the deposit requirement is one complete copy of the material, that is, the CD-ROM, the operating software, and any manuals accompanying it. If registration is sought for the computer program on the CD-ROM, the deposit should also include a printout of the first 25 and last 25 pages of source code for the program. In the case of works reproduced in three-dimensional copies, identifying material such as photographs or drawings, a deposit is ordinarily required.

If you're unsure of the deposit requirement for your work, write or call the Copyright Office and describe the work you want to register.

Effective date of registration

A copyright registration is effective on the date the Copyright Office receives all the required elements in acceptable format, regardless of how long it then takes to process the application and mail the certificate of registration. The time the Copyright Office requires to process an application varies depending on the amount of material the Office is receiving.

If you apply for copyright registration, don't expect to receive an acknowledgment that your application has been received (the Office receives more than 600,000 applications annually), but you can expect the following:

✔ A letter or a telephone call from a Copyright Office staff member if further information is needed.

✔ A certificate of registration indicating that the work has been registered.

✔ If the application cannot be accepted, a letter explaining why it has been rejected.

If you want to know the date that the Copyright Office receives your material, send it by registered or certified mail and request a return receipt.

Correcting and amplifying existing registrations

To correct an error in a copyright registration or to amplify the information given in a registration, file a supplementary registration form *(Form CA)* with the Copyright Office. The filing fee is $100. The information in a supplementary registration adds to but does not supersede that information contained in the earlier registration.

A supplementary registration is not a substitute for an original registration, for a renewal registration, or for recording a transfer of ownership. For further information about supplementary registration, request Circular 8, *Supplementary Copyright Registration.* Contact information is listed in the section "Contacting the Copyright Office," later in this chapter.

Paying registration fees

Table 7-1 lists the most common fees for various copyright services. For a list of all current fees, or for more information on various fees, contact the Copyright Office. Contact information is listed in the section "Contacting the Copyright Office," later in this chapter. (Note that copyright fees are subject to change.)

Table 7-1	Copyright Fees
Service	*Fee*
Basic registration (all forms)	$30
Renewal registration Form RE	$60
Addendum to Form RE	$30
Supplementary registration	$100
Special handling fee to expedite processing	$580

Your payment must be by check, money order, or bank draft payable to "Register of Copyrights." Do *not* send cash.

Fill-in application forms for your convenience

All Copyright Office forms are available on the Copyright Office Web site in fill-in version. Go to `www.copyright.gov/forms` and follow the instructions. The fill-in forms allow you to enter information while the form is displayed on the screen by an Adobe Acrobat Reader product. You may then print the completed form and mail it to the Copyright Office. Fill-in forms provide a clean, sharp printout for your records and for filing with the Copyright Office.

Contacting the Copyright Office

The Copyright Office is available to provide additional registration information and to help you with any questions that you have. You can access their office in the following ways:

- **Internet:** Circulars, announcements, regulations, other related materials, and all copyright application forms are available at `www.copyright.gov`.

- **Fax:** Circulars and other information (but not application forms) are available from Fax-on-Demand at 202-707-2600.

- **Telephone:** For general information about copyright, call the Copyright Public Information Office at 202-707-3000. The TTY number is 202-707-6737. Information specialists are on duty from 8:30 a.m. to 5:00 p.m. Monday through Friday, eastern time, except federal holidays. Recorded information is available 24 hours a day.

  If you know which application forms and circulars you want, request them from the Forms and Publications Hotline by calling 202-707-9100, 24 hours a day. Leave a recorded message.

- **Regular mail:** If old-fashioned correspondence is your thing, you can write a letter to the Copyright Office. Use the following address:

  Library of Congress, Copyright Office, Publications Section, LM-455, 101 Independence Avenue, S.E., Washington, DC 20559-6000.

The Copyright Office is *not* permitted to give legal advice. If information or guidance is needed on matters such as disputes over the ownership of copyright, suits against possible infringers, the procedure for getting a work published, or the method of obtaining royalty payments, you may want to consult an attorney.

Copyright Office records in machine-readable form catalogued from January 1, 1978, to the present, including registration and renewal information and recorded documents, are now available for searching from the Copyright Office website at `www.copyright.gov`.

Search of copyright office records

The records of the Copyright Office are open for inspection and searching by the public. Moreover, on request, the Copyright Office can search its records for you at the statutory hourly rate of $75 for each hour or fraction of an hour. For information on searching the Office records concerning the copyright status or ownership of a work, request Circular 22, *How to Investigate the Copyright Status of a Work,* and Circular 23, *The Copyright Card Catalog and the Online Files of the Copyright Office.* Contact information is listed in the section "Contacting the Copyright Office."

Transferring a Copyright

As an inventor, you're likely going to need to transfer a copyright at some point. Say, for example, that you hire a graphic artist to design your packaging. Unless you have the artist sign a work-for-hire agreement (see Chapter 10) in advance, he or she owns the copyright to the packaging design until you transfer it.

Any or all of the copyright owner's exclusive rights or any subdivision of those rights may be transferred, but the transfer of exclusive rights isn't valid unless that transfer is in writing and signed by the owner of the rights conveyed, or such owner's duly authorized agent. Transfer of a right on a nonexclusive basis doesn't require a written agreement.

A copyright may also be conveyed by operation of law and may be bequeathed by will or pass as personal property by the applicable laws of interstate succession. Copyright is a personal property right, and is subject to the various state laws and regulations that govern the ownership, inheritance, or transfer of personal property as well as terms of contracts or conduct of business. For information about relevant state laws, consult an attorney.

Transfers of copyrights, in whole or in part, are normally made by contract. Such transfers are tricky business and should be handled by a skilled copyright attorney. The Copyright Office doesn't have any forms for such transfers. The law does provide for the recordation in the Copyright Office of transfers of copyright ownership. Although recordation is not required to make a valid transfer between the parties, it does provide certain legal advantages and may be required to validate the transfer such as against third parties. For information on recordation of transfers and other documents related to copyright, request Circular 12, *Recordation of Transfers and Other Documents.* Contact information is listed in the section "Contacting the Copyright Office," earlier in this chapter.

Chapter 8

Mum's the Word: Keeping It Confidential

....

In This Chapter

▶ Using confidentiality agreements

▶ Protecting yourself

▶ Deciding whether to talk without an agreement

....

*P*rotecting your idea is an issue from day one. One of the most common tools you can use to help do that is a confidentiality agreement. A *confidentiality agreement* is a binding contract between you and the person or company that signs it stating that the other party won't disclose any details of your idea or invention without your express permission.

The hows and whys of having everyone — from your spouse, to the package designer, to the company thinking about licensing your product — sign a confidentiality agreement is what this chapter's all about.

Spilling the Beans about the Basics

The purpose of a confidentiality agreement is to put the other party on notice that you believe you have an idea or product worth protecting. If they want to see it or hear about it, they have to sign a document stating that they won't use or tell anyone about the information you're disclosing to them in any way without your approval.

The confidentiality/nondisclosure agreement should cover all proprietary information regarding your idea, concept, product, invention, process, or service. It should cover any trade secret you may divulge, internal workings, designs, drawings, and so on. It should cover everything that is not in the *public domain,* which means information already disclosed or readily available.

Use a confidentiality agreement whenever you believe your concept, idea, or product is at risk of being used or copied without your permission. Whether you ask someone to look at your invention or they express interest in seeing it, ask them to sign your confidentiality agreement.

Get help from a patent attorney in composing your agreement. You want to be all-encompassing and very specific — this isn't the place for generalities. Is the most important part of your invention the design, efficiency, or color? If you're uncertain, include it in the confidentiality agreement.

A confidentiality agreement also provides an opportunity for the other party to reveal any similar products that they're already in possession of or working on. Inventors all over the world are problem solvers and will develop solutions to common problems. There's a good possibility that the company you're approaching is working on a similar product. If so, they should let you know that upfront. Some confidentiality agreements are set up so that the signer must disclose this type of information; others simply state that the signer must be quiet about your invention. Either way, it's in the signer's best interest to reveal a competing product or idea to avoid future lawsuits and hassles.

One of the most important benefits a confidentiality or nondisclosure agreement gives you is time. Under patent law, discussing your idea with anyone without having a patent is considered public disclosure. You have just one year from the moment of that disclosure to apply for a patent or you lose patent rights. However, discussing your idea with someone who has signed a confidentiality agreement is *not* considered a public disclosure.

Using confidentiality agreements gives you time to fully investigate the market potential of your product before spending a lot of time and money on development and patent fees. You can use confidentiality agreements when talking with prototypers (to obtain model and tooling costs), manufacturers (to obtain production and volume costs), marketers, graphic designers, and investors. Just be cautious and take the time to cover all the bases.

In addition to a confidentiality agreement, get maximum protection for your idea or product by applying for a patent, trademark, or copyright, and determine what, if any, trade secret you have. The patent attorney who helps you with this process can also provide you with a good nondisclosure agreement to use, or you can use the samples I provide in Appendix A.

You don't need a confidentiality agreement if you filed a patent application to protect your idea or product. However, I encourage you to ask for one anyway just as an extra precaution. Sometimes, working around a confidentiality agreement is harder than working around a patent, depending on the type of patent. For example, a design patent basically only covers the exact appearance of the product and is fairly easy to work around.

After your confidentiality agreement is signed, you can tell as much as you like to that person or company. Use your good judgment and the knowledge of your patent counsel, and you'll come to the right decision of when to use these confidentiality agreements.

Sharing with the People in Your Life

You may wonder when and with whom to use a confidentiality agreement (sometimes called a nondisclosure agreement). The answer is quite simple — whenever and with whomever you disclose secret, proprietary, or protectable information important to the success of your idea, invention, product, or business.

Have any and all confidentiality agreements witnessed by trustworthy individuals.

Securing dinner-table talk

It may feel odd to ask your spouse and the rest of your family and friends to sign confidentiality agreements. If you need help making them understand that it's not that you don't trust them, just show them this section.

If someone wants to invalidate your intellectual property rights, whether that's a patent, or what have you, all they have to do is prove that you told someone about your idea without having a confidentiality agreement with that person more than a year before you applied for the intellectual property protection.

Ask your mate to sign an agreement; ask your children; ask your parents and grandparents; ask your aunts, uncles, and close cousins. Ask anyone you talk to who is a friend or acquaintance to sign a confidentiality agreement. The odds are against anyone close to you revealing the specifics of your invention, but the odds are quite high that if your invention is successful, you'll have to defend your rights to it. In a legal situation, the opposing party may ask for the names of people you talked to about your invention who didn't sign an agreement. Having signed confidentiality agreements with everyone you know helps prove consistency and fairness.

Signing on employees

During the development of your idea or invention, you may want or need to consult with various people who have expertise in specific areas. For example, you may consult with an engineer on design, a prototype builder on making a working model, a tooling expert to design production molds, a packager to create a container, and on through including the bookkeeper who helps track expenses. Each of these people is privy to proprietary information and each of them should sign a confidentiality agreement (check out Appendix A for a sample agreement that you can use).

Consultants often work with competing companies within the industry you sell to. They also may compete with you when they leave your employ. They may well start their own business with your inside information. They have the means and contacts to pass on your information, so it is essential that they sign your confidentiality agreement including a noncompete clause.

Make sure you get agreements with any subcontractors your consultants use. The consultants themselves may have confidentiality agreements with their subcontractors and those agreements help protect you, but don't assume that that's the case.

Sometimes, confusion arises as to who is the owner of the invention — especially who is the first inventor, which is what the United States Patent and Trademark Office cares about. Sometimes bosses, colleagues, or business associates attempt to say they are the owner or co-inventor. Make sure you keep good records (see Chapter 1) and use confidentiality agreements to protect yourself.

Zipping your lips at work

Especially if you're a professional or semiprofessional inventor or researcher, you need to be aware of the pitfalls of sharing the results of your work. I have nothing against collegiality or sharing knowledge, I'm just advising you to think before you speak — or write. Time and time again I've seen innovators in medicine, engineering, physics, and more lose the right to patent their innovations because they wrote about them for a trade journal or shared their findings at a seminar, didn't apply for a patent or other intellectual property protection within a year, and then found it was too late.

College and university professors are especially prone to the pressures of the "publish or perish" mentality of academia and don't realize that by discussing their research with a scientific journal editor they're setting the date for the first public disclosure of their findings and have just a year from that date to apply for intellectual property protection. Don't let this happen to you!

Of course, if you're a professional researcher, you may be bound by a confidentiality agreement you signed with your employer.

Talking to the big boys

Anytime you discuss or demonstrate your invention to a potential investor, licensee, manufacturer, or customer, a nagging concern is whether they'll try to copy your idea. After all, they probably have a large organization, ample funding, and a whole slew of lawyers on retainer. Getting them to sign a confidentiality agreement can help ease your mind and protect your rights.

Of course, getting a potential licensee to sign a nondisclosure agreement may be the hard part. Signing a confidentiality agreement places the company in a tough legal situation. It makes them vulnerable to a lawsuit if the company ever comes out with a similar product, and in our litigation-happy society, some so-called inventors and their attorneys are just looking for deep pockets (rich companies) to take advantage of. So, don't be surprised if the major retailer you're negotiating with is just as suspicious of you as you are of them.

One of the reasons companies may be reluctant to sign confidentiality agreements is that a well-known licensing company or large manufacturing firm sees hundreds, maybe thousands, of new products each year. When I was in charge of one of the largest publicly funded innovation centers in the country, I often saw several similar products each month. Each came from a different inventor located in a different city. They didn't copy or steal each other's inventions; they were simply solving problems and found similar solutions. Imagine the number of inventions that the major corporations review each month that are exactly alike.

Often, the corporate attorney has to review the agreement before signing. Other firms have their own standard agreement that they will ask you to sign before reviewing your product. (If they refuse to sign an agreement, you do have some options. Check out the "Running into Someone Who Won't Sign" section for more.)

 Make sure any agreement is signed by the proper people — on both sides. An agreement signed by an unauthorized person may be invalid. Find out ahead of time who the company's authorized representative is, and for your part, make sure your secretary or spouse doesn't sign the agreement on behalf of your company by mistake.

Running into Someone Who Won't Sign

What do you do when the party you want to disclose to won't sign your confidentiality agreement? You may encounter an investor who doesn't want to commit or a potential employee who doesn't want to be restricted. If a person refuses on his or her own behalf, I recommend not disclosing anything.

If a person or company can demonstrate that they've been developing something similar, a nondisclosure agreement with you doesn't give you any rights over their product or obligate them to abandon it. If the company or individual refused to sign the agreement, consider the ramifications if they don't sign and understand that you're making a public disclosure.

You're much more likely to run into resistance about signing an agreement with a large corporation. Many firms have a hard rule never to sign confidentiality agreements because they have been sued in the past based on a confidentiality agreement and something similar they have produced that they claim they did not know was in development. A company with multiple research and development labs can tell you in all honesty that they don't know if something similar is being developed in one of their many labs. A large manufacturing concern may state that they already process all the parts needed to make your product. An international licensing organization may have a policy of never signing confidentiality agreements. It is extremely difficult and expensive to enforce and defend international agreements.

In these cases, you have two choices:

- Not disclosing what you have, and thereby restricting the possibility of business with this party
- Trying to work out a nondisclosure agreement that has sufficient protection for you and for them

Before you make your decision, consider whether your invention is likely to be commercialized with that company and whether you can make a business agreement with them sooner or later. The company's reputation is another item to balance. A well-respected firm doesn't earn a good reputation with dishonest business dealings.

While there is always some level of risk, if you approach this disclosure problem in a businesslike manner, you can typically resolve the nondisclosure/confidentiality agreement issues. If not, you may decide to wait until you have sufficient patent protection to safeguard your idea.

Part III
Developing Your Idea

The 5th Wave — By Rich Tennant

"Okay, so maybe the Internet wasn't the best place to advertise a product that helped computer illiterate people."

In this part . . .

This part gives you some practical pointers on how to transform your invention from idea to actuality. In these chapters, I address issues that include getting a reality check on your idea before you get in too deep, having a model — or prototype — built, figuring out how to get your product produced, and taking on other people to help you accomplish all these tasks.

Chapter 9

Prototyping: Making It Work

● ●

In This Chapter

▶ Figuring out prototypes

▶ Knowing product-making options

▶ Keeping your ideas protected

▶ Making your product as inexpensively as possible

● ●

*Y*ou probably believe that your idea, concept, or new invention is definitely going to work. But you can't tell how workable it actually is until you test it out. After you determine that the process you used when innovating is a valid one, you need to design a working model, called a *proof of concept prototype,* to provide functional proof that your innovation works. Your prototype demonstrates to others that your novel idea actually does what you claim it does.

In this chapter, I explain what exactly a prototype is. I tell you all about the advantages of prototyping and I also walk you through the process of turning your concept into a prototype.

Understanding the Importance of Prototyping

Having a model or prototype in hand is a great asset. People love to see a product demonstrated. They want to see that your idea works or, in the case of a totally new concept, at least has the capacity to work. So having a prototype helps convince people that your idea has merit. Consider the following:

✔ You can show a prototype to private investors and bankers when seeking funding for further development.

✔ Because companies don't license ideas, you probably should plan to present a prototype to potential manufacturing companies and potential licensees in order for your idea to become a product. These companies may want to license your invention and pay you a royalty. (See Chapters 20 and 21 for more about licensing.)

✔ You can use your prototype to impress suppliers and wholesalers so that you can establish lines of credit.

If you have a prototype in hand, those who see it quickly grasp and assess the idea that you're trying to describe.

Obtaining Your Prototype

Basically, you can obtain your prototype in one of three ways:

✔ You can design and make your own proof of concept prototype if you have the talent and the facilities.

✔ You can hire a product designer to design the proof of concept model (prototype) and then make it yourself if you're capable, or have it made by a professional prototype shop.

✔ You can work with an existing manufacturing company to study your proof of concept drawings, make the prototype, and then fabricate an actual working model.

In this section, I discuss these options in detail.

Going through the process yourself

If you have an extensive knowledge of the prototyping process, and you have the skills and facilities needed to complete each step of the process, then by all means do it yourself. (Most people aren't able to go it alone, however, so don't feel bad if you have to get some help. Read this section to get an overview of the process and then read the sections that deal with hiring others to help you.)

Creating a prototype involves a variety of steps, called *phases.* Whether you decide to create your own prototype all by yourself, or you hire someone to help you with all or part of the process, you go through the following phases.

Design development
Oftentimes, a wild idea can lead to a mental vision of a new way of doing something or possibly a new machine that makes doing a task more efficient. Before you can convey your mental vision to someone else, you must make reasonable sketches or descriptions to first convince yourself that your idea will work, and then allow others to understand what you're trying to do.

Paper, pencils, and erasers are much cheaper than the materials and fabrication work it requires to make a proof of concept prototype. The better your preprototype drawings, the greater the chance of making an exceptional proof of concept prototype.

Schematic design

After you complete your basic preprototype sketches, you must project the entire design onto a drafting board and/or CAD/CAM (computer-aided drafting machine) to determine a logical, functional manufacturing process. This refinement of your original sketches is called a *schematic design*.

Your schematics drawings also reveal the various functional states of the expected operation to demonstrate how a consumer will be able to use your product. A schematic design and study model gives you an idea of the size, color, and shape of your product.

Your schematic drawing doesn't involve any aesthetics. You'll worry about that later. Plus, retail buyers ultimately approve the color, size, and packaging.

Study model

After the design drawings and functional schematics demonstrate that your concepts may be able to satisfy an existing need, have a prototype model made for the primary purpose of demonstrating your product's usefulness and marketing appeal. (You can make this model yourself if you have the skill and resources, but most people have to hire someone to actually build the model.)

Design rendering and graphic drawings

After the proof of concept study prototype has revealed that the concept can function optimally and reliably and has market potential, you now need to think about the aesthetics of your product's design.

Eye appeal sells products, so don't take this step lightly.

After the final aesthetics have determined your product's form, complete detailed graphic drawings to use in surveying potential users' opinions before committing to fund the expensive final preproduction prototype. Drawings are much easier to change than molds.

Preproduction model (s)

A preproduction model must ensure that you've reconfigured the product according to your findings from the previous proof of concept prototypes before committing to the final molds, or you may waste time and money on an inferior production model rather than a marketable product. One mistake in a mold drawing can cause the entire mold to become an expensive error.

Rapid prototyping

During the past few years, 3D computer aided drawing has advanced to the point where people can program a machine that creates a near instantaneous mold from a CAD/CAM drawing. Then an actual component part or small nonfunctioning prototype or model can be molded. Although this technology is very expensive, it requires only hours to provide functional prototypes that would otherwise take days, weeks, or months to manually accomplish. For example, if we want to make a kitchen blender, it might take over a hundred hours of manual labor to fabricate certain component parts from chunks of metal or plastic. Rapid prototyping can cut labor time to approximately 25 hours to complete a working model.

Final preproduction model

After you've tested your proof of concept prototypes and gotten input about the functionality and aesthetics, you use this information to design your final production model prototype. This prototype is the one that you'll show to potential buyers, investors, or licensees.

Hiring a prototype maker to do it for you

Prototyping involves creating several proof of concept models that lead up to a *market-ready version,* which is a preproduction model incorporating all the mechanical and aesthetics of the proof of concept prototypes. In working with a professional prototyper, you travel through each of the stages discussed in the previous section but at an advanced rate, which should save you aggravation and time.

If you're an idea person without the ability to design or make a proof concept prototype, you'll want to hire someone to create your prototype for you.

Deciding who you want

A professional prototype designer can create your prototype for you. You may also want to contact the nearest university to obtain technical assistance from the College of Engineering within that school. Universities, engineering schools, and similar technical schools have workshops where you can make connections to prototype makers. Local inventor organizations in your area and the national United Inventors Association (UIA) are also great resources for prototype connections. The UIA's Web site, located at www.iuausa.com, lists local inventors' organizations by state. These organizations can refer you to local prototype makers.

Prototype makers specialize their design development by industry. For example, if you have a medical product, you may want to search for a product designer who specializes in medical products. This person is probably already aware of the government rules and regulations in the medical industry. There are specific plastics, resins, and chemicals that can't be used in the development of a new product.

When looking for a prototype designer, select one with a proven track record. An experienced prototype designer has the ability to make suggestions and has contacts with manufacturers who may assist you in further development. A prototype designer works by reputation. He should be able to give you a list of successful products he's worked with in the past, as well as a list of individual references. Be sure to ask for references and thoroughly check them out before you hire someone.

Have all price estimates (for development and professional services rendered) put in writing. In fact, obtain price quotes from three different prototype makers so you can compare them, as well as find out additional information and obtain suggestions while talking with each professional.

Negotiating a contract

The cost for development usually ranges between five hundred to several thousand dollars, depending on the time involved in making your prototype. Professionals charge an hourly rate ranging from $50 to $125 per hour, depending on their experience, type of equipment, and product specialty.

Try to obtain a price estimate by the hour, as well as for the total job. (When you're charged by the hour, the prototyper's profit depends upon how many hours he spends on your job. This can encourage "time padding" if the prototyper is dishonest.) Every prototype is different, so it's difficult for a prototyper to bid a fixed fee for the job. However, you may be able to agree on an hourly fee with a price cap, to prevent the prototype maker from charging you for too many hours.

After you agree upon a prototype model, if you change anything before it's finished it will cost you a surcharge like a builder charging you for making changes when building a home. When your agreement is finalized with an agreed upon time to complete your model and price, stay away from the prototyper until the model is finished.

When working with a prototype maker, always use a work-for-hire agreement (see Chapter 10) as well as a confidentiality agreement (see Chapter 8). The *work-for-hire agreement* gives you, the inventor, the sole legal intellectual property rights to your product.

Many times, inventors pay professional prototype makers to do work for them and anticipate the professional making the product better and more efficiently and possibly suggesting improvements. If a professional prototype maker adds to your invention without a work-for-hire agreement, he can easily become a co-inventor on your patent. Be careful! You don't want another person whom you're paying on a short-term basis to be listed on your patent. Depending on the type of patent (see Chapter 2), you can end up being involved with this person for the next 14 to 20 years! When speaking with others, including the prototype maker, always use a confidentiality agreement so that discussing your product concept won't be considered a public disclosure.

The work-for-hire agreement simply states that you are the inventor and that you have hired the prototype maker to do work for you, including improvements. All intellectual property rights, including patents (see Part I), copyrights, trademarks, and trade secrets (see Part II) belong to you. The agreement states that the prototype maker has no legal claim to your invention.

A confidentiality agreement requires a company or individual to keep your product, invention, technology, or idea a secret. Getting a confidentiality agreement is extremely important and you should have one signed before you disclose your invention to anyone.

Professional designers, engineers, and prototype makers should be familiar with these prepatent agreements. If they create any hassle, save yourself a lot of trouble by walking away and hiring someone else.

Letting the maker do her job

Don't think that you only have to make one prototype. As the product develops, it changes. Many inventions require several changes during their development. It is common to have up to seven different prototypes as the product develops. Changes are made along the way by the recommendations of buyers, wholesalers, and consumers.

However, during each step of the product development, you must have iron-clad legal agreements relative to what the contractor of each phase is going to do for how much money, in a timely manner. If you intervene after the agreement is signed, the contractor has the right to charge you additionally for any changes you may want him to make. The contractor is only responsible for the quality of his work and not whether your idea is good or bad. This is why drawings and prototypes are called *proof of concept.*

Space cadets and prototypes

The National Aviation and Space Administration (NASA) funds the Space Alliance Technology Outreach Program (SATOP), an affiliate cooperative program designed to assist small businesses and inventors in solving technical challenges. This program offers up to 40 hours of free technical assistance from engineers, scientists, and related professionals. A group of 30 space industries, universities, colleges, and NASA Centers are involved. SATOP's goal is to provide resolutions in less than 90 days. SATOP help innovators and companies with machine design process engineering, materials selection, and many other technical issues. You may want to visit their Web site at `www.spacetech solutions.com`.

Prototyping with an existing manufacturer

Many times, a manufacturing company that makes similar products can make a prototype for you. They may not want to license your product and pay you a royalty, because they have their own products to develop. However, they may have slow times within their company when they can work with you on developing a prototype and possibly manufacturing limited quantities of your product. For example, bakery workers typically start about 3 a.m. and work until 2 p.m. to maintain fresh products. So the building and equipment they use are available after 2 p.m. until early in the morning. I once worked with an inventor who made an agreement with a bakery owner to contract the use of the facilities and equipment during the off time in order to produce their special fruitcakes and cookies that sold through mail-order catalogues.

I also worked with an inventor who had a medical invention. This inventor approached a medical manufacturing company to copartner with him on the prototyping and development of his invention. In return, the manufacturing company put approximately $50,000 into the development of this inventor's product for a percentage of the inventor's potential company. The inventor was able to obtain private investors, establish a company, and have a manufacturing company produce the product for him at a fair price. The manufacturing company then owned a small percentage of the inventor's business.

Often friends, colleagues, engineers, and technical people may be working on similar problems resulting in a solution that is a new invention. Bosses often try to claim ownership, as do faculty at universities who have graduate students work on the development of new technologies. Many companies and universities have employment agreements stating that if you develop an invention on their time, it becomes their property. In fact, some employment agreements state at any time you are employed at a company or university, the product is theirs. This is becoming more common as technology advances.

In certain instances, a company or university allows the inventor to develop the product if that company or university doesn't have an interest in that product. Most universities have licensing divisions that examine an employee's product or technology. After a review, they decide whether or not the university wants to keep the technology or sign off and give the rights to further development to the inventor. Companies have legal divisions that do the same. If you have an employment agreement with your employer, be sure to have them sign off on your new invention in writing, not just tell you they aren't interested at this time.

Protecting Your Ideas During the Prototyping Process

Memories fade over time. Nothing suffices over the life of the invention like a great written document.

Keep detailed and accurate information regarding your invention. For example:

- ✔ **Keep a journal regarding your invention.** Write down a clear description of your idea. Have this journal signed and witnessed by two trustworthy individuals — possibly friends or family members. Make sure these people not only witness your invention but understand it as well.

- ✔ **Take advantage of the United States Patent Office's Disclosure Document Program.** At a cost of only $10, this program assists you in establishing a *date of conception* (the date you conceived the idea).

- ✔ **Keep all receipts as you develop, build, and test your product.** If someone tries to copy your invention and claim it as his own, you will need all the detailed documentation to prove your ownership. The legal case that has the most convincing documentation and best-kept records wins.

The bottom line is that no one really cares about your invention until someone makes money from it. When you start making money, people will come from every direction and claim they helped or assisted you with the invention along the way, wanting to reap financial rewards from your hard work.

Cost-Effectively Producing Your Product

Prototyping can be very simple or quite complex depending on the nature and type of the product design. Each prototyper has an area of expertise, which may be primarily electronic, mechanical, chemical, and so on. Prototyping companies often specialize in a given area such as toys, housewares, electronics, games, medical products, and the like. Look for them in the Yellow Pages under "Prototypes."

Be sure to seek out a production company that has the expertise to design and develop your concepts into the prototype that you want and envision. When deciding who should produce your product, obtain information regarding the overall cost for making molds, tooling, and manufacturing the product. Obtain cost estimates for the raw materials. Get these estimates from at least three different manufacturing companies so that you can compare the costs. (You'll also have a backup manufacturing company in case larger-than-anticipated orders come in.) Include the costs for packing and shipping the product.

When trying to cost-effectively produce your product, you need to think about various considerations that will be of concern to potential buyers and retailers. This section discusses those considerations.

Meeting product safety standards

Any device marketed to the public must be scrutinized for overall safety, such as any possible way anyone can be injured by using the device. For example, a buyer reviewing a new stuffed toy may ask, "Can a baby pull the eyes off and possibly swallow them and choke?"

Each device must meet all applicable governmental codes. Safety standards are concerned with the normal function or potential malfunction of products when used as intended. They're designed to prevent personal or property injury or damage when using the product. Even so, more than 10,000 reports of product-related injuries and deaths by consumers are received each year.

The Consumer Product Safety Commission (CPSC) has jurisdiction over more than 15,000 products ranging from cosmetics to lawn mowers. The CPSC covers all manufacturers, retailers, importers, and distributors of consumer products regardless of their size, number of employees, or income. While working on your invention, be sure to contact the CPCS to find out the safety rules and regulations regarding your invention. The Web site is www.cpsc. gov. If you have a question and can't find the answer on the Web site, e-mail the CPSC at info@cpsc.gov or call the toll-free hotline at 1-800-638-2772.

Developing design control documents

You can't make or sell a product without specifications. Think of trying to fix a new automobile or figure out how to turn on the CD player without an owner's manual. So you should create a well-written user's manual.

After your final product design has been committed to production, you must document that the design conforms to quality control standards in order to meet applicable third-party, (that is, government) regulations such as electrical, health, and performance codes.

Furthermore, to enable the mass production to go smoothly, you must document each and every step of the manufacturing process in detail, with step-by-step assembly procedures. After the final unit is assembled, it must be checked out to ensure that it meets certain functional specifications. The bottom line is that everything must be made to specifications and industry standards, and you must conduct tests on your product to make sure those standards are met.

The primary source and leader in the U.S. of product testing and certification is Underwriters Laboratory, Inc. (UL). It is an independent, not-for-profit product safety testing and certification organization that was established in 1894. To obtain product liability insurance on many products is almost impossible without UL testing and certification. The Web site for UL is www.ul.com. The phone number is 1-877-ULHELPS. There are UL offices in Canada, Europe, the Middle East, Asia Pacific, Africa, Latin America, and the U.S. The UL web site lists specific contacts that may be helpful to you.

Considering graphic design and packaging

The packaging plays a major role in attracting the potential buyer to take a closer look and purchase the product. Look at the Pet Rock. Did this product sell because it was a major advancement to mankind? No, it sold because of unique packaging.

Graphic design imprinted on the carton can be eye catching or dull, depending on the details and color coordinates. Every individual has a unique favorite color. However, mass-market appeal, not logic, determines the color of the final product. Large companies spend millions of dollars conducting research to find out what consumers want to purchase. They know whether 3-year-olds like red better than purple. This knowledge is important when selling millions of products to a specific market. Have you ever wondered why wagons for children are red versus purple or yellow? Market research can tell you. Be sure to conduct a significant amount of research before selecting the final color for your product. (Chapter 17 discusses how to conduct market research.)

Make sure your packaging contains user-friendly instruction manuals that accompany the product. In addition, pay close attention to make sure that corrugated packaging meets U.S. Department of Transportation (DOT) interstate regulations.

Pricing your product

In order for a product to be successful in the market, it must meet certain *margins,* which is accounting speak for the markup between the cost of manufacturing and the price of the product that enables your bills to be paid with some money left over for reinvestment or pure profit. The nature of the product and where it's sold determines the product's markups. The minimum markup on a product is 4 to 1, meaning that the end purchaser (consumer) needs to pay four times what it costs to make and ship.

The minimum markup is typical for products that sell in mass merchandise stores, such as Wal-Mart. For example, if the consumer wants to pay no more than $10 for a product, then the manufacturing, packing, and shipping costs for that product can't be more than $2.50 or you lose money on it.

If a product sells on television in an infomercial, the product markups from the manufacturing company to the consumer range from 5 or 7 to 1. The average is 6 to 1. For example, for a new product on an infomercial that costs $19.99, the manufacturing, packaging, and shipping combined should not be more than $3.33 in order to make a profit. ($19.99 divided by 6 = $3.33). A product markup is determined by the industry where the product sells and ultimately how much people are willing to pay for the product. All industries have price points. If you mark up the price too high on the product, say 10 or 20 to 1, then people don't buy it. The product markup is what the market will bear and consumers will pay.

Ask a prototype maker to refer you to a variety of manufacturing companies for product estimates.

Don't make the mistake of calculating the manufacturing, packing, and shipping costs and then multiplying times your given markup factor so that you can then tell consumers what they will pay for your product. This mistake is made quite frequently. You must first ask the potential consumers, through conducting market research, what they're willing to pay for the product, then divide that amount by your markup factor. If your product costs come in over that number, drop the product until you can find a way to produce it for less.

Choosing the right manufacturing materials

The majority of commodity products in today's marketplace are molded from plastic materials. Vast arrays of plastic resins are available with various resistances to thermal stress, scuff, compression and expansion, and rough handling. (Your prototype maker should be able to help you figure out what type of resin you need). Most of all, each plastic resin has specific molding factors, which greatly influence molding costs. The cost of the resin versus the cost of molding is always a major consideration.

During recent years, the plastic resin manufacturers have become very competitive. They provide a wide selection of available plastic resins to meet the requirements of various products. For example, your telephone is made of a rugged ABS material with a rubber additive, so it's less brittle if dropped or otherwise abused. This material might cost $6 per pound. The thin plastic boxes your blueberries came in at the grocery store are made of Polyprop, which is a cheaper, more brittle plastic that costs about $2 per pound. A reusable hospital device might be made of a thermoplastic material, which can withstand continuous heat sterilizations between hospital patient uses, costing about $9.50 per pound. Therefore, you need to determine the final material used on your product based upon how it will be used and possibly abused.

Manufacturing costs of the finished device is based in part upon the prorated cost of the mold, the cost of the plastic resin, and the cost of molding. You must carefully select a plastic compatible with the intended use of your invention.

Although the use of plastic technology in product function, appeal, and cost factors is the current predominant manufacturing consideration, there are many other products that lend themselves to fabrication from wood or metal combinations. There still are many manufacturing plants with metal stamping, turning, welding, and milling facilities in addition to woodworking and plastic facilities. Therefore, your product can be made of a material most suitable for its intended application.

Chapter 10

Hiring Helpers and Working with Work-for-Hire Agreements

*U*nless you're a master of all trades — inventing, engineering, and designing, to name just three relevant skills — you need to hire people to help develop your invention and design packaging for it. In most cases, hiring professionals to assist you in the development process can help you move your invention to market quicker and more efficiently. There are many experts out there to work side by side with you.

Of course you want people with up-to-date experience that's relevant to your project in size and scope. You also want people who are contractually obligated to keep your ideas confidential and respect your intellectual property rights.

In this chapter, I tell you about various types of people you may need to hire along the way, and I also discuss how important work-for-hire agreements are and how and why you should require prototype builders, manufacturers, designers, and others to sign them.

Hiring Professionals to Turn Your Idea into a Reality

You have an idea, so now what? To turn your idea into reality you need the active help and practical advice of a whole army of people. Forgetting the financial and marketing people for a moment, you need prototype builders, mechanical designers and engineers, package designers, and so on to undertake all the practical jobs related to turning your idea into a reality. You may also hire a custodial or payroll service and other professionals to perform tasks that contribute to your product's success.

Some of the types of helpers you may hire include the following:

- ✔ A prototyper or product designer to make the product for you
- ✔ A graphic artist to design the artwork and wording on your package
- ✔ A bookkeeper or accountant for financial matters
- ✔ A writer to put together an operations manual that explains how your product works
- ✔ In-house regulatory personnel to assure compliance with government rules and regulations
- ✔ Trainers to show people how to use your product
- ✔ Sales people who can assist you in selling your product

Make sure that anyone and everyone who has access to or knowledge of your idea (its structure, mechanics or any aspect of it) and anyone who is privy to financial information signs a confidentiality or work-for-hire agreement (which I explain in the "Working Out Work-For-Hire Agreements" section later in this chapter). Each person you hire carries valuable information and know-how in some fashion. For example, you don't want your bookkeeper, who's not bound by the same professional rules of nondisclosure as an accountant is, to discuss your financial information with their family and friends.

I talk about a couple of the more practical professional types you may need to hire in the next sections.

Picking a prototyper

You have an invention that you believe has commercial potential, but you're still in the idea stage and don't have a functioning model or prototype to determine whether your idea really works. If you don't know how to take your idea and make it into a working model, consider hiring a professional.

A *prototyper* builds a functioning model of your invention. After the prototype is built, any design flaws or engineering difficulties become clear. The process lets you determine the best materials to use and may help you refine your design. When (and if) you get a functioning prototype, you use that model to work out the specifications for any molds, dies, and stamps you need to mass-produce your invention.

Plus, you benefit from the prototyper's expertise. A professional prototype builder is apt to be aware of health and safety regulations about the types of materials to use. He should also know about current government standards and be familiar with the *Consumer Product Safety Commission's* rules and regulations for new products. This agency oversees approximately 15,000 different types of products from coffee pots to earrings.

You have to be careful about infringing on other inventors' intellectual property rights through the prototype builder. The prototyper may bring knowledge of intellectual property from other jobs and apply them to your new product. On one hand, you want the prototyper to use her expertise, but on the other hand, you have to be careful of potential patent infringement. (Flip back to Chapter 9 for detailed info on finding and hiring a professional prototyper.)

Many great ideas fail in the prototype stage because the prototype, which is created to see whether an idea works, proves that it doesn't. You may pay a pretty penny to develop this worthless prototype, but don't be bitter; you would have spent many times the amount you spent on the prototype had you moved on to the even more expensive patent application process. And at least you know the truth.

Arranging for packaging personnel

Packaging is an extremely important aspect of your marketing plan. Packaging sells products. I cover the ins and outs of packaging in Chapter 12, but in this section, I want to talk a little about the people who get your invention into its box, bag, or hang-tabbed, bubble-wrapped, talking, dancing display unit.

Proper packaging, by which I mean profitable packaging, requires a variety of skills. You may end up hiring a few packaging professionals. For example, you may need:

- ✔ An engineer to make sure your packaging stands up to shipping abuse *and* stacks easily on store shelves
- ✔ A technical writer to explain what's in the package and how it works
- ✔ A sales writer to make sure the correct, customer-attracting words are on the package
- ✔ A graphic designer to create an eye-catching, visually appealing home for your invention
- ✔ A silent store shopper to scan what's currently selling on store shelves, study pricing, packaging, color schemes, competition, and space limitations of retailers' shelves

Any and all of these people can claim rights and demand additional compensation for their work unless you bind them with a work-for-hire agreement.

Protecting Your Idea and Your Product

Unless you're a CIA agent working deep undercover, you talk about what you do at work to your spouse, friends, even people you just met. Think how easily such innocent conversation can reveal information your boss or company wouldn't want known. And realize that someone involved with your invention may think they're making simple conversation at a cocktail party, but in reality they're disclosing trade secrets to your competition. You need to prevent such conversations in the first place and protect yourself from the damage such a conversation may do if it should happen. The best way to do this is by using confidentiality agreements (see Chapter 8). Having employees and contractors sign a confidentiality agreement at least makes them think before they speak, and at worst, offers you some protection should loose lips lead to litigation.

A cautionary tale

A game developer came up with a theme for a fabulous video game. Developing the story-board and doing the research took months. The developer hired a software writer to develop the software that would follow the game theme. During the process, the developer came up with a terrific name for the product, easily recognizable and understood.

The software was completed and the developer paid for the work. The developer took the software to the patent counsel and filed a copyright TX (a specific type of copyright on software) application for the software as well as a trademark for the name. The inventor/developer thought everything was done properly.

The video game was a tremendous success. It was licensed to one of the largest manufacturers for a 5 percent royalty, which was the norm at the time. This translated into millions of dollars in *potential* royalties.

But then the problems came. The inventor/developer/licensee received a cease-and-desist letter and lawsuit claiming he didn't have the rights to license the product software or the name. When the lawyers met around the boardroom table with the inventor/developer, in came the software writer. The inventor and patent counsel brought their original copyright TX and trademark for the name — and so did the software writer and his patent counsel. The inventor was confident he had the rights. He didn't. The software writer had filed a TX copyright on the software and it was filed and dated before the inventor's patent counsel's document TX copyright was filed.

You ask, "How could this happen?" This happened because the software writer completed the software and prepared the copyright filing and filed before giving the software to the actual inventor/developer. There was no work-for-hire agreement and the patent office always goes with the first submission. No one could prove otherwise. What was the outcome? With millions of dollars at stake and the market ready, not to mention potential fraud from the licensee toward the licensor, the royalty fees were split and both the original inventor and software writer each received half the royalties.

In another scenario, say you develop and produce your invention and your wildest dreams come true — your product is selling like hotcakes. Your bank account is growing and you're well on your way to easy street when you hear a knock on your door and then are served court papers stating that there should have been a co-inventor listed on your patent. You're thinking, "What in the world are they talking about?" Then you read the name of the proto-typer who helped work on the development of your product. You may not have heard from this guy since you paid his fee, and naive inventor that you are, you thought that was the end of the story. It's not.

You may have sweat blood, borrowed money from your family and friends, begged money from people you don't know, mortgaged your home, and denied yourself (and your family) vacations to turn your idea into a thriving business. Now, the nice professional who made your prototype years earlier comes along and wants a piece of your action. To this end, she claims status as a co-inventor and co-owner and wants half of your royalties and half of your sales income. To add insult to injury, under the United States Patent and Trademark Office's defi-nition of a co-inventor, the prototyper may have a good case, despite the fact that you paid that person a fair price for her professional services at the time.

Another potentially troublesome scenario involves the graphic designer who works on the packaging for your product. That nice lady who designed the beautiful box your product is displayed in may come along and demand you pay her copyright fees for each unit you sell that is packaged in the box she designed. Unless you've secured an agreement to the contrary, the artist owns the copyright to her work. (See Chapter 7 for more on copyrights.)

You can prevent this unhappy picture from becoming your own nightmare by following these tips:

✔ **Negotiate all the terms right at the beginning when you're poor and just starting up and put them in written, signed agreement.** Money attracts people who want it, and your success may look like a free ride to someone who knew you or your invention in its early stages.

✔ **Document every step of the process.** Record when and where you met with designers, lawyers, financial advisors — and what was discussed. If you think of a name for your product, seek trademark protection for it immediately.

✔ **Insist on confidentiality agreements.** Have anyone you speak to about your invention sign a *confidentiality* (or *nondisclosure*) agreement, com-plete with a noncompete clause, *before* you disclose information on your invention to them. If you want to bounce ideas off a friend or colleague, have them sign a nondisclosure agreement. Chapter 8 has more on how to keep your invention confidential.

✔ **Get signed work-for-hire agreements.** If you want anyone to do any kind of work with your invention or idea, product, or software, which may result in the subject matter of a copyright, whether they work on drawings, prototypes, packaging, or any other aspect, always have them sign a work-for-hire agreement along with nondisclosure and noncompetition agreements. A signed work-for-hire agreement can stop a lawsuit in its tracks.

Many inventors confronted with a lawsuit over patent ownership immediately want to blame their patent attorney, which is probably a natural inclination, but not effective or logical. A patent attorney's job is to get you a patent, not necessarily to protect all your interests every step of the way. You need to do your own homework and inform yourself of your rights and how to protect them.

Working Out Work-for-Hire Agreements

A *work-for-hire agreement* states that you're the inventor who has come up with an idea, and you're hiring the professional services of a person to work with your invention. By signing this agreement, the prototyper or manufacturing company or whomever you've hired relinquishes all rights as a co-inventor, even if he or she must be named as a co-inventor, and the packaging or label designer gives up any copyrights.

Work-for-hire agreements are typically made between an employer and an employee or between an independent contractor and a person who needs the contractor's professional services to do a specific job.

Employers often require employees to sign a work-for-hire/noncompete employment agreement upon hiring, and for good reason. Imagine you own a software development company and hire computer programmers to develop new software to add to your company's product line. You pay the programmer a salary and provide health insurance, vacation, sick time, and holiday pay. You assume the financial risk — it's your money on the line. The programmer went for security. From this perspective, it's only fair that the programmer signs an agreement assigning all intellectual property rights to you, as well as agreeing not to compete with your company for a certain length of time after leaving your employ. You don't want the programmer taking trade secrets and know-how gained on your dollar and starting a competing business.

Some of the key components to consider when negotiating your agreements include:

✔ **A warranty or indemnification against patent infringement.** Suppose that an old, established company hires a young engineer directly out of college to work on an assigned project. The novice engineer learns from the other engineers along the way while being paid a full-time salary with no risk. How does the company prevent him from taking the acquired ingenuity and potential trade secrets with him to a future competitor for more money and benefits? Well, by having the engineer sign a work-for-hire agreement, including indemnification against patent infringement, the new engineer can't include trade secrets or any other type of intellectual property information he discovered into the new projects he'll work on, if he gets a job with a competitor in the future.

✔ **The length of the term of the agreement.** You want to make sure that your project has a beginning and an ending. You want to know when your work will be complete.

Why? Say that you've revealed your product to the general public; therefore, under patent law, you only have one year to apply for a patent. During that year, you're working on your prototype and want a working model in order to conduct some market research with potential consumers. Because you may go through several prototypes in the developmental stages, you absolutely want to state your prototype must be finished in say 60 days, 90 days, or whatever time frame that you and your product developer agree upon. You don't want an open-ended contract. Some developers drag a project on for several months or even years and run up a lot of bills in the meantime. Get your time frame set and move forward. Your contract should have a definite beginning and end.

✔ **Stipulation that you're the owner of all variations and revisions leading up to the completed project, including concepts that were considered but not used.** This includes prototypes that didn't work.

✔ **Extended coverage to include any subcontractors the person you hired used.** You may hire a printer to make the box for your product to be placed in, and the printer may subcontract with a graphic artist who's a part-time student to design the artwork. Many times, design and engineering firms subcontract various work to outside firms or individuals in order to curtail employee overhead costs.

✔ **The payment schedule, which should be based on delivery.** An agreement for a prototyper, for example, may stipulate that one-third of the fee is paid up front, one-third when technical drawings are completed, and final payment made upon completion of project.

Be sure to address how expenses such as travel, material costs, and subcontractor fees are paid.

✔ *Scope creep* **— quite often the development process ranges far and wide as you consider and reject idea after idea.** Document your expectations in very clear terms and include a specific process that addresses any change of direction or broadening of the scope of the original project.

For example, your original concept had one wheel but now you realize that you need four. You should also include the reverse situation, in which you specified one wheel and the developer used four.

Keep in mind that every project is different, and that the associated agreements can be simple or extremely complex. Your legal counsel may be able to provide you with other elements to consider, based upon your specific situation.

Appendix A provides you a sample agreement, which you may feel free to modify to fit your situation whether you're hiring a prototyper or graphic artist, but I strongly suggest that you involve your attorney. This process is too important and things can go afoul quickly. You want to fend off as many potential problems and lawsuits as possible and hire an attorney at the beginning.

Always, from the beginning, have everyone sign a nondisclosure and noncompete and always have a work-for-hire agreement. *Never* leave anything to chance or prepare to give half or more away. I usually tell my clients to negotiate when they're poor, because when you're successful, many people are going to want a piece of your profits.

Chapter 11

Evaluating Your Invention's Potential

Getting a new product to market takes lots of money and lots of effort from lots of people. So you want to make sure that your invention has a reasonable chance of making it in the marketplace before you expend all that money and effort. Helping you figure out how to determine your product's chances is what this chapter's all about.

Answering Questions about Viability

You must travel a long road between waking up with a great idea and getting your invention into the market. Each step toward a marketable product is one of denial and challenge. You may go down the road of invention any number of times before you hit on an idea and an invention that can make it in the marketplace. Rarely is a first invention a marketable invention. As an inventor, you have to be willing to try, try again.

As the creator, you may need outside help to evaluate whether your idea (your baby) has what it takes to make it in the cold, cruel marketplace and is worth the time, effort, and money to get it to that point.

Before you get to the multitude of marketing issues, you need to address a handful of basic questions about your invention — questions I explore in the following sections.

Is your idea original?

Obviously, if somebody has already come up with and produced an item as good as or better than your invention, you shouldn't pursue a similar idea any further. You'd only be wasting your time and money. So, your first step is to find out whether your idea is actually original.

You can look in many places to find products similar to yours. If you have an idea for a consumer product, check stores, catalogues, and the Internet. Conduct a patent search (see Chapter 3). Check trade associations and trade publications in your field. Visit trade shows relevant to your idea. Look in the business and popular press. Ask people in the field if they've ever heard of anything along the lines of your idea.

You don't have to be afraid of someone stealing your idea when it's still just a gleam in your eye — all the hard work still has to be done. Of course, you want to keep your questions general and keep the details of your idea to yourself. Don't forget that your patent rights in major foreign countries may be jeopardized if you disclose your patent claims before you file a patent application in the U.S.

If you don't find an existing product at first glance, you eventually have to do a patent search (check out Chapter 3 for tips on how to do this). You can do that in this early stage, but it's probably a better idea to hold off until you've taken a look at your idea in the light of the questions posed in the next two sections. (For more on international copyrights, see Chapter 2.)

How will your invention be produced?

Many inventors just think of an idea and patent it and then assume that big companies are going to contact them to license their patent. I'm sure I don't have to tell you that this isn't going to happen. (Usually, only the rip-off marketing firms make these kinds of promises and predictions.) Inventors need to think the entire process, including production, through, along with their options and who's going to do the work — themselves or someone else or some other arrangement. As an inventor, you need to consider whether producing the invention will be cost-effective or even possible.

The first impulse many innovators have is to take their ideas to a big national company. Provide the dazzling idea, they think, and let the giant work out the details. After all, the national company has the money, the production capability, and the marketing know-how to make this surefire profit maker succeed. Unfortunately, the big companies are almost never interested in ideas from outsiders. They have what's called the *not invented here* (NIH) syndrome. Whether because an outside invention is considered a long shot or simply because large corporations need potential sales of an item to be in the tens of millions dollars, the chance of selling your idea to a major corporation is slim.

On the other end of the scale, you may be able to produce your invention yourself, manufacturing it in your home (or garage!) and selling it by mail order. This method can be a good way to get started, but after a while you may find yourself getting tired of having 200,000 better mousetraps stashed in your garage. Of course, if you can start a company or already have your own company, you have a tailor-made platform for producing and distributing your invention.

Another option is taking your idea to small and medium-sized businesses. Many smaller firms are interested in producing quantities that are far below a larger company's threshold. A small firm may lack the marketing and distribution expertise of a larger firm, but you can at least get the ball rolling (or the mousetrap snapping).

Will your invention make money?

Whether your invention can make money is a question designed to keep you up at night. Unfortunately, no one can answer with any assurance. After all, even major corporations that do massive market studies hit clinkers all the time. Remember New Coke?

You certainly can and should do research to determine whether your invention has a market (see Chapter 17 for details). You need to figure out your profit ratios to make sure that you can take in enough money to make it worth your while. When checking into the costs of manufacturing your product, if you find that it can't be cost-effectively produced, don't waste your time. (Of course, even if you find that you can make money from your product, weighing the profit margin after production and distribution costs against your personal efforts, expenses, time, and travel away from home may cause you to think twice before traveling down this adventurous road.)

One indication you can use to help judge your invention's marketability is whether other people are interested in investing in it.

Ultimately, though, you make your best guess and either abandon ship or pull out the stops and charge full steam ahead.

Asking for Evaluations

Just because *you* think that your invention is the greatest thing since sliced bread doesn't guarantee that everyone else will. And because you won't make money selling your product to yourself, you need to know what other people think about your invention.

Getting some free advice

I recommend hiring a professional product evaluation service, but even people who aren't professionals in commercializing new products can be an excellent source of feedback and information for you. Some of the laypeople you may want to speak with to obtain pertinent feedback are:

✔ **Buyers and salespeople who buy and sell products similar to yours:** They work with the public every day and have a vast amount of experience. The manager of a large retail department story is likely to have 10 or more years experience in the business and be familiar with pricing, warehousing, distribution, packaging, and more.

✔ **Engineers and technical people:** They can give you advice as far as product design.

✔ **Packaging designers and companies:** Packaging sells products.

✔ **Professors and students studying your industry:** Teachers and students can give you additional insight into the current market and they probably have information on the latest research.

✔ **Entrepreneurs:** They can tell you what it's like running a business and give you tips on what to do right, share what they did wrong, and advice on what they'd do differently.

If you don't know people in these areas on a personal basis, find someone who does. You don't know the consumers who will buy your product on a personal basis, but you'll have to figure out how to get to them. Plan and target whom you want to talk with and follow through.

The best time to solicit these opinions is before you've spent a lot of money developing your invention. The best people to ask are anybody and everybody you can convince to talk to you.

Hiring a professional evaluator

The Commissioner of the United States Patent and Trademark Office (USPTO) advises inventors to have a professional, nonbiased evaluation conducted before applying for a patent. That's great advice, and I recommend the same. I highly recommend having a professional, nonbiased product evaluation conducted before committing yourself to the patent application process. You may not want to spend the money on a patent unless you can show that your invention has commercial viability.

Make sure that you have a signed confidentiality agreement with the person evaluating your invention (see Chapter 8). If you don't have a patent and disclose your idea without using a confidentiality agreement, you have only one year from that disclosure to apply for a patent before you lose your patent rights.

Take care in hiring an evaluator because a number of invention promotion companies are nothing more than scams. See Chapter 17 for more on invention promotion companies.

You also need to protect yourself against inexperienced and incompetent evaluation services. Before hiring a company or person to evaluate your invention, get references and check them. Find out who's conducting your evaluation. Some organizations, including universities and nonprofit associations, use undergraduate college students and other untrained or inexperienced staff as new product evaluators. The evaluation system the company uses may be great, but the experience of the evaluator or evaluation team is what counts. Trained and experienced product evaluators can spot technical and commercial flaws that others cannot.

Ask the company how many products they give a high rating to in comparison to the products that get low ratings, and don't be put off if the company gives you a report that points out a lot of flaws in your product. That's exactly what you're paying them to do. Finding out the negatives before you spend money on getting patents or on producing your invention can save you big bucks whether you decide to proceed or not.

Some reputable professional invention evaluation services companies include:

- ✔ Innovative Product Technologies, Inc., 4131 N.W. 13th Street, Suite 220, Gainesville, FL 32609; phone 352-373-1007; fax 208-265-4482; Web site www.inventionevaluation.com. Also a second location at: P.O. Box 817, Sandpoint, ID 83864; phone 208-265-5837. (This is my company!)

- ✔ Innovation Institute, Center for Business Research & Development, SW Missouri State University, 901 South National Avenue, Springfield, MO 65802-0089; phone 417-836-5751; fax 417-836-7666.

- ✔ United Inventors Association, P.O. Box 23447, Rochester, NY 14692; phone 585-359-9310; fax 585-359-1132; e-mail UIAUSA@aol.com.

- ✔ Wisconsin Innovation Service Center, 402 McCutchan Hall, University of Wisconsin-Whitewater, Whitewater, WI 53190; phone 262-472-1365; personal phone line 262-472-1366; fax 262-472-1600; Web site http://academics.uww.edu/busines/innovate/innovate.htm; e-mail malwicd@uww.edu.

Bracing for feedback

As the inventor, you already know your invention's good points (though you won't mind hearing them repeated). What you need from evaluators, however, is a clear idea of whether your invention is worth pursuing down the long and costly road to the marketplace. You want solid information that helps you avoid mistakes and costly errors.

Look for and listen to the suggestions for improvement and constructive criticism. I can assure you that making changes before you go into production is much cheaper than making them afterward.

Any type of professional evaluation should give you

- ✔ An overall assessment of your invention's commercial viability

- ✔ A heads up about problems that may arise as your product moves through the different production stages

- ✔ An indication of whether a prototype will be necessary and useful to present your invention to others

- ✔ A pathway to determining what additional information is needed to further investigate your invention's overall feasibility and marketability

An honest, unbiased product evaluation report and documentation of any action you plan in response to it can help you attract investors, potential licensees, and others who can work with you in bringing your product to market.

Invention rip-off marketing companies are able to snatch inventors' money because people *want* to be told that their products are winners and that they'll make millions of dollars. Ask everyone who tells you that your idea is worth millions to invest in it — this is a good reality check. After all, you wouldn't want to deny them the opportunity to invest in a multimillion-dollar deal, would you? If they balk, you know what they really think.

Looking at evaluation techniques

Having your idea evaluated for viability can bring you several types of responses:

- ✔ **Simple *yes, your idea is great* or *no, your idea stinks* evaluations from one or more evaluators:** This type of evaluation is simple but useless. Even if you're just asking your friends, have them tell you *why* they think your invention has a shot or not.

- ✔ **An in-depth individual analysis by one or more specialists who have technical and/or marketing expertise in your invention's area:** This is a dream evaluation, but it costs several hundred to several thousand dollars per evaluation, making it impractical.

> ✔ **A systematic analysis by a cross section of people who represent a broad range of technical and commercial expertise.** This type of evaluation is just right. It gives you the level of detail you need to make decisions about your invention and its costs are within reason (usually less than $500).
>
> Major manufacturing companies generally have their own evaluation systems for products, not necessarily ideas. Other evaluators use the licensed PIES system, which I explain in the "Cutting into PIES" section.

Any evaluation system you use should, at a minimum, accomplish the following:

> ✔ Identify ideas and inventions worthy of further development
>
> ✔ Recognize ideas and inventions that don't have the potential to become successful innovations
>
> ✔ Point out potential trouble spots or areas requiring special attention before development or commercialization begins
>
> ✔ Suggest strategies for further development and/or commercialization

Realize that predicting whether a product has what it takes to succeed while you're still in the early stages of the innovation process is hard to do. Too many unknowns are out there for even a professional to accurately predict success. Very rarely, an idea or invention has such clarity of technical and commercial feasibility that its potential for success is obvious. However, most ideas and inventions require astute development and marketing in order to become successful products. The professional evaluation service doesn't know how you plan to market your invention, what it will end up looking like, or any of a hundred other key factors that contribute to your product's success or failure. An evaluation can help you make the decision about whether to go ahead with development, but it cannot guarantee or even predict whether your invention will make money.

Cutting into PIES

I highly recommend using the PIES system to evaluate your invention's viability. PIES stands for *Preliminary Innovation Evaluation System*. This system was developed by Dr. Gerald G. Udell in 1974 under a National Science Foundation Grant and is now in its 11th generation. Various changes and improvements to this system have been implemented over time in response to the experience gained from evaluating more than 30,000 ideas and new products from all walks of life.

PIES evaluates your invention from a variety of perspectives, all of which are helpful for you to consider on your own. I talk about the broad categories in the following sections.

Health, safety, and welfare

If your invention is subject to government regulations of any kind, you need to be sure you can meet them. Think through safety issues by considering the potential hazards of using your invention.

Take environmental impact into account. Does manufacturing your invention require scarce or fragile resources? How ecofriendly is the manufacturing and disposal process? Can your invention promote destruction or misuse of natural resources?

Ask whom your invention benefits. You want to make a positive contribution to society as well as to your pocketbook.

You also want to take care of your own welfare by determining whether you can protect your intellectual property with a patent, trademark, or copyright.

Development, feasibility, and function

Evaluating what stage your invention is at helps determine what more you have to do and gives you an idea of whether it's worth pursuing further. If you're just at the idea phase and things aren't looking good in other evaluation categories, you can cut your losses or switch directions if possible.

You also need to do a reality check. Your idea may be earth shaking, but if it doesn't work, isn't practical, or can't be produced or replicated, you won't get very far.

Beyond the theoretical questions, you need to get a firm grasp on what exactly your product is, what it does, and what purpose it serves. Does your product fill a psychological or physical need for the consumer or is it a gimmick? The answer itself isn't as important at this stage as just knowing what the answer is.

You also want to know what potential there is to adding additional products or additional styles, qualities, and price ranges. Some products will spin off other ones. For example, a new life preserver for boating may also be developed for uses in aircraft for pilots. Then you may want to add additional products to your product line for both the boating and aircraft industries, because you'll be talking to the same buyers and industry reps.

Look at your invention and compare it with existing products in terms of attractiveness, durability, price, and value. Judge whether your product is compatible with existing attitudes, methods, and uses. Can potential consumers readily recognize its function and usefulness?

If your product requires frequent service and parts, estimate the cost and determine who pays them — the manufacturer or the consumer?

Costs

You have to consider costs all through the process.

Get an idea of how much it will cost to get your idea to the production stage, including the research and development aspects, the market analysis, legal costs, and so on. Beyond production, you need to consider distribution costs and weigh potential problems you may encounter when establishing distribution channels.

Think about whether your invention needs investors to bring it to fruition and if so, how much and who.

How many resources and how much money and time will it take to promote the advantages, special features, and benefits of your product?

Think about how your invention can be made profitable. You need to get an idea of how and when your invention would make enough to pay potential investors off and bring you some profit.

Market matters

You need to determine what kind of market research is required in order to investigate the commercial viability of your invention. The search tells you what the overall market is and the potential sales volume. You want estimates in terms of local, regional, or national sales.

Look at the existing competition for your invention. Is your invention distinctive enough to break into the market? List the advantages it has over similar products and look for ways to offset any disadvantages. Even if your product has a shot at taking on the competition, you need to anticipate the appearance of competing products and evaluate how well you can do against them.

Look for barriers to entering the market. For example, does your invention require that you educate consumers about what it does or how it works? Is your invention a supplement to something else, and if so, what happens if that primary product takes a nose dive?

Gauge how stable the demand for your invention is likely to be and whether it is likely to remain constant, grow, or decline. Try to anticipate seasonal or other market fluctuations. You need to figure out how long your invention's life cycle is. How long can your product be profitably sold before the market shifts or your invention is replaced by a new product or technology?

Management issues

Judging how much technological, financial, and general management talent your product requires is an important evaluation step. Knowing who the players are and how they can help your idea succeed is key to weighing its chances.

If your product requires a significant amount of technical expertise, it helps if you have access to that expertise. Likewise, a knowledgeable financial person on your team is an asset in getting your invention to market.

Risk factors

Consider competition, difficulty of distribution, cost of reaching your target market, financial investment, and technical needs to determine how risky your venture is. Starting any business or introducing any product to market is risky, but you need to assess whether the anticipated return for your investment in time, energy, and money is worth that risk.

Maximizing the Results of Your Evaluation

Product evaluation shows that your idea is worth spending time, sweat equity, money, and energy on. Use the evaluation to the fullest extent by showing it to potential investors and your banker, insurance agent, and accountant. Remember, these people probably know people who have money to invest.

The results of your invention's evaluation may reveal a short product life cycle. A short life doesn't necessarily mean a profitless life, however. Fad items can make their inventors a fortune, if they use certain financial, product, and marketing strategies to maximize their profits. In this type of situation, the evaluation system can be a useful mechanism to help avoid obvious mistakes. Unfortunately, even the most sophisticated marketing-oriented firms make mistakes that could have been avoided had the firm conducted a more comprehensive initial evaluation of a new product.

Even after the evaluation is completed, do more research on the industry and on similar products. Get some professional assistance and advice to explore intellectual property protections such as patents (see Chapters 2 and 3 for patent info).

Chapter 12

Looking at the Production Process

· ·

· ·

*H*ow many would-be inventors progress beyond the dream of product conception to the reality of a functioning product? Fewer than you may think. The few who persevere and develop their invention into a functional product are the true entrepreneurs. If you want to be one of the successful ones, you must avoid the countless traps set to snare you. You have to be or become an inventor with hands-on, practical knowledge of what it takes to be a manufacturer.

In this chapter, I outline the manufacturing issues you need to be aware of whether you make the product yourself or subcontract the manufacturing process. (For details on subcontracting, see Chapter 16.)

Focusing on the Process

The production process starts with you — you conceive the product and possibly patent it. After that, someone else (usually) designs it, the government may inspect it or regulate it, and, finally, a manufacturing plant produces it.

In this section, I explain the process and how it works.

Whether you subcontract the manufacturing or make the product yourself, you should know what's involved in producing your invention. You must be able to discuss manufacturing components and understand the costs of the production process so that you can make intelligent decisions.

> ## Ruling in Uncle Sam
>
> As any area of public involvement serving the public matures, governmental agencies exploit the area, primarily to seek revenues.
>
> For example, if you make electrical products, you're required to have your product approved for public safety by agents such as the Underwriters Laboratories, the Consumer Product Safety Commission, or the Bureau of Fire Underwriters. If you develop a medical device, the Medical Device Section of the U.S. Food and Drug Administration must provide you with approval or a marketing release.
>
> If you manufacture your product in the U.S. and want to ship into the European Common Market countries, you need to secure a CE *(Community*
>
> *of Europe)* approval in addition to your required U.S. ISO *(International Standards Organization)* manufacturing and design approvals. The cost of meeting regulatory standards for your products can often add up to 20 percent or more of the cost of your product.
>
> You may want to talk with someone in your local Small Business Development Center, SCORE *(Senior Core of Retired Executives)*, or the U.S. Small Business Administration to find further contacts on what type of approvals that you specifically need when manufacturing and distributing your product. Do this before you go into production, not afterward, to save yourself money, time, and a lot of aggravation.

Examining product cycling

Everything in life has a beginning and an end. Sometimes those starts and finishes are hard to see, but you don't have that fuzziness in the production process — you start with a collection of raw materials that don't add up to anything and end up with something you can see, touch, and, most importantly, sell.

Product cycling refers to how fast your product can be made, shipped, and sold before a reorder comes in. It's also known as *turnaround time.* Product cycling requires all contributing factors to be properly addressed before the cycle starts. A tremendous amount of preparation is required before an assembly line can start producing something as simple as a key ring or as complex as an automobile. One thing out of place — raw materials aren't up to standard, or there aren't enough workers to run the production line, for example — and the whole process breaks down. Planning is crucial for any endeavor, and for a production operation, planning is everything.

The greater the number of diverse components in the final assembly process, the more critical long-range planning becomes. Manufacturing processes are extremely varied depending upon your product and its level of sophistication. Today, you have a wide variety of plastics, resins, metals, and molds to deal with in order to make even a simple product.

For example, say you develop a new toy using a special lead acid battery (a miniature of your car battery); it also uses several different light bulb assemblies. Your toy requires molded plastic parts, metal parts that need to be turned on a lathe, and some stamped metal parts. You also need the special battery, the light bulbs, and maybe a battery charger made and assembled. And you need a number of nuts and bolts to hold all the parts together. On top of keeping track of all the components, you may have the different components made by different companies in different places, so you have to coordinate getting all the materials to the right manufacturer at the right time and then everything assembled at the right place. You can see how production scheduling can cause ulcers.

Your ulcers only get worse because your invention is a toy, which has a definite high-selling season — before Christmas. You may plan to make 12,000 toys the first year in 12 production runs of 1,000 each. However, to accommodate Christmas sales, you need to have 5,000 units delivered to your wholesalers by — but not before — August 15. So you have to figure out how to schedule your production runs to meet your Christmas deadline, without needing to warehouse your toys before you're allowed to ship them. (Stores won't accept merchandise too far in advance — they have space management issues of their own.)

Subcontracting

Most amateur inventors who want to mass-produce an invention subcontract the actual manufacturing. Unless you're already in the production business, you're far better off farming out production of your invention. If you're not already knowledgeable about the ins and outs of manufacturing, I strongly recommend that you pay an experienced manufacturer (or two or three) rather than try to master a very complex process in what's bound to be too short an amount of time.

Whether you subcontract or do it yourself, it pays to have a general knowledge of the production process for your invention. To start out, you have to evaluate candidates for one or more aspects of the production cycle, then you have to troubleshoot snags in the process at some point, and you must evaluate your contracts with your suppliers, producers, and distribution vendors periodically, so it pays to know what you're talking about with all these people.

You have to carefully consider the ability of a manufacturer to be an effective subcontractor of your invention. Subcontracting manufacturers are available in all physical sizes for both short and long runs. The size and complexity of your product directly relates to your subcontractor's performance.

When shopping around for a subcontractor, the first consideration you should make is the ability of the management to run a tight, efficient shop. Some of the issues you need to address are

✔ **Financial stability:** A production plant with huge loans outstanding may be poorly managed or on the verge of foreclosure. Get references from banks, if possible, and from long-term customers.

It sounds strange, but be wary of a bid that's significantly lower than other bids for the same job. The manufacturer may be poorly managed or so strapped for cash that they're looking to get cash any way they can. They either won't be able to continue to offer the low price or won't be able to pay their own bills and can very well leave you in the lurch.

✔ **Overall capabilities:** How efficient is the manufacturing process? How quick? How many components of your product can one plant handle? (Generally, the more components you have made at one place, the more cost-efficient the process is for you.)

How does your product fit into the production schedule in relation to the plant's bread-and-butter products? Is there room in the schedule to do additional runs if your product sells out quickly? (Work out contingency plans to cover such a situation — and the reverse — in the contract you sign.)

You don't want to have labored for years to conceive and develop your invention only to discover that you can't meet the required sales volumes, because your subcontractor doesn't have enough capacity.

✔ **Ability to meet standards:** Your subcontractor must meet not only your quality standards, but perhaps government rules and regulations, also. Make sure that the plant manager is aware of and familiar with any regulations your product is subject to.

Check around, get references, and know what you're getting.

The manufacturer should know how to set up an efficient mass production line. How the production line is designed is based upon the volume, whether short or long runs. The cost of setting up and breaking down an assembly line between product runs can have a major impact on the final cost of your product.

Remember that some manufacturers who make seasonal products take on other products during their slower production times. For example, a boat manufacturer may also manufacture hot tubs for another company during the off-season.

Take the time to physically visit a manufacturing company if you're thinking of signing on the dotted line for that company to make your product, even if the plant is overseas. I'm amazed at the number of inventors who don't make this simple check. Especially with offshore production facilities, you need to make sure the facilities are up to your standards. I know of many inventors who paid foreign manufacturers in advance for 10,000 units or more, only to find that those units were not at all up to the standards promised. And trying to get your money back in a situation like that is a story in itself. Always visit the companies that you're planning on doing business with.

Chapter 16 is all about subcontracting with a manufacturer, so flip over to that chapter for more details.

Making Up the Materials

Molds, tools, dies, and raw materials are a major part and a major expense of the manufacturing process. Figuring out where to get your raw materials and how much you have to pay is an important step in the production process.

Figuring out what you need

Before approaching any manufacturer, you must have a production-quality prototype as well as a CAD/CAM drawing of your product. (CAD/CAM stands for *computer-aided design/computer-aided manufacturing*.) This is a mechanical drawing constructed on the computer instead of the ol' fashion drafting board. Many times, research can be conducted with consumers to see if there's a market by using the CAD/CAM drawings instead of spending money on a prototype if funds are limited. The prototype and drawing together detail each individual part used in making your product. Each mold drawing should be complete to the point where mold makers can figure how much it would cost to make the mold in various materials so that they can bid on costs of tooling each component part, based upon the expected level of volume. (Your projected sales volume figures come from your market research; see Chapter 17.)

Different materials are used for different purposes. For example, an aluminum mold may make 20,000 units; whereas a steel mold, costing a few thousand dollars more, may make 200,000 units before wearing out. So, whether you anticipate relatively few sales of a high-priced item, or high-volume sales of an inexpensive product helps determine what you need to spend on molds. You should be able to develop a cost for each component as part of the overall tooling costs.

If you do short production runs, you have to figure in time to set up the assembly line. You spread the costs of setting up the line over the number of units produced during a specific run. Remember that the unique components of each setup must be stored during their inactivity. Consider how and where you can store them to maintain a state of readiness.

Some of the factors to consider when determining the production facilities and equipment that you need include

✔ **Material:** What type of material — resin, plastic, metal, wood — or combination does your invention require?

✔ **Cost:** How can you get the quality you need at the cheapest cost? (See the section "Calculating Costs" later in this chapter for more on costs.)

✔ **Source:** Where can you get the raw material?

✔ **Quantity:** How much of the raw material do you need to have in stock at all times, and where are you going to store it?

✔ **Storage:** Are there special requirements involved in the storage? For example, chemicals and resins, food related products, and so on may need certain storage conditions.

You may consider listing a variety of sources, thus giving yourself price estimates for the cheapest cost with the best production. In other words, create options for yourself.

Taking on tooling

To make things easier on yourself, look for a manufacturer who's making a product similar to yours. That way, the subcontracting manufacturer has people skilled in developing the jigs, fixtures, stamps, and molds needed to produce your invention.

The overall efficiency of any production line is directly related to the design of the tooling required to make the components. The tooling determines the quality of parts that come off the production line.

Finally, the design and flexibility of the jigs and fixtures determine mass assembly and packaging costs. The more efficient the design and tooling of your product, the cheaper it will be to make your product. Most manufacturers have an in-house packaging division due to cost efficiency. Because manufacturing is so specialized nowadays, sometimes if you're a start-up or small company, it's less expensive to have your product made by one company and then packaged by another.

Controlling inventory

You aim to achieve a rapid turnover on your inventory because the fewer dollars you tie up in raw materials and finished goods, the more dollars you have to reinvest in your business, or take out in profits. Good inventory control means balancing goods and materials coming in with goods and materials going out so that you have neither shortage nor overabundance.

The main purpose of installing and keeping on top of a good inventory control system is to save money. Everything costs money, especially in the business world. If you receive the raw material to make your product before the production line is ready to use it, it costs you money to store it. If you receive the material too late, it costs you money in lost production time, missed schedules, and so on.

To maximize your inventory control, you need to figure out how many days your product spends in inventory. To do this, use the following formula, which shows the average number of days it takes to sell your inventory.

$$\frac{\text{Average Inventory}}{\text{Cost of Goods Sold} \times 360 \text{ days}} = \text{Number of days the product sits in inventory}$$

$$\frac{5,000 \text{ keyboards}}{\$1.25/\text{unit} \times 360 \text{ days}} = 11.11 \text{ days}$$

Look for trends that indicate a change in your inventory levels. Then, compare the calculated days in inventory to your *inventory cycle* — how quickly inventory moves out of your possession. Compare that timing to industry standards. If sales aren't good, inventory is basically sitting and costing you money while it sits. If your inventory cycle is high, you're selling and your product is moving from the manufacturer to the consumer at a fast rate. Reorders are coming in. You want to compare how fast your products are selling to the industry average for similar products.

Calculating the number of times that you turn over (or sell) inventory during the year tells you how quickly your inventory is selling. You use this information to predict how many products to manufacture and how many production runs to schedule. The following formula shows you how to calculate turnover.

$$\frac{\text{Cost of Goods Sold} \times 360 \text{ days}}{\text{Average Inventory}} = \text{Number of times you turnover (sell) your inventory during the year}$$

$$\frac{\$1.25/\text{unit} \times 360 \text{ days}}{5,000 \text{ keyboards}} = 9 \text{ times per year}$$

Generally, a high inventory turnover is an indicator of good inventory management and that your product is selling. But a high ratio can also mean a shortage of inventory. A low turnover may indicate overstocking, or obsolete inventory. Compare these to industry standards, which are usually found in trade magazines related specifically to your product.

Packaging for profit and protection

The packaging of a potentially breakable product must be scientifically evaluated relative to the type of shipping container, which is designed to comply with the various applicable regulations of the shipping service. Just like when you ship a package via the U.S. Post Office, you have to follow its rules and regulations regarding not only packaging, but even for letter size. The same goes with your product's packaging when you're sending it by train, truck, ship, or mail carrier. All have specific packaging requirements, so be sure to check before attempting to send several thousand units to a warehouse or store.

How many times have you received something you ordered from a catalogue in pieces? You may be inclined to blame the delivery service instead of placing blame where it belongs; with the person who designed the packaging. In reality, about everything you use is breakable. If you don't believe me, give your invention to a 12-year-old kid and discover the many ways it can be broken. If you were making high-tech electronic equipment, you'd want to make sure that the equipment was safely packed, most likely with foam molding around the product so that it wouldn't be able to move and break while being transported.

Packaging has to work on a number of levels and serve a variety of purposes. It has to be sturdy yet attractive, stackable yet easily separated, make people want to pick up your invention, and able to take lots of handling.

When packaging your invention, you have to accept the fact that it will be frozen, baked, dropped, kicked, and abused in every possible way. Therefore, if it is broken in shipping, it reflects back upon the overall manufacturing process, because packaging is indeed a component of that process.

The cost of packaging can easily exceed the cost of the product it is designed to protect. For example, a large, thin-walled glass vase made in Timbuktu at a cost of one dollar has to travel by mule to a distant harbor, be transported by steamship to the U.S., where it is picked up by truck, delivered to a warehouse, and later transported from the warehouse to the retailer's shelves. Obviously, the costs of packaging this vase far exceed the cost of the vase itself.

Keep in mind that you must package well, but packaging costs can literally wipe out your profit margin if they're too high. For instance, if you have a product that retails for 99¢ and the cost for packaging the product is 79¢, you've got a problem. To avoid spending too much, get estimates from various packing companies. You can find such companies by doing an Internet search. Go to your favorite search engine, such as Google, and type **packing companies**.

Shipping news

Shipping containers serve two functions. They contain your product and protect it. Containing is important, but protecting is paramount. Consider the way you treat shipping containers yourself. If you ever received a box at home or at your job, you may have dropped it, sat on it, stepped on it, rolled it, kicked it, shook it, and generally abused it in every possible way. When you design shipping containers for your invention, keep people like yourself in mind.

Shipping crates are also exposed to extremes in temperatures and weather conditions, so you have to make sure the container can withstand heat, cold, humidity, rain, snow, sleet, and gloom of night.

How would you like to be in a small airplane and have a large bottle of exotic perfume break in the cargo hold and literally fumigate the whole airplane? Obviously, bad packaging can affect many lives.

The most common methods employed in getting goods from one place to another are listed here. Remember, your product may use one or more of these options at different stages of delivery:

- **Corrugated cardboard box with cardboard separators:** Used for the bulk shipping of wine bottles and/or canning jars, as well as other multi-pack items.

- **Hard plastic shell that supports and seals in the product:** This works great for computer cords, but not for breakable glassware.

- **Liquid foam packaging:** A liquid expanding foam is sprayed into a container, and then covered with a plastic paper sheet. The device is then placed and pushed down into the container. Finally, another plastic sheet is used to cover the device, followed by a second application of liquid foam over the top. At this point the corrugated box is then closed and stapled. The foam continues to expand, firmly encapsulating the device within the container. This is probably the most expensive but effective method of shipping any device, usually reserved for expensive, potentially breakable devices.

- **Pallets:** Employed for heavy devices, which are placed and strapped to a wooden base plate *(pallet),* designed to be handled with a forklift for loading. Often a cardboard box covers the device, which is positioned by stapling the base pallet. Palletizing is often employed to stack and ship a number of square boxed items in multiple to a warehouse.

- **Paper insertion packing and wrap, in a box with crushed paper suspension:** This method can work to pack light household items and is possibly a good way to use old newspaper, but isn't very practical.

- **Paper wrap shipped in the middle of a box filled with soft plastic balls:** A reliable method of shipping.

- **Plastic air bags:** Used to protect and separate mixed items that are prepackaged.

- **Plastic bubble wrap:** Very convenient and effective but quite expensive.

- ✔ **Preformed Styrofoam:** This encapsulates the product and is designed to snuggly fit the corrugated container and/or other containment box.

- ✔ **Weatherproof shipboard containers:** Generally used for large bulk shipments from overseas.

Some commercial delivery services may require your product to be packaged a specific way. FedEx, UPS, and other carriers each have specific packaging requirements. Make sure that your product conforms before spending big bucks on packaging. Some products, such as high-quality medical or electronics products, require foam packaging to be injected around the product. Otherwise, they won't pass inspection by the commercial carriers and won't be insured. Having a safe type of packaging for your product to prevent damage during the shipping process is definitely to your advantage.

The U.S. Department of Transportation (DOT) codes the durability and capacity of corrugated containers. Standards have been developed due to breakage in the past. Boxes are tested by their manufacturers and are designed for height, weight, flexibility, and durability.

Shipping a new product from the manufacturer to the retailer is a major cost. For example, if your product is made in the Pacific Rim, you may not be able to afford airfreight if you have a bulky, heavy product with a low cost value. Sea freight is a better option as it's much lower in cost; however, if time is a factor, it can be a major consideration, especially if your product involves perishable goods. In order to ship products from the west coast to the east in the U.S., it requires either trucking or railroad with trucking taking several days as opposed to several weeks by rail. Ports along the Mississippi River provide a north to south freeway for your product. You can also use this river via the Port of New Orleans to enter the European market by sea freight. After arriving at dockside, the shipments must be delivered to a warehouse by railroad and or auto freight (depending upon volume and location).

Delivering the goods

Where your production plant is physically located in relation to where the customer is located can often mean the difference between the success or failure of your company. The cost of domestic transport may equal or exceed the total cost of the delivery, even from overseas. Costs vary according to whether you're delivering to a warehouse or to a retailer. Obviously direct deliveries to the retailers' warehouses save you considerable handling and transportation costs.

Storing things away

Warehousing can be a major expense. Consider the following costs:

> ✔ The space itself
>
> ✔ Transporting goods or materials to your warehouse
>
> ✔ Loading, unloading, and reloading
>
> ✔ Fire, damage, and theft insurance

If your product has special storage needs (for instance, it requires cool temperatures), you have to accommodate — and pay for — those also.

About now, the possibility of licensing your product for a royalty may look very good when you start realizing the cost and effort it takes to move your product from a prototype stage to the store shelf.

Inspecting Facilities

Finding a space in which to produce your product is a complicated and challenging process. If you own your own manufacturing plant, you have questions on top of questions to consider, but even if you're *only* subcontracting the production of your invention, you have plenty to think about. In the following sections, I talk about the building and equipment.

Finding housing

Sometimes inventors visiting a huge manufacturing plant are overly impressed with the facility itself. Remember that bigger is not necessarily better and that the size of the factory has nothing to do with the overall cost-effectiveness of your product. Basing your decision about a subcontractor on the physical space is a mistake. What's inside the building is what really counts.

A huge building may be impressive to look at, but the company may be deeply in debt trying to pay for the space. The more money the manufacturer owes, the more interest they have to pay and the less competitive they are.

On the other extreme, beware of a bare room. To facilitate quality work, each production line table, or work bench, should be equipped with overhead lighting as well as drop down utilities; such as electrical services, compressed air, inspection devices, and so on.

Neither too big, nor too small; you want your production facilities to be just right, and have potential for expansion should your invention take off and warrant increasing production runs or expanding the plant.

Other issues to take into account when you're searching for a facility include:

- **Storage space:** You more than likely need to store either raw materials or finished product or both. Make sure the space you need in the condition you need it is available either at the plant itself or nearby.

- **Shipping facilities:** You need to get materials and possibly partially assembled components to the manufacturing facility. You also need to get the finished product to its next destination. The plant needs to be able to receive and send your product safely and efficiently.

If you're looking to buy production space, you have a few additional issues to concern yourself with. If you're going to manufacture and sell, you need to find out about local zoning and other restrictions and you have to consider space for parking and facilities for employees — including bathrooms and break rooms.

When you have a manufacturing facility, it must comply with the Occupational Safety and Health Act of 1970. You can obtain a copy of *Standards for General Industry* from the Superintendent of Documents, U.S. Government Printing Office, Washington, DC 20402, or a field office of the Occupational Safety and Health Administration.

Molding methods

Molding lends itself to a variety of techniques and qualities. For example, injection molding is capable of making parts almost as precise as those machined out of metal. On the other hand, blow molding is quite inexpensive — perfect for parts that don't have to be precise, such as milk jugs.

The quality of the molded part is determined by the skill of the mold maker and accuracy of the molding process, which I explain here:

- **Injection molding:** Beads of resin or plastic are melted in a heated cylinder at about 340 degrees Fahrenheit. When the cylinder is filled with melted resin, the material is pressed out and injected into a mold that's closed on all sides. The mold is then cooled rapidly and the material hardens. You can use different types of molds to get a variety of products — like using a set of cookie cutters to make a variety of cookies.

- **Vacuum molding:** A sheet of plastic is laid over the bottom of a form. The top of the form presses the plastic into place. The plastic is heated and becomes soft. Then a vacuum is formed on one side that sucks the soft sheet material into the design of the mold that forms a part. The part is then ejected from the press and the excess material is cut off.

- **Blow molding:** A hot glob of melted resin is forced into a mold that is the shape of the desired part. The air pressure within the glob of melted resin forces the resin out around the mold.

Lining up your equipment

The equipment you need to produce your invention comes in all shapes and sizes; unfortunately, it all comes with a pretty expensive price tag. But you need the equipment that's best for your invention and even if you can skimp on equipment, doing so isn't worth it in the long run.

If you're subcontracting the production of your invention, ask the plant manager about the equipment available and make sure the factory has what you need. If the plant has to install new machines in order to manufacture your product, be very careful. Make sure that the workers know how to handle the equipment efficiently and correctly — you don't want people experimenting on your baby. How fast the equipment works is a relevant issue, as well as how old it is, how adaptable it is, and whether it can handle the type of material your product needs.

If you're doing your own production work, you need to determine whether you want to buy or lease your equipment. Let me tell you right now that unless you already own a factory with the right equipment, you want to lease. A lease provides you the use of equipment for specific periods of time at fixed rental payments. The vast majority of businesses go the leasing route, because it makes the most sense for novices. The benefits of leasing equipment are numerous:

- **Leasing is flexible:** Companies have different needs, different cash flow patterns, and different and sometimes irregular streams of income. Therefore, your business conditions — cash flow, specific equipment needs, and tax situation may help define the terms of your lease. Leasing allows you to be more flexible in the management of your equipment. Many times when leasing, you can upgrade to newer, better equipment. If you own your equipment, you most likely pay for it over time and can't afford to buy the newest equipment.

- **Leasing is cost-effective:** Equipment is costly. If you lease your equipment, you're less likely to get caught with old equipment because most of the time you can upgrade or add equipment to meet your company's needs. Also, your equipment needs tend to change over time as your company diversifies. Leasing allows you to stay on the cutting edge of technology with modern equipment.

- **Leasing has tax advantages:** Instead of dealing with depreciation schedules and Alternative Minimum Tax (AMT) problems, you can simply deduct the lease payment as a business expense.

- **Leasing helps conserve your operating capital:** Leasing gives you financial flexibility while keeping your lines of credit open. You won't be as cash poor as you would be if you had to meet loan payments every month. You can avoid large cash down payments.

Although leasing does provide benefits to business owners, there are hidden costs to deal with, and business owners need to be aware of such costs. Some of the disadvantages are:

- ✔ **Non-cancelable agreements:** When entering into a lease contract, the business owner agrees to make all the lease payments to the end of the term. You can pay off the lease early, but even if your invention doesn't fly in the marketplace and you stop using the equipment, you have to pay off the lease. In some cases, though, you can sublease your equipment. Read the fine print in your lease.

- ✔ **Document fees:** These administrative fees are due upon signing the lease and range from $50 to as much as $350 or more, depending upon the complexity of the lease contract and size of the transaction.

- ✔ **UCC-1 fees:** Required in virtually every state, this one-time fee is due upon signing the lease documents.

- ✔ **Taxes:** In most states, you pay a tax on goods you buy or lease. Some states tax at 5 or 6 percent, or more. The tax is factored into the lease payments, so be prepared to calculate this cost, as it can increase your monthly lease payments by $20 or more per month, depending upon the total cost of the equipment and the state of purchase.

- ✔ **Insurance:** Any lease agreement requires that you insure the equipment against fire, theft, flood, and so on. If you own or are buying the building the leased equipment is housed in, the insurance on your building should cover the contents also, but you need to make sure. Depending on the type of equipment, you may need additional insurance.

Read the fine print to know what is and isn't covered in your policy. And consult with your agent to make sure you understand everything thoroughly.

Calculating Costs

In order to get a complete picture of your overall business costs, you have to know how much your production costs are. Measure the costs of your day-to-day operations to ensure that your profits aren't eaten away through delays in processing or production downtime and so on. In order to determine the final cost of your product, you have to calculate the fixed costs and variable costs on a per-unit basis.

- ✔ **Fixed costs** are prices that remain relatively stable over time, such as rent and utilities. Even if your variable costs increase, your fixed costs remain the same, or close to the same.

- ✔ **Variable costs** are prices that fluctuate according to usage or market changes. The cost of materials and labor are examples of variable costs.

Periodic production reports allow you to keep your finger on potential drains on your profits and should also provide feedback on your overhead expenses.

Don't get carried away and imagine that your invention will immediately put you on easy street. If you don't carefully plan your production costs, manufacturing your product may just as well put you in the poor house.

Without understanding the costs, you definitely won't understand whether or not you're making a profit. Understanding your ongoing operational costs on a daily basis can ultimately determine success or failure, regardless of how good your product is.

Finding ways to save

One way or another you pay for every aspect of the production process, from raw materials through the production run to transportation. You figure your operating costs on how much each unit costs to make. You want to first negotiate the best deal up front — the lowest price per production run. Other ways to save include:

- ✔ **Order raw materials and components in bulk:** If you order and receive shipment on mass quantities of resins or nuts and bolts, you can negotiate a substantial discount. Of course, you need to make sure storing the material doesn't cost more than the amount you save. You also need to be confident that you'll use the entire order.

  To get a feel for how volume can affect price, consider sending a bid sheet out to five suppliers in different geographical areas for different quantities of materials. You'll be amazed at the difference in costs between different vendors, as well as the decease in unit prices as batch volume increases.

- ✔ **Buy early:** Many manufacturers offer discounts or dated billing as incentives to buy early. This is important to manufacturers because of production planning and the lead time necessary for ordering raw materials. If suppliers know they can count on your order, they reward you for giving them peace of mind. You pay less than usual, or pay later than usual and can use your money longer.

If you place a last-minute order, be prepared to pay a premium. The manufacturer charges the extra worker and equipment time to you.

Most businesses operate according to the just-in-time principle. Supplies, goods, even employees are scheduled to arrive right when they're needed and not a moment before. Production facilities make use of just in time to form a seamless on-time assembly process. The lack of one component part can cause an expensive interruption of the assembly process, as well as the loss of a time-sensitive order.

Judging economies of scale

Economy of scale basically says that as volume increases, the cost per unit goes down. So, in producing your invention as well as in selling it, you want to maximize production and sales volume in order to minimize costs.

An illustration of economies of scale: Say you're freezing cherries. To prepare the cherries for freezing, you have to remove the pits. To do this, you have a number of options: removing the pits one at a time with a kitchen knife, purchasing a cherry pitter that pits each cherry individually, or purchasing a cherry processor so that you can dump a large number of cherries into the hopper that come out with the pits removed.

If you plan to freeze only a small amount of cherries, it makes sense to spend a little extra time and use the kitchen knife. If you're freezing several pounds of cherries, buying the handheld single pitter is probably worthwhile. If you're supplying cherries for a bakery that makes dozens of cherry pies each week, you have to process hundreds of pounds of cherries. You now must rationalize the cost of paying workers to remove the cherry pits, which becomes a consideration. You can invest the hundreds of dollars required to purchase the automatic cherry pitter because of the high volume of processing required during each seasonal processing operation.

You also consider time, which as we all know, is money. In this case, the volume justifies the increased cost of buying the tools. In the end, the tooling investment decreases the cost of removing each cherry pit. Another consideration is the time it takes to set up your cherry pitting production line. After the line is set up, though, you don't incur that cost anymore and the less each cherry costs to pit.

Working with People

Consider the type of labor skills needed to run and maintain the equipment you use. A frequently overlooked critical consideration is the quality and the know-how of production line employees.

You may want to take the time and list the specific types of workers you'll need individually, as well as the number of people you need. Then figure the average wage rate plus benefits and gasp at the cost of skilled labor.

You need to be sure that you can hire enough of the specific type of manufacturing workers you need — including machinists, assemblers, packing people, molders, sheet metal workers, metal turners, metal stampers, platers, blow molders, vacuum molders, injection molders, quality control agents, and so on. Do your homework and find out what you need.

Access to the skilled labor you need is crucial to the success of your venture. When multimillion-dollar corporations consider relocating, they take the time to fully investigate the labor pool for available workers. You may want to call your local job service agency and speak with an employment specialist to help you. Ask around until you find the answers to help you make educated, cost-effective decisions.

You also need to consider the indirect labor you need to keep your facility up and running — landscapers, janitors, and so on. What are the skill classifications, the number of people needed, the availability of the labor pool, and the average wage rate for these individuals?

Checking Quality Control

Consumers have many options in purchasing new products. If your product is poorly made, you lose the customers you have and don't gain new ones. An important rule of merchandising is: "It doesn't matter what you say about your product, it's what others say." You need to check quality at every step of the process to ensure that you're making your invention the best it can be.

Good quality-control checks that the product is manufactured in the most cost-effective way and is of the finest quality it can be. To ensure quality you need high-quality raw materials, skilled workers, and a smooth assembly process. A product needs to be manufactured without flaws the first time. No bubbles, no cracks, no tears, no speckles, no sharp edges, no breakable parts.

Set up several checkpoints along the way on the assembly line. Without good component parts, the final product is compromised. The final assembled product must be tested over to make sure it performs to all standards. Your production system itself is the primary component of having a great quality control system in place.

When a product fails performance tests, shipments are held up, inventory is increased, and a severe financial strain can result on the manufacturer, as well as others along the way. When the quality of a product is poor, you can be assured that the waste and spoilage on the production line are greater than they should be.

For various types of products, government approvals are in place and are mandatory. Manufacturers must meet a variety of approvals and regulations to produce a product, as well as to be able to stay in business.

When a product is of poor quality, all departments and companies who carry the product suffer. For example, if you purchase a poorly made shirt, your opinion of the brand and the store that sold it goes down.

If product quality is so compromised that you have to recall it, you end up paying big bucks. If you want to salvage any goodwill, you give customers a full refund, and with the costs of delivering that refund and replacing the damaged merchandise, you're out quite bit of money. Not how you want to be remembered.

Part IV
Commercializing Your Invention

RIDIN' HIGH IN THE ERGONOMIC SADDLE

©RICHTENNANT

"I don't care if this is better for my back, I'm startin' to feel ridiculous."

In this part . . .

All the work you do in thinking up your idea, testing it, studying it, and producing it, has been for nothing if you can't sell it. The chapters in this part help you decide which method to use to do just that.

Whether you start your own business to produce and sell your invention, subcontract out the manufacturing part, or sell your rights in return for a percentage of the proceeds, the chapters in this part give you advice and tips on how to be successful.

Chapter 13

Developing a Business Plan

A business plan is the first step you take toward turning your invention into a marketable reality. Like any other well-thought-out plan, a business plan goes a long way toward helping you succeed in your business.

In this chapter, I take you through each section of a business plan and tell you what information to put in that plan. I also point you in the direction of other chapters in this book that may help you get that information.

Many potential investors understand a business proposal much better than they understand the technology of an invention. Business people usually look at the profit-and-loss possibilities differently than the way you look at them. Business people want to see your action plan. A business plan gives you a road map to follow.

Realizing that You Need a Business Plan

You have your great invention. You're taking steps to protect your intellectual property. Now you're thinking about how to make money from your invention.

The first step is to write up a *business plan* — a step-by-step, section-by-section account of your invention; how you plan to produce, market, and sell it; how you propose to raise the money you'll need; how you intend to make a profit (as well as how much and how soon); and who the key people involved are.

You may think this plan sounds like a lot of work, and it does take time and effort. But you absolutely need to spend that time and exert that effort. If you don't have a business plan, you don't know where to start to get your business rolling or your product off the ground. Furthermore, without a business plan, you don't know the next steps through the growth stages and what to do if your idea succeeds, and you can't take full advantage of a success you're not ready for.

Even if you're planning to license your invention, working up a business plan forces you to consider all aspects of the deal and gives you a heads up on what to expect.

A business plan helps you set out your goals and objectives. And, I'm sorry, but "I want to make a lot of money and be rich" doesn't give you enough information. Until you determine how much money you want to make and how rich you want to be and formulate a plan to get some of those riches, you don't stand a chance of achieving anything. You face the tough job of figuring out your goals and objectives and how to accomplish them, but this book is here to help.

Setting goals and objectives is one of the most important steps you have to take to sell your invention. So you need to translate those goals into concrete action with a business plan. All the pieces of your business plan help you define your goals very clearly and, better yet, help you structure your goals so that those goals become a reality.

Working Up a Business Plan

Think of your business plan as a road map showing the way to your goal. It's a step-by-step plan to build your idea, invention, or service into a profitable business. So you have a written day-by-day guide to help you reach your goal.

Creating a business plan takes you through a number of steps in which you analyze each and every aspect of your idea, from creation to profit.

What your plan can do for you

A successful business plan demonstrates that you know your product thoroughly and that you've studied the industry and competition. Investors and clients consider a good business plan a primary indicator of future success with a well-organized company.

Businesses create many, if not most, business plans for the primary purpose of attracting funding. But you can also use business plans to attract business partners, advisory or corporate board members, or even potential customers. A business plan should, first and foremost, keep you on track. Your business plan is your road to success. After all, you wouldn't build your house without a plan.

Be clear about what you want the plan to accomplish and who you're aiming that plan at, and tailor certain sections to meet your goals or your audience's needs:

- A business plan aimed at raising funds lays out the amount of funding required, what's offered for those funds, and the potential payback for the investors. A plan written primarily to get funding needs an emphasis on *financial projections* (projections of monies needed and outlaid, considering the costs of goods sold and profit margins over time), *break-even analysis* (how many units sold until you cover the cost of your expenses), and *capital structure* (the type of business you have, how it's funded, and how the profits and losses will be distributed).

   Private investors, venture capitalists, and other financial types who see hundreds and hundreds of business plans are probably your audience. For this audience, you want to make your plan reflect solid information and realistic and attractive potential.

- A section of your business plan written to attract experts in the field to join a board of directors should focus on university affiliations, government regulatory approvals or applications, patent positions, and ongoing research and product development. Your plan will need to be very well written to attract the kind of people you need to have on your board. In the past, many people were flattered to be asked to serve on a board. This is no longer true with sophisticated experts because of recent changes in federal regulations and scandals such as the Enron affair. Director liability will cause many experts to think twice about serving on your board.

- A part of your business plan may be targeted toward attracting a partner to manufacturer your product, a marketing group to assist you in bringing your invention to market, or investors to help you fund your invention. The plan will help you attract those who can work with you along the way. Sometimes, they will work for you on a percentage basis. The plan, if written well, can lay out a path for their investment of time, resources, and money.

Who should write the plan?

You should put the business plan together, as much as you can, yourself. You're the one with the idea, invention, product, or service, and you know more than anyone else about it. You know what you're selling, who your customers are, and why your customers buy.

Every buyer, lawyer, banker, investor, manufacturer, chain store representative, and government authority asks you questions that a well-thought-out business plan answers. The more detailed your plan, the better you can use it to respond to questions about your invention and business.

A mistake I've seen too many times is inventors and entrepreneurs hiring a large consulting firm to write their business plans for them. When the inventor takes the business plan to potential investors and the investors start asking detailed questions, the inventor often can't answer questions regarding his or her own company, its projects, competition, goals, and plans. Hiring someone to write your business plan for you is like hiring someone to write your future and mission.

If, for some reason, someone else does write your business plan, make sure that you're familiar with every aspect of it so that you can answer any and all questions about it — both long term and short term.

For some of the financial and legal sections, you probably do need professional help. Have the accountant, lawyer, or consultant you hire help you polish your plan.

Breaking Down Your Business Plan

The following sections offer section-by-section information about what goes into a business plan. Figure 13-1 lists all the sections of an effective business plan. Your plan may or may not include all these sections, but this template can help you get started.

Making your plan look presentable

The *Cover Page* of your business plan should indicate the name of the company and give your company's contact information. Often, the Cover Page also indicates the *Purpose of the Plan*.

Try to decide your Purpose of the Plan before you write it. Occasionally, you can write the body of the business plan and emphasize a certain aspect afterward, but keeping the goal in mind as you write certainly makes your plan more focused.

Sketching it out

Face it; some of your readers may have 20 business plans sitting on their desks at any one time. Of course, you want yours to be the one they read. The next section talks about hooking them with the Executive Summary, but you get your first chance to spark interest in your proposal with the outline.

The *Outline* should be simple, no longer than one or two pages; it's basically a table of contents. It tells readers what to expect and shows them that you've given appropriate consideration to all the relevant areas.

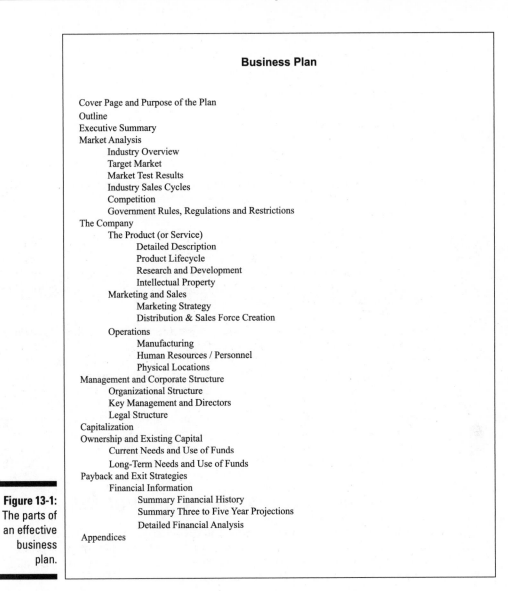

Business Plan

Cover Page and Purpose of the Plan
Outline
Executive Summary
Market Analysis
        Industry Overview
        Target Market
        Market Test Results
        Industry Sales Cycles
        Competition
        Government Rules, Regulations and Restrictions
The Company
        The Product (or Service)
                Detailed Description
                Product Lifecycle
                Research and Development
                Intellectual Property
        Marketing and Sales
                Marketing Strategy
                Distribution & Sales Force Creation
        Operations
                Manufacturing
                Human Resources / Personnel
                Physical Locations
Management and Corporate Structure
        Organizational Structure
        Key Management and Directors
        Legal Structure
Capitalization
Ownership and Existing Capital
        Current Needs and Use of Funds
        Long-Term Needs and Use of Funds
Payback and Exit Strategies
        Financial Information
                Summary Financial History
                Summary Three to Five Year Projections
                Detailed Financial Analysis
Appendices

Figure 13-1:
The parts of an effective business plan.

Writing an Executive Summary

The *Executive Summary* is exactly what the words imply — a few pages that succinctly sum up your entire business plan. It exactly states your product, invention, service, or idea and how you plan to bring it to market.

The Executive Summary is the most important part of your business plan. It's what potential investors read first, so it has to attract every reader in its very first paragraph. It should make your reader immediately want what you're offering, or to invest in your product or business, or to call you to ask if they can get involved.

Think of the Executive Summary as the coming attractions preview of your plan. You want the summary to highlight the best parts of your plan so that your summary entices the reader into wanting to see the rest of the show. If your Executive Summary is dull and boring, forget about anyone reading the rest of your plan.

Along with your concise but captivating introductory paragraph, the Executive Summary should sum up each of the major sections in your business plan. Imagine that your reader has only 15 minutes to glance at your business plan. Pick the highlights or most important points from each of the other sections and put them in the summary. For example, the synopsis for the Product section should answer the primary questions about why you developed this product and why its features are superior to the competition. The synopsis for the Capitalization section should explain the current ownership structure, the current funding needs, and the potential payback.

Keep in mind that the Executive Summary should be able to stand alone. You can present it to interested parties and follow it up with the complete business plan only to people who indicate further interest. (In such a case, you then seek to qualify their interest by obtaining a nondisclosure/noncompetition agreement, which legal counsel can help you draft. See Chapter 8.)

If the Executive Summary is a snooze, you can forget about anyone reading the rest of your plan. If your reader isn't excited by the summary of your plan, he or she isn't likely to get excited about your product or business, either.

Putting your research on the market

The *Market Analysis* section provides the details of all your market research. In general, the Market Analysis reviews the potential market for your product and that product's potential position in that market. In this section, I detail the parts and contents of the Market Analysis.

You really have to do your research to write this section. If your product is a board game, then you need to assess the toy industry in total and figure out what portion of the purchasing dollars go to board games. You have to find out which other board games are selling, both new board games and those games that have been around and successful for years. You need to look at how businesses market board games and design a marketing plan for your game.

In my dreams . . .

I'm waiting to see the Executive Summary that starts out, "We have discovered a cure for cancer. It's a teaspoon of tea that costs 25¢, and we have applied for the patent." or "We have discovered new fruit that brings you to your ideal weight if eaten daily for six months. This fruit grows only on my farm, and I have 11 agricultural patents in process. Would you like to invest?" Okay, okay — you don't have these products, but your invention can be as good for your product, idea, or service. That's the reason you're making a business of it.

You must know everything there is to know, not only about your product, but also about the industry in which your product competes. You must work up a profile of your purchaser and know how to make your product appeal to his psychological needs. Your business plan can't just say, "Everyone is going to buy my board game." It's just not going to happen. You have to fight for shelf space against some of the largest toy companies in the world who have multi-million-dollar advertising budgets. Just because your product is new, patented, or available doesn't mean people are going to buy it. Find out who your customer is and how to target his needs, desires, and pocketbook.

Some of the many sources you can use to assist your Market Analysis include:

- ✔ **Business Periodicals Index:** A cumulative subject index for articles on business policies, management, accounting, advertising, marketing, banking, finance and investment, labor, taxation, and specific businesses, and industries and trades.

- ✔ **Census of Manufacturers:** Data on employment, hours, payroll, inventories, assets, expenditures, costs, contract work, product shipments, and selected characteristics for manufacturing companies.

- ✔ **Census of Retail Trade:** Data on kinds of business sales, payroll, organization, employment size, and specialized data for 100-plus kinds of business classifications (basically, establishments selling merchandise to consumers).

- ✔ **Census of Wholesale Trade:** Data on kinds of business, sales, payroll, employment, organization, size, expenses, inventories, and specialized data (info given for a specific industry for statistical and analytical purposes).

- ✔ **Country Business Patterns:** Useful for analyzing market potential, measuring the effectiveness of sales and advertising programs, setting sales quotas and budgets, analyzing the industrial structure of regions, and making economic studies of small areas.

- ✔ **Data Sources for Business and Market Analysis:** Provides marketing information available from and/or relating to trade associations, advertising media, mailing lists, periodicals, abstracts and indexes, and information on centers and business firms.

- ✔ **Encyclopedia of Associations:** Lists names, addresses, activities, and publications of national associations. This encyclopedia provides you with valuable information about the industry your product is going to sell in. You must not only know about your product, but also how and where similar products are sold, manufacturers, wholesalers, the industry, and your potential competitors.

- ✔ **Sales and Marketing Management:** A survey of buying power. It reports population, effective buying income, and retail sales estimates. It also gives you metro market populations.

- ✔ **Simmons Reports:** Provides customer profiles (demographic information) for purchasers of consumer products.

- ✔ **Small Business Sourcebook:** Gives information on various types of businesses, including start-up information, primary trade associations for your product, organizations that may be interested in your product, educational programs, reference works, sources of supply, statistical sources, trade periodicals, and consultants.

- ✔ **Thomas Register:** A national directory of manufacturers.

Because many of these sites are not available on the Internet, and the ones that are require you to pay a fee, I would advise you to go your nearest public library where you can likely obtain every one of these sources in the reference section for free and simply copy the pages you need.

Put the results of your research into a quantitative form that your reader can easily understand. The best Market Analysis sections convince the reader that the market is sufficiently large for you to have a chance of entering it successfully.

If the market for your product isn't especially large, you need to show that your product has a good chance of capturing a high percentage of the market that does exist.

Looking at the industry's big picture

The *Industry Overview* is crucial to your Market Analysis because it shows the total market for your product and your product's potential within that market. The more information and data you show here, the more credible your overall plan appears to the reader.

Every product has an industry and any number of sources for data about that industry. Some of these sources include the government, the Internet, trade magazines, trade associations, and trade shows, along with annual reports from companies in the product line, and, of course, the people involved in the industry.

Your Market Analysis must show all the data you've collected regarding your research of the industry. For example, if your product is an item for the ski industry, you must show sporting goods industry dollar sales as a whole because each dollar spent on any sport other than skiing is a dollar not spent on your product. Then you must show total dollars spent on items for the ski industry as a subset of the total sporting goods industry. This comparison shows the potential size of the industry and the size of your specific market. Remember that you have to define your market by the product category for that product. Say you developed a new ski pole; you should probably find out how many ski poles retailers sold in the previous market season.

You can often find this type of information in trade industry magazines or articles about large companies in your products' industry. If an article reports that company XY-Ski sold $2 million worth of ski poles and that they had 25 percent of the ski-pole market, then the total market for ski poles, as defined by the article, is $8 million.

Aiming at the right people

As part of the Market Analysis, you need to indicate your *target market,* or the likely end user of your product. You use the data from your Industry Overview to show who your actual consumer is likely to be. Continuing the ski pole example, you show that your target market consists of skiers in various regions of the world. Because nearly every skier uses ski poles (you're not interested in those daring but slightly crazy skiers who don't use poles), you need to show the total number of skiers in the world by country. You should also indicate how often skiers purchase ski poles — for instance, with every set of skis or not.

You also need to show the number of customers in your target market who can purchase your ski poles and how often they do so.

The more data you show about your target market, the more likely it becomes that your audience can see the potential of your product selling to that market. Again, you can gather much of this data from specific trade magazines, trade associations, and even secondary sources. The trade magazines for the ski industry show the number of skiers. The articles about ski pole manufacturers may show volume or number of customers, and the trade associations may have data on the number of skiers who visit ski resorts annually. In addition, many advertising articles and magazines have marketing and advertising data that may be helpful to you. The number of subscribers to ski magazines gives you a number of potentially serious skiers (though not the whole market). Advertising magazines also indicate advertising budgets, and if your research turns up the ad budget for a ski pole maker, you may discover that a certain percentage of total sales goes toward the ad budget.

Be as complete as possible in defining your target market for your business plan reader. From there, you explain how you plan to capture part of that market. (Read on to find out how.)

Presenting those research results

After you have defined your target market, you need to do some *primary market research* in order to fill out this portion of your plan. This is the type of research that you get by talking one on one with potential customers. It's frontline action.

You can use a couple of different primary market testing methods to determine whether customers may be inclined to buy your product:

- ✔ **Questionnaire:** You can actually survey potential customers with a well-designed questionnaire that indicates whether or not the customer would actually purchase your product.

- ✔ **Focus groups:** You can assemble focus groups specific to your target market and ask the group members for their opinions about your product and its features.

Ideally, you hire a market research company to conduct surveys at malls or other public venues or to gather a focus group. The research company then compiles and analyzes the data for you. Using a market research company in your primary research is expensive (about $5,000 to $8,000), but you get data specific to your product and specific to your potential customer.

If you have limited funds, consider making use of students at the nearest community college or university. Often, students majoring in Business Administration at a university can get class credit for helping you do market research or write a business plan. If need be, you can offer to pay them; even so, a student costs a fraction of what a professional firm charges. The college or university may be able to provide a wealth of assistance. Make an appointment with the head of the department. If they find your request appropriate, they may assign the task as a student project.

The following list matches your needs with the academic department likely to help you:

- ✔ Advertising materials, videotapes — College of Journalism

- ✔ Business plan — Entrepreneurial Center/College of Business Administration

✔ Marketing materials — Marketing Department in the College of Business Administration

✔ Packaging design — Graphic Arts Department

✔ Prototype design — Engineering Department

✔ Technical evaluation — Engineering Department

Secondary market research can come from data collected on similar products from market tests published by other people. (Consider secondary info as existing information on a product or industry. For example, if your invention is a new tent spike, secondary information would be information on the number of campers, campgrounds, number of tents sold, costs of similar existing products, as well as monies spent by consumers for their camping equipment.) You can gather data about a product that has many of the features of your product or a product you believe you will compete with in the future. Many sources have this research data, (see the section "Putting your research on the market" earlier in this chapter for a list of sources), and those sources may give you a good indication of the potential success of your product, based on the information gathered on a similar product test.

Secondary market data is much less expensive than primary market data and can often give you valuable information. Secondary data may give credibility to primary data about the feasibility of selling your product, and it may also assist with projections for those sales.

Knowing your industry's cycle

Every industry and the products within that industry have marketing and sales cycles. You must be ready and able to fit in with these sales cycles for your product to have a fighting chance in the market.

Continuing with the ski industry example, in the Northern Hemisphere, retailers of ski equipment order products for the next season from January through March. Providers deliver ordered products between September and late November, and the retailers sell those products from November though March. So, if you intend to sell to the ski industry, you must have your product manufactured to meet the *lead times* (the buying season and time allowed to get the product through all its distribution channels) for marketing and sales in January through March and then produce to deliver by Thanksgiving.

Clearly, you need to know and contract lead times to create a successful product and demonstrate to your business plan reader that you've taken sales cycles into consideration.

The other guys

To write a credible Market Analysis section, you must acknowledge your competition and quantify that competition as best you can.

Competition exists whether you acknowledge it or not. You're always competing for the consumer's dollar, whether in a head-to-head battle with a similar product or in a more general lobby for consumers' *discretionary dollars* — the money they have left after paying for essential needs.

This section of your business plan needs to show why consumers should spend their hard earned money on your product over all the other competing products. Your market research examines the target market, number of customers, and how often those customers consume a similar product. Outline each competitor, explain how the features and pricing of your product are better than that competition's product, and give the consumer good reason to buy your product. Many plans have a *competitive analysis chart,* which shows a matrix of every competitor and the features, pricing, service, and so on of its product.

Be thorough! You lose credibility if your business plan reader knows of a competitor that you don't mention. The reader simply assumes that you've made other mistakes, and that reader becomes disinclined to support you.

Abiding by the law

In writing this section of the business plan, you demonstrate to your readers that you have researched the appropriate regulations and have complied with them, as necessary.

You must comply with all the regulatory requirements for your product's industry in order to legally market or sell, or perhaps even advertise, your product in the United States. A couple of examples of the government agencies and the types of products they have jurisdiction over are:

- ✓ **The Food and Drug Administration (FDA):** Any medical device must have FDA approval before you can advertise, commercialize, or sell it.

- ✓ **The Federal Communications Commission (FCC):** Any device that emits radio waves must comply with FCC requirements.

Most industries have some form of regulatory compliance. Often, industry trade associations can help you determine what you need to do to meet any requirements. Your manufacturer may also be able to help you figure out what you need to do. Of course, if you hire a patent lawyer or advisor — some inventors hire a firm specializing in regulatory advice — your advisor should be aware of applicable regulations.

If you do not comply with the governmental rules and regulations, you may be subject to fines, having your product confiscated, and even criminal prosecution. And although the government may not notice your noncompliance right away, your competitors feel a civic duty to point it out — and then you have more trouble.

Introducing yourself

This section of your business plan sets forth your company plans and relates your operating method. You lay out your company's structure and the administrative resources and skills required to operate each part of the business here.

If you're planning to license your product to an established company, this part of your business plan is fairly limited.

You need to show that you understand what your business must do to succeed. You demonstrate that you have the ability to locate customers and sell your product at a sufficient profit to stay solvent, at the least. Of course, you fervently hope that you can make millions, and you should certainly show in detail that such an outcome is possible.

If you're writing your business plan to raise capital, this section must prove your ability to operate the business with sufficiently trained personnel.

Often, your lawyer assists in developing the company structure preferable for the industry and for your purpose (see Chapter 15 for info on various business structures). Investors typically favor certain structures for their investments, and you need to be able to accommodate the most-accepted structure.

Your brilliant idea

The *Product section* (or *Service section*) should give a complete account of how you discovered or developed your invention and include a very detailed description of the product itself — without disclosing any proprietary secrets. (Hopefully, you have already applied for a patent, trademark, and/or copyright to protect what you've developed. See parts I and II for info on intellectual property.)

Your Product section needs to thoroughly educate your audience about your product. In doing so, you

- ✔ Discuss any technical advancements your product features
- ✔ Explain how and why your product is better than any similar product(s) on the market
- ✔ Prove that the product is worthwhile
- ✔ Relate the history of your product's development
- ✔ State the problem your product solves

Good visuals showing the product design and the project in action make up a key component of this section. Include diagrams and photographs as appropriate, and if possible, refer readers to a Web site where multimedia features show the product in use.

Include information, such as rough costs, packaging, price, size, and color, and all technical specifications. Check similar products' descriptions, as well, and make sure you've made your product description complete. Go to stores where your product can be sold and check out where those stores shelve similar products. See how much those products sell for and how manufacturers have packaged them — the colors, size, and shape. Look at who does the manufacturing, as well as the distributing, of these products. A large toy company pays millions of dollars to find out if 3-year-olds like the color red. They do their market research, and so should you.

What in the world is that?

You may find this section of the business plan the easiest for you to do. Why? Because here you just describe your product, and you should be able to give that description better than anyone.

To write a detailed description of your product, you simply need to provide answers to questions readers may have:

- ✔ What exactly is your product?
- ✔ What does it do?
- ✔ How does it do it?
- ✔ What are the functional specifications?
- ✔ Have you tested the product to make sure it works?
- ✔ If a prototype exists, who constructed and tested it?
- ✔ What are its size dimensions?
- ✔ How much does it weigh?

If you kept a journal while you developed the product, use some of the interesting points in the development process to describe your product's function. If you have a technical product, describe the technology involved and why that technology works and how you can maintain your developmental lead.

Keep in mind that the person reading your business plan probably isn't an engineer, so don't get so technical that you bore or confuse a right-brained person. In fact, most people don't care how the product does what it does. They care that the product does what you say it can do. If you're like me, you don't care how your cell phone works, you just care that your calls go through!

Labeling failure a success

3M researchers were trying to develop a type of paper that would stay stuck firmly to all surfaces. They thought they'd failed when the notes they developed didn't stay permanently stuck. The research department threw them out. Fortunately, the accounting department found them and started using them. They wrote notes and stuck them to papers, easily detaching those notes later. And thus, Post-it Notes were born.

You may want to include a chart describing each function of your product compared with the functions of similar products, much like those consumer evaluation magazines print. List all the features available, and then compare your product and your competitors in each feature category. Also have a section for price comparisons.

The life and death of your product

Every product has a *life cycle,* typically defined as how long the product functions under normal use and conditions. The life cycle dictates how often a consumer has to repurchase a product. You need to know and share your product's life cycle, which, like a chain, is only as good as its weakest part.

The *planned obsolescence* theory holds that some manufacturers build a shortened life into their product to hasten the day it needs to be replaced. The opposite holds true, also. The first Honda Civics ran virtually forever if you changed the oil, making their life cycle longer than every other car of that period.

The general public now knows the life cycle of most products and industries well. You should build to meet or exceed this life cycle and utilize parts that help you meet that life cycle. You don't need an expensive part that lasts 15 years for a product that you design to last 5 years.

Consider life cycle as you develop and enhance your product. Customers always look for something newer, cheaper, and with better features at the end of the original product's life cycle.

And you continue to grow . . .

Initially, research and development generates your new product. Research discovers a solution to a problem that leads to the development of a new product.

Explain here how you used research and development to create your new product and how you intend to continue to enhance your current product and to find new products. You want to demonstrate that you have ideas for future growth and for the enhancement or replacement of your product.

Claiming what's yours

Investors and lawyers study this section the most. Although they may not understand the process or technology you used to create your new product or service, they certainly understand if you have applied for or acquired a patent, trademark, or copyright protection from the United States Patent and Trademark Office.

Protection of your intellectual property increases the value of your product because it secures market protection for 14 years or more depending on the type of patent. A grant from the Patent Office also shows that you have a unique product protected by law.

Planning to reach, and keep, the customer

Your business plan audience knows that no company becomes successful overnight, but they want to be reassured that you have a realistic plan for making money. The Marketing and Sales section of your business plan should demonstrate that you know the potential customer profile (including age, race, sex, income, and shopping patterns) and how to reach those customers, as well as your competitors, timelines, and the typical growth patterns of companies in your industry. It must also show that you're thinking beyond the first dollar in the door.

Mitsubishi of Japan takes a very long-term view; their planning documents cover the next 1,000 years. You must take the long-term view, as well (though you don't have think a thousand years ahead). Tell readers where your company will be in one, five, and ten years.

The marketing language in this section should remind the reader of the pertinent data you presented earlier in the Market Analysis section and show her how you plan to make use of that data to best sell your product.

Your product needs the Marketing and Sales plan to actually get sold, and therefore your plan must be convincing to you and your readers. Turn to Chapter 18 for more information on marketing.

Crunching the numbers to find the best bargain

What is a marketing strategy? Well, it's not just saying, "I'm going to hire a telemarketing firm to sell my product." Strategy is choosing the best, most economically feasible method to sell your product, including how you're going to advertise, who's going to sell and buy your product, and how and where the sellers and buyers can meet each other. Basically, you're laying out a courting strategy.

In this section of your plan, first remind readers of all the valuable data and observations you provided in the Market Analysis section. Then show them that you can make the tough choices, based on your analysis of this data. Say your data suggests that elderly people buy your product more than young people. Part of your Marketing Strategy section explains that you plan to advertise in the crossword section of the newspaper rather than on billboards because of this fact.

The marketing plan shows that you know your customer, your potential sales, and at what price point your consumers agree to purchase your product. You must show your plan to enter the market, the trade shows where you'll exhibit, and your knowledge of the global market for your product. You must show how you plan to achieve sales and by what methods.

Using others (in a good way)

In the sales section, walk the reader through how you intend to actually sell your product. Address issues such as

- **Distribution:** Every industry has specific and well-defined distribution channels. Working within these channels usually gets your product to market faster and more easily than building your own distribution network, which is a time-consuming and costly undertaking. Tell readers which channel works best for your industry and your product, keeping in mind that a product that falls outside conventional distribution channels often isn't accepted.

- **Sales force:** Tell readers whether an established sales force and salespeople who sell similar products represent your product or you're building your own sales department. Then convince your audience that you made the right choice for your product.

If you're planning to license your product to an existing company within the industry (see Chapter 20), tell readers why you've made that choice and explain the licensing company's strategy for your product.

Explain clearly how you plan to use suppliers, distributors, and wholesalers both as channels of distribution and as customers. You need to have a well-thought-out channel distribution discussion for both your sales and purchasing.

How your business runs

The operations section outlines the day-to-day operations of your business and shows the reader how those operations make the company profitable. Your operations section should discuss the tasks of each department and show how the departments relate to each other and to the outside world.

This section of your plan also details how many people you need on staff to accomplish each task and whether you plan to hire people to work in-house or plan to outsource some operations — a customer service line, for example.

Use this section to point out any competitive advantages your operations give you. If you're selling your product in Latin America, having a major office or distribution point in Miami gives you a competitive advantage. You can find a competitive advantage almost anywhere inside your company — your employee base, your manufacturing process, your management team, your organizational structure, or even your reputation. You may have seen Hewlett Packard's (HP) advertising campaign that shows the HP logo next to the word "invent." HP is trying to suggest that they have a competitive advantage in the fast-changing technology world because they're inventors, not followers. If this mindset really exists in the company, it can certainly be a competitive advantage.

Of course, I'm waiting to see a company logo with the words *we follow* next to it. Don't laugh! You can get as much of a competitive advantage from following as from inventing. Low-cost generic products are stealing profit and market share from all those folks inventing.

Putting your product together

The Operations section of your business plan can address all types of processes that need to be carried out within the company, but it most commonly discusses manufacturing.

Don't think you can skip this section if you're offering a service and not a product. Rather than describing actual nuts and bolts, you describe the figurative nuts and bolts needed to manufacture your service — the personnel, facilities, and so on that you need to make your service operational.

Even if your invention just improves an existing product and you're going to license that improvement to a third party, you have to explain how your invention adds value by enhancing the existing product.

The people who make it all happen

An important subsection of Operations addresses human resources needs. You explain your company's organizational structure in Management and Corporate Structure (see the "The corporate bigwigs" section later in this chapter), but this section addresses personnel from a raw operations standpoint. Given what you describe about manufacturing, research and development, and sales and distribution, how many people do you need and how soon?

You may have a tough time writing this section because you need to demonstrate that you've researched the labor market from which you plan to draw employees to determine what competitive salary ranges for the qualifications you need, the benefits your employees expect, and how much those benefits cost. You need to explain whether you plan to have employment contracts and noncompete agreements with your product engineers. Set forth your thoughts on employee motivation techniques, whether you plan to offer commissions or bonuses, how often you do employee reviews, and where and how you can find employees. Even if you're the only employee, show the reader that you're thinking ahead to a time when your successful business expands.

Bragging about your digs

This section can be short (depending on your business idea), but don't leave it out. The smallest company has a headquarters (even if it's only your garage), and you need to tell readers where it is, what relevant equipment it already has (copier, fax machine, phone line, and so on), and what it needs. Show your readers that you've thought ahead. You can include a paragraph that starts, "When the company reaches $X million in sales, we will need to expand to a new location because . . . "

Some businesses need larger versions of this section than for others. If location is key to your business's success, you need to present an in-depth discussion of how you have chosen or will choose locations for business.

The corporate bigwigs

Management and Corporate Structure are so crucial to a business's success that many investors refuse to invest in a company that doesn't have an experienced management team. Business history shows that a good management team is more important than a good product. My personal experience says that products fail more than people. When making judgments on what to invest in, I choose the person or team behind the product. You can work with a great entrepreneur who has a good product much more easily than a marginal entrepreneur with a great product. That marginal entrepreneur causes many problems in the long run.

You must show that your organization and management team has the capabilities to carry out the purpose and reach the goals of your company.

How your ducks look in a row

The *organizational structure* of a company shows the chain of command and responsibility for specific functions within the company. Often, an organizational chart depicts the company's structure and all the functional responsibilities within that company.

The structure of a company depends on the type of business operations involved and the industry in which it operates. A manufacturing company, for example, needs manufacturing and product development departments, along with the standard accounting, finance, human resources, marketing, and sales sections. The economy also plays a role in business operations. Internal structures become smaller and tighter in difficult economic times and expand in periods of economic growth.

Even if you don't provide an organizational chart, make sure that you provide clear descriptions of information flow to your reader. Direct, formal communications as well as more informal company newsletters or weekly staff meetings build morale and inform employees how they can do their jobs better.

You can't forget the importance of external communication to customers and suppliers, and you should carefully design this communication to obtain the results you want for the company.

The players and their pieces

In this section of the business plan, you should discuss the key players you already have on your team and the spots you want to fill. The *key players* in any organization are those experienced people who can get specific tasks done. Examples of key players include

- ✔ The inventor or entrepreneur — probably you! — is a key player, especially at the start. Other key personnel may come on board as the company grows.
- ✔ A well-known scientist may be a key player in an organization selling a medical device.
- ✔ The person attracting capital to the venture is often a key player.

Key players also usually have a network they tap into for advice and help — they know other key players in the industry.

Putting a key player on your Board of Directors is a smart move — he or she adds experience and depth to the company.

You want to show how you rely on each of your key players and what you expect of them.

Make sure to include the biographies of your key players or team members, either in synopsis form in this section or as part of the appendix. Disclose any family relationships between key players, also. If you and your spouse are the two key players, investors can infer that you're skilled in managing at least one relationship. Also mention any employment contracts and noncompete clauses you have secured with your key players in this section.

Staying on the up and up

You probably need professional legal and accounting advice to set up your legal structure. These professionals help you determine whether you should form a corporation (and if so, what type of corporation), or whether some other business agreement suits you better. The decisions you make about what type of business entity you form have accounting, tax, and legal ramifications for the short and long term (see Chapter 15).

You should have everything settled before you write your business plan, though you may want input from your advisor on the language you use in your plan and how to explain why your decision is the right choice for your company.

Indicate the name of the firm you retained as your corporate counsel, if you've done so.

The money

This section of the business plan should describe the funding behind your idea. The detail required in this section varies greatly depending on the purpose of your plan. For example, if you're sending your plan to a venture capitalist (see Chapter 14) or other potential investor, you provide detailed specifics, such as ownership percentages. If you're sending the plan to a potential strategic alliance partner, you can make this section a little more general, letting readers know that you're the major stockholder and mention other relevant stockholders.

Who's putting money in and who's taking money out

In this section, especially when you present to potential future investors, include a table showing all the owners, with the amount of money each has invested and what percentage of the total ownership each possess.

You may want to show your fundraising timeline — "The two founding partners contributed $30,000 each in January and raised an additional $25,000 from family members in March," for example.

Provide a paragraph for each loan or lien (including real estate) the company has outstanding. This paragraph should detail to whom the loan is owed and the terms of that loan (particularly rate, payment, and collateral requirements).

Each state has specific rules as to ownership and issuing of shares, and your readers want to know that you have complied with regulations by hiring a good corporate counsel to assist you.

What you need now and how you plan to use it

This section lays out all the company's funding needs for the next six months. You present the budget for each department and state how much money you need to meet your obligations for payroll, taxes, rent and utilities, production costs, marketing and sales expenses, and everything else the business has to spend money on. Have a good accountant help you put the cash flow projections together, and make sure the chief financial officer of the company reviews it.

The *Use of Proceeds* section tells readers how you plan to use funds. A Use of Proceeds table shows investors how you plan to utilize the capital they invest and what result the company hopes to achieve in production and sales. You don't have to explain why you need the amount you do for a specific area — you do that in the "Laying down the numbers" section later in this chapter — but the amounts should make sense to the reader if you've done a good job in the other sections. For example, if you're manufacturing an electrical component that requires some very expensive raw materials, readers shouldn't be surprised to see that the price in the raw materials category is high.

Looking for funds far down the road

In this section, you put forth the company's long-term capital requirements. You typically provide three-to-five year projections in the Financial Information section (see "Laying down the numbers" later in this chapter), but you use the section to address where you expect your funds to come from.

You typically include a sources-and-uses table in this section that shows where you expect to get your money and how you expect to use it.

All the figures in this section must match up with the figures you provide in the long-term projections in your Financial Information section.

Getting even and getting out

This section details how and when investors get the return on their investment they're looking for. You summarize the amount of capital you're seeking and the amount others have already invested. You may also remind readers of your long-term projections — "If things go as planned, we will reach the break-even point by the end of year two and have cash flow of $X by the end of year five," for example. Then bring up the projected payback to investors.

Investors want to know when they can expect you to return their capital to them, and you need to present an appealing *exit strategy,* which is another way of saying when you expect to be able to return their investment and at what level of profit. They don't want to be married to you and your product forever, and you don't want their input forever — you *both* want an exit plan.

The details of your proposed exit strategy often determine the structure of the original investments. An investor may loan the company money with a specific interest rate and payback date. Alternatively, the investor may loan money with an option for the investor to convert the loan to equity in the company instead of being repaid.

Again, seek advice from a financial and legal consultant knowledgeable in this area.

A smart reader may check the Financial Information section to judge whether you have a reasonable chance of turning your idea into a reality. You want to make this section optimistic (you believe in your idea, don't you?) but realistic. The more work you've put into the previous sections of the business plan, the easier writing this section becomes.

Make sure the numbers in this section correlate to the story you've already told in the qualitative part of the business plan.

Handing over your financial story

The company must have good accounting records and financial history. Typically, financial history includes past and current financial statements, tax returns, and revenue analysis for each year the company has existed. If you're a brand-new company and don't have past financial records, just say so.

If you have a patent, copyright, or trademark, you can assign a value to it here.

Companies fortunate enough to show a number of quarters or years of increased earnings happily show their financial history, but even those companies with less stellar results should show their past history (though you can provide some discussion of any obvious setbacks the figures show).

Keep in mind that readers compare your financial history with your current funding request and projections, so make sure the numbers seem reasonable.

This section also should list any professional firms involved with your accounting and financial management.

Telling your future

Three-to-five year projections have become a requirement of the fundraising process. The projection of expenses and revenues often gives potential investors a good idea of what you believe potential revenues will be. A five-year business plan also helps you plan where you want your company and product to go in the near future.

In some cases, you may want to include multiple scenarios in this section. For example, you may be trying to break into both domestic and foreign markets. In such a case, you may want to show what may happen if you enter just the domestic market. Or consider the case of a product that's very dependent on outside factors — you may want to show separate scenarios for favorable and unfavorable conditions. If, for example, you invent a new snow shovel, you can forecast what may happen if your market area receives record snowfalls and what would happen in an unusually warm winter. What you're really trying to do with this section (and all others) is to demonstrate that you're presenting a well-thought-out business plan.

Testing your plan for numbers consistency

The detailed financial analysis reviews the projections, any historical and current financial data, and the sources and uses of proceeds. The information in this section compares what you've said in each preceding section of your business plan with the others for consistency.

This section also provides you with an opportunity to explain any costs or projections that fall outside the norm. You can explain your assumptions about the raw material cost of each of your products or why you project that next year's travel and entertainment expenses will actually go down.

Stuff tacked on at the end

You should reserve the Appendices for data or materials pertinent to the success of your idea that don't fit into an easily readable format. Very detailed documents that have too many pages to put in the body of the business plan often end up in the Appendices. You can often find these kinds of documents in business plan Appendices:

- ✔ **Advertisements:** If you have already produced some advertisements for your products or services in print form, including a sample is always a good idea.

- ✔ **Contracts in hand:** Include any contract, purchase order, or letter of potential use here. Contracts and purchase orders are valuable when backing up projections. If you want to keep your clients' names confidential, you can block out their names or assign them generic names (client A, client B, and so on).

- ✔ **Employment and noncompete contracts:** If you recruit valuable personnel, you should have employment contracts with them that show how long you expect them to work with the company under what rules and regulations. Also include noncompete clauses signed by key personnel that prohibit those personnel from competing with you and from taking product concepts to another company. (See Chapter 10).

- ✔ **Insurance policies:** Most investors look for general, key-person, and product liability policies to ensure that you're protecting the company's assets.

- ✔ **Lease agreements:** Include copies of any leases for space or major equipment.

- ✔ **Owner agreements:** Include any agreements among the owners of your company involving equity in the business, the business property, or any other business-related issue.

- ✔ **Patents, copyrights, trademarks, and trade secrets:** Consider including copies of your intellectual property to allow readers see what you've accomplished and to save them the time of getting these documents from the Patent Office.

- ✔ **Pictures or recent presentations:** Photographs or a good PowerPoint presentation really help you get your point across. Pictures can show the management team in action, the product's production process, the physical location, or other graphics that may give readers a visual image.

Computer accessory stores and office supply stores have PowerPoint presentations available for purchase. These prepackaged presentations allow you to insert information about your specific product or company.

✔ **Research statistics:** Include all the results of your research studies, including both primary and secondary research on your product's potential market. This appendix may be very long, but it also may be at the heart of your technology or scientific invention.

✔ **Product liability insurance and agreements:** Product liability insurance promises that you stand behind your product if it causes injury to anyone.

✔ **References:** You can include detailed references, including personal and business references, here. Not only does this section show your references, it includes contact numbers. You should include testimonial letters about your product here as well.

✔ **Resumes of the management team and board of directors:** Some people choose to simply include bios in paragraph form in the Key Management and Directors section (see "The players and their pieces" earlier in this chapter), which works, too.

What you include in this section is really up to you; think about who you want reading the plan to decide what you can't leave out.

Chapter 14

Finding Funding

*Y*ou can sum up this chapter's theme with the simple saying: It takes money to make money. You may have the greatest idea in the world, but without some sort of financing, reaping the rewards of your idea is next to impossible. Although poor management most commonly causes businesses to fail, inadequate or ill-timed financing runs a close second. Whether you're starting a business around your new invention or expanding your product line, sufficient ready capital (in other words, having enough money readily available) is a must.

The success of your business rests on having enough money to keep that business running smoothly. Your cash flow affects all aspects of the company, from operations to your ability to deliver a final product or service. But having sufficient financing isn't enough; you have to be knowledgeable about money, too. Securing the wrong type of financing, miscalculating the amount of money required, or underestimating the cost of borrowing money all can hurt your business.

In this chapter, I discuss the various ways that you can obtain needed funding for your invention or your business, alerting you to the risks associated with each option for you and the investor. I also point out the different sources you can look to for that funding.

Not many inventors consider raising capital their favorite task; they want to be inventing new products or services. If you identify with that philosophy, consider hiring or partnering with someone who enjoys asking investors for money to keep on top of your funding needs. There's a big difference between an inventor and an entrepreneur. Investors and companies don't invest in inventors; however, they do in vest in entrepreneurs.

Determining How Much and For What

You certainly need money to launch your invention into the marketplace. But before you solicit investors or apply for a loan to fund your business expansion, ask yourself whether you really need more money or just a different strategy.

All your funding needs tie directly to your company's cash flow, the most critical element of every company's day-to-day operations. *Cash flow* is the amount of money you pay to meet your expenses (acquiring raw materials to manufacture; supporting administration, marketing, and sales personnel; and so on) and the money you get from sales of your product or service. Insufficient or erratic cash flow can cause the obvious financial problems, and it can also result in poor company morale (have you ever seen how an employee works when he doesn't know if he can get that paycheck at the end of the week?). Many funding needs come from a cash-flow problem.

Before starting a search for funds, know how much you need, why you need it, when you need it, and what you need it to do for you. Before trying to find funding, answer the following questions:

- ✔ **Do you really need more money, or can you manage what you have more effectively?** Do you know what it will take to get started? Have you sat down with a pencil and paper to figure it out, or are you just assuming that you automatically need more money from credit cards, investors, or bank loans? Take the time to plan a strategy and look at your options whether you're going to sell your patent rights and license your inventor or whether you're going to start your own business. Consider your personal strengths and weaknesses and talk with your spouse or partner about his or her dreams and vision as well. Sometimes you can cut corners in your spending habits without going into debt or automatically getting partners and investors when first getting started.

- ✔ **Why do you need money?** Are you trying to introduce your product to market, expand your product line, or do you simply want a cushion? When investors invest in a product, they want to know how you plan to spend their money. They want to make sure that you aren't going to buy new cars, build new buildings, or take extended vacations to Europe. They want to make sure that you're going to spend their money wisely.

- ✔ **How urgent is your need for funding?** Do you need money to meet immediate obligations and, therefore, have resigned yourself to paying higher financing costs, or can you wait and negotiate favorable lending terms?

✔ **How will you use the money?** Are you trying to have a prototype made, hire people, pay distribution costs, or expand your product line? You should realize that your need for funds is most critical during your product's transitional phases. You may think that you'll need money only in the start-up phase, but find that you need funding in different stages as your product moves through its life cycle. Also realize that any lender requires that you request the capital you borrow for very specific needs.

✔ **How does your need for financing coincide with your business plan?** Any potential funding source will want to see your business plan. If you don't have a business plan, write one! (See Chapter 13 for tips on how to do that.)

Looking at what you need money for

Before you go running off to talk to a loan officer or some other financial type, take a close look at your current finances situation and think specifically about what you need money for.

If you're looking to start a company to make and sell your invention, you need a detailed breakdown of all your expenses, from renting or buying space to hiring workers to getting your product to the customers. Perhaps a new assembly process can turn out your product more quickly and efficiently (and thus more cost-effectively), but you don't have the funds to pay for the new technology right now. Maybe your business is growing, and you need help with the initial payroll costs after adding more workers to handle the load.

Whatever you need or want money for, make sure that you have a detailed explanation of how you plan to use the money and how that plan ends up making more money for your investors. Even if you're getting the money from your mom and dad, you should be able to reassure them that you're not just upgrading the sound system in your car.

Sometimes — not often, mind you, but sometimes — taking a close look at your financial situation shows you that you don't really need more money at all. Delving into your income and expenses may reveal that you're spending money on a service or machine that you're really not using or that you can do yourself. You may find an expense that made sense at one time but isn't necessary any longer can be taken out of the budget.

Determining how much you need

Logically, how much money you need depends on what you need it for. If you're looking to start a new company, you need more money than if you want to upgrade your production process.

I'm sorry to say that this section doesn't include a handy list that tells you that you need $X to start a company from scratch, $Y to expand into a new market, and $Z to advertise your invention. You have to find the numbers by doing some research into the going rate for the services or supplies you need.

Doing the explorations, market research, and comparisons you need to write a business plan gives you probably the best way to figure out how much money you need. Some investors and lenders require a business plan, and even if the money folks don't need to see that plan, working one up familiarizes you with all aspects of your business. If you haven't written a business plan yet, do it now. Chapter 13 walks you through the process step by step.

Give yourself some margin of error (whatever you feel comfortable with) when you're figuring out how much cash you need.

Figuring Out the Types of Financing

Don't worry, I'm not about to start spouting off about the ins and outs of convertible debt, dividend protection rights, preferred equity, seed capital, put options, or other unintelligible topics. I am giving you enough financial knowledge so that you can at least understand the language your financial advisors and financial backers speak. The big-picture issues are pretty simple, and as the person in the driver's seat, you need to have a grasp of them.

In this section, I define and briefly discuss various financial terms you're likely to run into, and I show you how investors rate risk and return when deciding on whether to fund a company or project.

Defining the terms

The two main types of financing are debt financing and equity financing. *Debt financing* is like taking out a loan — you promise to repay the money within a certain time period and with a certain amount of interest — and with *equity financing,* you're basically selling stock in your company — you share your profits (and losses) with the investors. Debt financing poses the lowest risk for the investor (along with the lowest return potential), and equity financing poses the highest level of risk for the investor (but with an infinite return potential). Other forms of capital fall somewhere between these two forms. (For more on risk and return, see "Rating risk and return" later in this section.)

The following list defines the types of funding options available for debt financing and equity financing:

✔ **Secured financing:** Like a loan guaranteed with collateral, secured debt is backed by some asset. If you don't pay off the debt, the investor keeps the asset, so this is a low-risk investment with a low return rate to match.

✔ **Unsecured financing:** Riskier for the investor than secured debt, this financing method is basically a loan without collateral. For the higher risk involved, the investor expects — and gets! — a higher return rate.

✔ **Convertible financing:** This form of financing starts out as a regular loan-type arrangement, but if the company does well, the investor may choose to convert some or all of the loan amount to shares in the company (explaining where the *convertible* part of the name comes from). The risk factor here is sort of 50/50. If the company does well, the investor converts the debt to stock and potentially reaps large rewards; if the company does bad, the investor most likely gets the investment amount back with just a small amount of interest.

✔ **Preferred stock:** These stocks are shares in a company that pay the investor a fixed dividend before the company pays dividends on common stock. This investment has a fairly low risk rate — after all, preferred stockholders get their money before anyone else does. But the set dividend rate means that the investor doesn't benefit much if the company does really well.

✔ **Common stock:** Shares in a company that give the owner a vote in how the company runs and entitles the stockholder to receive dividends. Probably the riskiest investment type, common stock also has the most potential for a spectacular return.

You should hire expert lawyers, accountants, and financial staff to deal with the details.

Any form of debt is an obligation that the company must pay back in the future. You show what you owe in the long-term debt section of the company's balance sheet, and investors consider all debt a liability. Debt financing is a costly form of capital because you have to pay the interest, in addition to the capital you originally borrowed, and you often have to decrease your cash flow to meet your repayment deadlines. Too much debt can burden your company because paying off the debt uses cash that can't be used for other operations. A potential lender looks at the ratio of debt to equity as a barometer of a company's financial health. Too much debt sends up a red flag for a potential investor.

When looking for money, you must consider your company's *debt-to-equity ratio* (the comparison between the dollars you've borrowed and dollars you've invested in your business). The more money you personally have invested in your business, the easier attracting additional financing becomes.

Rating risk and return

To get a good idea of how to look at your capital, funding, or financing (terms I use interchangeably in this book), think like the investor. If you had money, and some inventor like yourself asked for some of it, what questions would you ask? These three questions drive every financing structure you encounter in raising money:

- When will I get my money back?
- How much will I get back?
- What happens to my money if things go bad?

The answers to these questions determine the level of risk for the investor and the conditions you place on yourself.

Table 14-1 answers investors' main questions for both debt and equity financing.

Table 14-1	Comparing Debt and Equity Financing Returns	
Investor question	*Debt*	*Equity*
When will I get my money back?	A specific time in the future	Uncertain
How much will I get back?	A fixed amount over the original investment	Uncertain
What happens if things go bad?	You usually get some of your money back	You'll be lucky to get any money back

You're thinking that the equity column in Table 14-1 looks a little thin. An equity investment — buying a share of stock — may or may not pay off. So why would you ever buy stock? Well, I'm sure you already know the answer: because you're hoping for a high return. The *most* you can earn by giving someone a loan is the loan amount and whatever interest you agreed to. But the same amount invested in stock in a company that takes off may theoretically yield an *infinite* amount of money (or at least more than you'd know what to do with).

Just as you can guarantee a loan with *collateral* (something of value that you forfeit if you don't pay the loan) or sell the same kind of stock to all your investors (*common stock*), you can choose (or the investor chooses) from a range of financing options with different levels of risk for the investor and obligations for you (see the previous section, "Defining the terms," for details on your various options). Figure 14-1 shows the range of options on a scale from low risk, low return to high risk, high return.

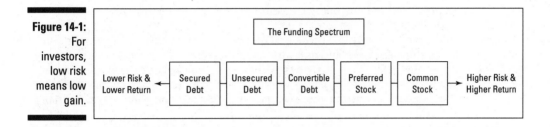

Figure 14-1:
For investors, low risk means low gain.

The Funding Spectrum

Lower Risk & Lower Return ← Secured Debt | Unsecured Debt | Convertible Debt | Preferred Stock | Common Stock → Higher Risk & Higher Return

When starting a company (so you can market your product), you should probably seek debt financing in the form of loans if your company has a high debt-to-equity ratio. However, if your company has more equity than debt, increase your ownership capital (equity investment) for additional funds. The more funding that you personally put into your product, the larger your percentage of ownership in the company. Remember — ideas are cheap; products are expensive.

Make sure that you get proper legal advice before you attempt to sell stock in your venture.

Seeking Out Sources of Capital

You can go to any number of sources to finance your business — banks, commercial finance companies, individual investors, the *Small Business Administration* (SBA), venture capitalists, and more. In addition, many state and local governments have developed programs in recent years to encourage the growth of small businesses in their regions because small businesses build the local economy and create jobs. In this section, I cover the basics for each source.

You're doing nothing wrong by asking people to invest in or lend money to you. Many people are looking to do exactly that! Venture capitalists exist to fund new businesses. They're rooting for you to succeed so that they make money in their investment. So, yes, their interest is a little self-serving, but as long as it serves you, too, you both come out winners. Even successful companies that go public and generate billions of dollars in revenues still have cash flow problems sometimes and seek to borrow additional funds.

The most important source — you!

If you're like most inventors, your primary and initial source of capital is your personal financial resources. You may pay for the materials to build your product with a credit card. You may take out a home equity loan or withdraw money from savings to finance your company.

You can reasonably use these first steps to get your idea off the ground, but these steps are risky and don't provide long-term solutions. If your company or product fails, you still owe the credit card company or mortgage company and may not have the cash to pay them. You may lose your savings. On the other hand, not putting your own money into your company tells potential investors that you aren't willing to take the same risk you're asking them to take.

All your company's investors and lenders, even suppliers and customers, want to see that you, as the inventor, put your money where your mouth is. You may feel that the years you spent on your product should count as your investment. All inventors have this so-called *sweat equity*, and unfortunately for you, this kind of investment doesn't carry a lot of weight with investors because they want to see you put your own bucks, as well as time, into your invention.

If you want people to invest in you and your product, you have to show them that you're confident enough to put your own money at risk. If you're not willing to risk your money, why should they? I always ask inventors who come looking for funding how much money they've personally invested in their product. Believe it or not, I've gotten this response on several occasions, "Do you think I'm stupid enough to spend my own money on this product?!" Needless to say, none of those people received any money from me.

Taking advantage of corporate credit cards

Grab on to the dramatic changes credit card companies are making after they discovered what a gold mine small businesses can be. Credit card issuers run all over each other to woo low-risk small companies away from using their personal cards to an assortment of new business services.

Credit card companies used to regard small companies as high risk and thus set up restrictions that excluded many businesses. Nowadays, those companies are aggressively pursuing small-business owners such as yourself — an estimated $75 billion to $100 billion market — in hopes of selling you on corporate credit cards. The credit card companies offer perks, like including discounts from popular vendors, to get your account. And, of course, they charge a variety of fees — annual fees, fees for extra cards, and so on — but at least you're not overextending your personal credit.

You want to be smart about investing in yourself and evaluating how much money you can risk. Keep in mind both your business's day-to-day startup cash needs and your own personal needs. Borrow from your lowest cost sources first — get a home equity line of credit instead of charging everything to your credit cards and paying astronomical interest rates.

Keep track of all the money you invest in the company (even $20 on your credit card at the office supply store). You want to get paid back some day. After all, you put this money at risk, so you should get a return on it.

Getting a little help from your friends

Friends and family, your soccer teammates, former coworkers, and fellow book club members — start looking at all of them for your start-up money. You can more easily test your idea out on your closest buddies and get their criticism than approach professional investors. The same theory of personal investing applies here: If you can't convince your sister that your business will work, how will you ever convince somebody else?

You see your nonprofessional investors, like your friends and family, for the rest of your life. And you don't want them to hate you if you lose their hard-earned investment.

You may also receive more advice than you need from folks who aren't shy about commenting on any or every aspect of your business. Some of this advice may be helpful — after all, your family and friends may have useful contacts — but ask yourself if you can deal with your retired Uncle Joe showing up at the office every week telling you his latest idea about how to run the company.

Going the conventional route with bank loans

Most businesses borrow money at some point in their life cycle, and traditionally, small businesses use banks as their major source of funding. The bank's principal role is that of a short-term lender, offering loans for building, machinery, and equipment, and providing lines of credit for seasonal or unexpected expenses.

Banks only reluctantly offer long-term loans to provide the full cost of starting a small business, though you may find a bank an attractive lending option after your business is up and running and has a proven track record. At that point, you can probably get a loan without using personal assets to guarantee it. In fact, banks may compete to make loans to you. Shopping around for the best rates and terms makes sense.

Taking out either a business or personal loan means putting your personal assets at risk. Often, a bank lending to a start-up business requires some sort of collateral, like your house or personal property, to guarantee the loan. If your company can't repay the loan, the lender comes to you to make good on it. You may have to forfeit the collateral you pledged or pay off the loan according to a schedule the lender sets up. So, before you apply for a loan, do a careful assessment of the risks involved. Can you handle the worst-case scenario?

Interest payments mean cash out the door today that you never see again. Don't borrow so much that you can't make your current cash payments. When you get in over your head, the dream dies. If you can't seem to get the sales of your product going or establishing a market share, sooner or later, sales will start to decline. The lack of sales added to increasing debt payments make businesses close their doors.

Before you approach a bank, make sure that you have all your ducks in a row. You want the bank to see a well-run, well-managed business that is executing an up-to-date business plan.

Don't forget to have your lawyer read the fine print of any loan documents. The documents are usually pretty standard, but you especially want to know what kind of rights the bank has if you don't make your interest or principal payments on time.

The Small Business Administration (SBA) encourages banks and nonbank lenders to make long-term loans to small businesses by guaranteeing loans and thereby reducing the lender's risk. The SBA's programs have been an integral part of the success stories of thousands of firms nationally.

Calling on angels

Private investors who bankroll businesses are known as *angels,* and who doesn't want an angel involved in a new enterprise? Certainly not you.

Angels are typically successful inventors, professionals, and entrepreneurs that have money to invest. In addition to financial support, these private investors may offer to share their knowledge, experience, and contacts, so that you get even more bang for their bucks.

Private investors come from every industry and all walks of life. But they all have money and extra capital to invest. You can find them through your banker, your lawyer, your insurance agent, or your accountant; you may find an angel or two through an investment club, your small business owners networking group, or any other organization with a financial aspect.

Planting the seeds of invention

Seed Capital typically comes in the form of early stage funding from an angel, individual investors, and occasionally venture funds. The investor gets ownership in your company by receiving equity, and the funding that comes into your company doesn't have to be repaid. Investors consider their investment *paid-in capital,* and that investment becomes an asset of your company. Seed capital is early-stage, high-risk, and high-cost equity. You want to obtain seed capital investment rather than debt capital, if you can, because obtaining funding that doesn't have to be repaid shows a greater commitment toward the company. If you can't find seed capital and debt capital is all that your company can obtain, then you obviously have to go with debt capital.

But remember, this capital is called *seed* for a reason. It gets the plant from the soil to the sunlight, but it's not the end of the funding story.

Don't be shy about letting people know that you're looking for investors. Approximately 85 percent of private start-up funding comes from people either connected to or referred to the business's owner. Money is crucial to business — everyone knows that. Ask anyone and everyone for money and contacts. Go to churches, charity events, organizational meetings, country clubs, golf courses, schools, and conferences — in other words, go anywhere people gather — and you may find someone to talk to about funding opportunities. Tell people about your product and your company and ask if they know anyone who may invest. (And always have a copy of your business plan available to pass along.)

Even if a potential investor says no, that noninvestor may give you someone's name or offer to contact a person who turns out to be your biggest backer. So be sure to follow up on any referrals.

Angel investors and venture capitalists seek to add value, in addition to capital, to the companies in which they invest so that the company grows and the investors achieve a greater return on their investment. To accomplish this big return, these investors often insist on being actively involved in the company. And almost all angels want, at a minimum, a seat on the Board of Directors.

Letting employees invest

Employees who show their faith in the company by agreeing to work there may also have enough faith to invest in the company. Setting up a program whereby your employees contribute a portion of their salary for shares in the company can improve the company's financial situation because you don't have to pay the employee the amount she invests, and your employees get a greater stake in making the company successful. If you're doing a good job, your employees shouldn't need to be convinced that a dollar invested in the company may be worth a lot more than a dollar in the future.

Employee programs may or may not go into a retirement fund account and may or may not qualify for matching shares from you. (Talk to your financial advisor about setting up this process.)

If employees' investments fund their retirement accounts, you may want to set a limit on how much of their retirement money they can invest in company stock so you can keep the account diversified. If the company goes belly up, you don't want your employees to lose all their retirement savings like the unfortunates at Enron.

Acquiring funds though acquisitions — If you can't beat 'em, acquire 'em!

You just started your own company, so why am I talking about acquiring another company? Well, in some cases, buying another company improves your bottom line. Say that you have a great new condiment dispenser to sell to restaurants, but your manufacturing cost estimates are way too high. You're convinced that your product can be made for a lot less money. Rather than building your own manufacturing facility, think about buying an existing facility.

But how can you consider buying something a form of financing? Well, you can spend about $10 million to start your own manufacturing facility. You find a manufacturing plant whose owner is willing to sell it to you for $5 million. You can retrofit the plant for $4 million, and instead of needing to find $10 million, now you're a million ahead — even more if you can continue to produce the plant's original product during the transition. So, though you can't start a business this way, you can certainly improve the financial situation of your existing business with judicious acquisitions.

Venturing over to venture capitalists

Venture capitalists are institutional investors who provide start-up capital to new businesses. Venture capitalists are professional investors with a mandate to invest other people's money in high risk, high return start-up or spin-off companies. A venture capital firm may be a group of wealthy individuals, a government-funded or -assisted organization, or a major financial institution. Most venture capital companies specialize in a few closely related industries, such as medical products or energy-related technologies. If you have an invention that's going to revolutionize its field, venture capitalists want to fund it.

Paying the bills on your time

As your company grows, you may find your cash-flow situation tightening up — your customers pay you slowly and you have to pay your bills quickly. Don't worry, quickly growing companies often have negative cash flow — it's perfectly normal.

But if you can arrange to pay your creditors after you get the money from your customers, you can ease the cash-flow squeeze. Industry competition often dictates when you have to pay your bills or when you're paid for your products. If you sell to a giant distributing company, the company may tell you that they pay invoices 45 days after they get them — and it's just too bad if you want them to pay in 30 days.

Your supplier may give you 30 days to pay, and you usually pay the bill in 20 days — you can change some payments around to make that work for you. Say you owe a certain supplier $30,000 a month and have an outstanding loan with an interest rate of 8.5 percent. If you pay your supplier in the required 30 days (rather than 20 days), you can pay off your loan 10 days earlier each month, thereby reducing your total interest payments. You save $850 a year in interest payments and come out ahead of the game.

You can also try to get people who owe you money to pay sooner and improve your cash flow in both directions.

Your financial advisor can help you determine what makes sense in your situation.

The right venture capitalist can make the difference between failure and success, growth and major growth.

Approaching a venture capital firm

No one finds approaching a venture capital firm easy. You have to seek them out; they don't come looking for you. Several books in the reference section of your local library list the names, addresses, and phone numbers of venture capitalists. These books include:

- *Pratt's Guide to Venture Capital Sources* (Venture Economics)
- *The Directory of Venture Capital* (Wiley)
- *Vankirk's Venture Capital Directory* (Online Publishing)
- *Fitzroy Dearborn International Directory of Venture Capital* (Fitzroy Dearborn Publishers)

Try to approach a venture capitalist before you need capital, not at the last minute. They typically invest in existing businesses that want to expand, and they tend to shy away from new start-ups. If you don't need the funding immediately, you can negotiate from strength. If you need money to make payroll, however, the venture capitalist has more power and can demand more concessions. Remember, the more you need the financing, the more it costs your company and management in the amount of control you have to give up.

Knowing what to expect

Various venture capitalists have different approaches to managing the business they fund and invest in. They generally prefer to take a very passive role in the day-to-day operations of a business; but if the business doesn't perform as expected, they may take an immediate and active role, insisting on changes in management or strategy.

Venture capitalists bank on the possibility that your company may go public and start trading on a stock exchange. If you envision a family-owned company, don't look for funding from venture capitalists.

You may see a few clauses in an agreement with a venture capitalist that you don't see in contracts with other types of funders, including

- ✔ A large interest in the company, sometimes more than half.

- ✔ A substantially higher rate of *return on investments* (ROI).

- ✔ The right to assume control of the company in certain situations — if the company's financial position plummets, for example.

- ✔ The option of buyback rights for you so that you can regain full control of your company. The venture capitalist generally likes this type of agreement. The investors are looking for a good return on their investment, so if your company is doing well enough that you can buy back the venture capitalist's investment, you're in a win-win situation — investors make money; you get control of your company.

You should always include a buyback option in your negotiations upfront. That way, when you pay back the original money you borrowed, you have an option to take back control of your company. When a restaurant was getting started, the entrepreneur needed $1 million dollars. He had $400,000 of his own money, so he needed $600,000 additional funding. Twenty investors put in $30,000, and each investor owned 3 percent of the company. The investors owned a total of 60 percent of the company and the entrepreneur only 40 percent. When the entrepreneur paid back the investors their initial investment for their high risk, each of the investors then still owned 2 percent of the company, thus owning 40 percent, rather than 60 percent. The entrepreneur gained control ownership back in his company.

Looking at the pros and cons

Venture capitalists have a lot of money and a lot of contacts that can aid you in a lot of ways:

- ✔ They can jump-start product development and the regulatory process.

- ✔ They may have established relationships with production and manufacturing facilities that can make your production process less expensive.

- ✔ They have established an effective business system you can adopt immediately.

✔ Their ranks may include experts in your field who can assist and advise you. (Probably at least one member of the venture capital group will sit on your company's board of directors.)

✔ They may run an *incubator* — a place where a lot of start-ups come together to take advantage of economies of scale by sharing common overhead costs, such as rent, a receptionist, legal and accounting services, internet connections, office machines, and so on.

All the money, expert advice, and experience venture capitalists offer do come at a price:

✔ They typically want a significant portion of the ownership in your company — often the majority stake. When someone else owns 50 percent or more of your company, you no longer work for yourself (thus, the importance of the buyback option).

Sometimes, a venture capital group creates a structure whereby they assume majority ownership only if your company or product doesn't get off the ground or if things go badly.

✔ They almost always want at least some representation on your board of directors. Make sure you can live with the representative who may show up at your office offering advice way more often than you may like.

✔ They may pull out if the company doesn't meet certain milestones. Sometimes, the venture capitalists phase in the investment over time based on predetermined milestones, and if the company doesn't reach a milestone in the allotted period, the venture capital group may stop funding you.

✔ They may force a sale or merger in order to reap the profits they expect.

The pros and cons must be weighed against your opportunities to obtain financing from other sources. Don't forget to consider the noncash contributions venture capitalists can make that end up saving or making you more money.

Obtaining a government loan

The government has some a variety of loan programs for small businesses. The SBA is the leader in these programs. It is important to note, however, that the SBA is primarily a guarantor of loans made by private and other institutions.

The SBA's primary business loan program is to help qualified small businesses obtain financing when they might not be eligible for business loans through normal lending channels. It is also the agency's most flexible business loan program, because financing under this program can be guaranteed for a variety of general business purposes. Please check out the SBA website at www.sba.gov to investigate the rules and regs on a variety of loan programs.

Some are as follows:

- **Basic 7(a) Loan Guaranty:** This loan program is the agency's most flexible business loan program, because financing under this program can be guaranteed for a variety of general business purposes.

  Customers on this loan program are start-up and existing small businesses. Funds for the loans are delivered through commercial lending institutions. SBA also offers multiple variations of the basic 7(a) loan program to accommodate targeted needs.

- **Certified Development Company (CDC), a 504 Loan Program:** This loan program provides long-term, fixed-rate financing to small businesses to acquire real estate or machinery or equipment for expansion or modernization. Typically a 504 project includes a loan secured from a private-sector lender with a senior lien, a loan secured from a CDC (funded by a 100 percent SBA-guaranteed debenture) with a junior lien covering up to 40 percent of the total cost, and a contribution of at least 10 percent equity from the borrower. The maximum SBA debenture generally is $1 million (and up to $1.3 million in some cases).

  The typical customer on this type of loan is a small business requiring basic "brick and mortar" financing. Funds for loans for this program are delivered through certified development companies (private, nonprofit corporations set up to contribute to the economic development of their communities or regions).

- **Microloan, a 7(m) Loan Program:** This loan program provides short-term loans of up to $35,000 to small businesses and not-for-profit child-care centers for working capital or the purchase of inventory, supplies, furniture, fixtures, machinery and/or equipment. Proceeds cannot be used to pay existing debts or to purchase real estate. The SBA makes or guarantees a loan to an intermediary who, in turn, makes the microloan to the applicant. These organizations also provide management and technical assistance. The SBA does not guarantee the loans. The microloan program is available in selected locations in most states.

  A customer for this type of program is typically a small business or not-for-profit organization such as a childcare center needing small-scale financing and technical assistance for start-up or expansion. Funds for this program are administered through specially designated intermediary lenders (nonprofit organizations with experience in lending and in technical assistance).

- **Loan Prequalification:** This SBA loan program allows business applicants to have their loan applications for $250,000 or less analyzed and potentially sanctioned by the SBA before they are taken to lenders for consideration. The program focuses on the applicant's character, credit, experience, and reliability rather than assets. An SBA-designated intermediary works with the business owner to review and strengthen the loan application. The review is based on key financial ratios, credit and business history, and the loan-request terms. The program is administered by the SBA's Office of Field Operations and SBA district offices.

A typical loan customer for this type of a loan is a small business. Loan funding is delivered through nonprofit intermediaries such as small business development centers and certified development companies operating in specific geographic areas.

Getting Free Money from Your Uncle Sam

Apple Computer, Federal Express, and Nike Shoes all received financing from government programs at critical stages in their growth. The government and government agencies have a number of grant programs designed to help small businesses and thereby help the economy.

A *grant* offers you free money. It's not a loan, not a trade for a share of your business, not anything but free. Sounds good, doesn't it? But just because it's free money doesn't mean you can just sit back and let the dollars roll in. You have to apply, meet the rules and qualifications, and be selected for a grant.

Don't let the thought of a little paperwork put you off, though. Applying for money from a bank, private investor, or venture capitalist requires a substantial amount of paperwork, too. And if you get a grant, you don't have to pay the money back or give up any ownership in your company.

The U.S. government and various local and regional agencies sponsor all kinds of grant programs to support the development and commercialization of new ideas, products, and technologies. Technology-based innovations receive most of the federal grant money, but local-, regional-, or state-level grants often target improving the local economic and employment base by building jobs (and those grants aren't picky about what kind of jobs you can give).

Keep in mind that your tax dollars fund a lot of grant money. Taxpayers, like any investors, want the best bang for their buck. The administrators of government-funded grant programs want to please the taxpayers, so don't be surprised at the high standards you have to meet to qualify for these grants. You don't want your tax dollars given to just anybody.

Locating local grants

To locate local grant givers, try these sources:

- ✔ **Your local Chamber of Commerce or state Department of Commerce.** They can often tell you where the grant money is at the local level.

- ✔ **A nearby university.** Speak with someone in the Office Of Technology or the College of Business. Universities and colleges can be great sources of information.

- ✔ **Local inventors and entrepreneurial organizations.** Many times, inventors and service providers who attend the monthly inventor and entrepreneurial meetings know of resources you can make use of for funding.

Going to the SBA

The first place to go when you're seeking free grant money from the federal government is the *Small Business Administration's* (SBA) Web site at www.sba.gov. This Web site provides invaluable information on the primary types of federal grant money available to you and a listing of state, regional, and local grants available.

The SBA offers two primary types of federal grant programs — the Small Business Innovation Research Program (SBIR) and the Small Business Technology Transfer Program (STTR). These programs actually work. Several of my clients got free money for their new products and technologies through either the SBIR or the STTR, so keep them in mind for your invention.

Saluting SBIR

The SBIR (Small Business Innovation Research) program is designed to encourage small businesses to do technological research and to help them make money from any new invention or technology they develop. SBIR grantees report their results to the SBA, so the government gains from information submitted by hundreds of company research programs across the nation and from the economic benefits when new products stimulate the marketplace.

Realizing that small companies are often the most innovative, and also realizing that small companies probably can't afford to conduct serious research and development programs, SBIR targets entrepreneurs like you for grant awards and sets aside a percentage of federal research and development money to fund small business programs or services, which stimulates the U.S. economy.

To qualify for the SBIR program, your business must have

- ✔ American ownership
- ✔ A for-profit focus
- ✔ Independent operation (you can't be a subsidiary of a larger corporation)
- ✔ No more than 500 employees

The SBIR system works through federal government agencies, such as the Departments of Agriculture, Commerce, Defense, Education, Energy, Health and Human Services, and Transportation. SBIR also works through the Environmental Protection Agency, National Aeronautics and Space Administration, and the National Science Foundation. Each agency posts the type of research it's looking for, accepts proposals, and awards grants.

The SBA collects and publishes the specifications for each agency's research in a *Pre-Solicitation Announcement* (PSA). The PSA also lists deadlines for proposal submissions. For more information on the SBIR Program, please contact: U.S. Small Business Administration, Office of Technology, 409 Third Street, SW, Washington, DC 20416; phone 202-205-6450; Web site www.sba.gov/sbir.

If the SBA awards you a grant, you enter a three-stage process:

1. **Start-up phase:** You get up to $100,000 for approximately six months to discover whether your idea is technically feasible and valuable.

2. **Phase 2:** If your preliminary research shows promise, the SBA gives you a grant of up to $750,000 for as long as two years to expand your research and evaluate your product's potential in the marketplace.

3. **Phase 3:** You get no more grant money and have to find your own funding to move your product from the laboratory into the marketplace.

Sharing in the Small Business Technology Transfer Program (STTR)

The STTR's mission is to encourage scientific and technological innovation. It fosters research and development opportunities in partnerships between small businesses and nonprofit research institutions.

Not-for-profit research laboratories produce high-tech innovations very well, but these laboratories rarely put their innovations to any practical use. That's where you, the small business owner, come in. The STTR combines the strengths of pure research and commercial appeal. Researchers get to research with a purpose, you get to make money, and Uncle Sam gets a stimulated economy — everybody wins.

Just as for a SBIR grant, your business must be American-owned and independently operated and have no more than 500 employees, if you're a for-profit company. The chief researcher may or may not be one of your employees.

Your partner research facility also has standards to meet. It must be located in the U.S. and be a nonprofit research organization, a college or university, or a federally funded research and development center.

Just five federal departments and agencies participate: the departments of Defense, Energy, Health and Human Services, the National Aeronautics and Space Administration, and the National Science Foundation. These agencies designate the topics they want to have researched, and they accept proposals and hand out awards bases on their criteria.

The STTR program also has three phases:

1. **Start-up phase:** You get up to $100,000 for up to one year to research the scientific, technical, and commercial feasibility of your idea.

2. **Phase 2:** If the start-up phase results look promising, you may get up to $500,000 for as long as two years in order to develop the product and look at its market potential.

3. **Phase 3:** Your product moves from the laboratory into the marketplace during this phase, and you get no more federal funds.

Complete all three phases, and you should have a well-researched, well-financed, and very marketable product to sell.

Chapter 15

Keeping Control with Your Own Business

· ·

In This Chapter

▶ Making sure you really want to start a business

▶ Making the decision

▶ Planning the structure

▶ Understanding the rules and regulations

▶ Supplying Uncle Sam

▶ Locating sources of assistance

· ·

Starting your own business is almost a birthright in the United States. Being your own boss and having creative freedom to follow your goals to financial independence is part of the American dream. Small businesses make up the major portion of the economy, and small business owners form the backbone of this country.

However, just because you can doesn't necessarily mean that you should. Being an entrepreneur is a tough job, and one you should consider carefully before taking it on.

If you do decide to start a business, you're in for an exhilarating (if exhausting) ride. You get to plan your business structure and figure out the specifics of not only your venture but also how to keep on the right side of state and federal laws and regulations. You can also decide whether to work for Uncle Sam and figure out how to get help from him and other contacts. This chapter runs through all these issues, so strap yourself in and prepare for the ride of your life.

Considering Carefully

If you come to me and say, "I want to start my own business," don't be surprised if I look you straight in the eye and ask, "Why?" To start a business to sell your invention, you need a whole range of skills that very few people have. As an inventor, you're certainly creative, and if you've gotten to the stage of being ready to market your invention, you're persistent and determined. But are you also a financial wiz, a marketing genius, a winning salesperson, an efficient production manager, an empathic human resources manager, and a reliable truck driver all rolled into one? Of course, owning and operating your own business can be incredibly rewarding, too. You just need to be as sure as you can ahead of time that starting a business is the right decision for you.

Consider whether you have what it takes by going through the following sections.

Asking yourself some basic questions

Entrepreneur means many things to many people. I can tell you a few things it's not: It's not having a safety net, a retirement plan, sick leave, vacation leave, or paid holidays. It's not going home at 5 p.m. every day and leaving work at your desk. It's not a stress-free life in which you never get a call in the middle of the night with some business crisis. Not to discourage you from building our tax base or anything, but first off, you may want to consider some basic questions:

✔ **How deep is your commitment?** Are you willing to put in 60 to 80 hours a week or even more? Especially in the early years, small business owners often eat, sleep, and breathe their businesses. You may not get to take a vacation, and you sure can't call in sick. Do you have enough enthusiasm and commitment to your invention and to every aspect of getting it produced and selling it that devoting your life to making it happen sounds like fun? If you're cringing just reading this paragraph, business ownership isn't for you.

✔ **Do you have the support of your mate and family?** Aside from your commitment, your spouse and other family members have to share some level of commitment to your invention. You'll be dedicating your energies to the business, and I guarantee that you won't have as much time or energy for your family as you'd like to have.

You also put your family in a risky financial situation. Your family may have to adjust to a lower standard of living and do without vacations or that new car or summer camp or college for the kids. Any problems will be exacerbated, and the good times will shrink. Consulting a couples or family counselor before launching a business is a smart investment of time and money.

✔ **Is your knowledge base broad enough?** If you're going to design, manufacture, sell, and distribute your product, you better know more than a
little bit about all aspects of the process. As the head honcho, it's up to
you to troubleshoot when the production line hits a snag, transportation gets waylaid, or any other problem crops up. If you don't have a
clue about things mechanical, your production line snag may become a
major headache. Likewise, without some familiarity on distribution systems, your transportation trouble may run off the rails.

Of course, you gain knowledge as you go, but you need to have basic
familiarity to get started.

Now, things are already starting to make sense, or you're beginning to have
doubts. Either way, listen to your feelings and trust yourself. In the end, these
are only tools for you to use in your evaluation process, nothing more and
nothing less.

People talk about putting *sweat equity* into a business — in other words,
increasing the stake in a business by working in it. Well, just as the business
is real, you can know for a fact that you'll be putting gallons of real sweat
into it.

Evaluating your skills

Start out by evaluating your strengths and weaknesses as the owner and manager of a small business. Sit down and ask yourself the following questions:

✔ **Am I a self-starter?** It will be entirely up to you to develop projects, organize your time, and follow through on details. If someone has to pounce
on you to get you out of bed and motivated in the morning, think twice
before starting your new adventure.

✔ **How well do I get along with different personalities?** Realize that business owners typically need to develop working relationships with a variety of people, including customers, vendors, buyers, staff, bankers, and
professionals such as lawyers, accountants, and consultants. Can you deal
with a demanding customer, an unreliable vendor, or a cranky receptionist and maintain a productive relationship?

In selling your invention, you come into contact with the general public.
Ask any restaurant server or business receptionist whether the general
populace is even tempered and unfailingly polite. My experience says
no. But, you may be a people person who enjoys humans no matter their
mood or attitude. Just be aware that you will encounter every mood and
attitude and be prepared to make the best of it.

✔ **Am I good at making decisions?** You have to make decisions constantly
as a small business owner — some with large consequences and some
not so large; some in an instant and some after taking time to explore

options. You may have an advisor to bounce things off of, but you're the final authority and must make many decisions all by yourself.

✔ **Do I have enough physical and emotional stamina?** Running a business can wear you down. You put in long hours six or seven days a week. You're not home enough to get nourishment from your mate. You have commitments to vendors and customers and employees and responsibilities to meet here, there, and everywhere — the buck stops with you. Strong motivation can help you survive ups and downs in your business and personal cycles.

✔ **Am I good at planning and organizing?** Many business failures can be attributed to poor planning. Good organizational systems throughout the company improve those systems and help make planning easier also.

You can, and should, have help if you're planning to start your own business, but you also can, and should, have some basic resources within yourself if your business has a chance of success.

Realizing that most small businesses fail

Success is never automatic. Business success depends primarily on your foresight and organization — and a little luck never hurts. Even then, you have no guarantees. According to the U.S. Small Business Administration, over 50 percent of small businesses fail in the first year and 95 percent fail within the first five years.

To give yourself and your business a shot at being one of that successful 5 percent, try to avoid the top reasons for failure:

✔ **Poor management:** Lack of experience, faulty systems such as inventory control.

✔ **Money troubles:** Insufficient capital, inefficient use of capital, disadvantageous credit arrangements, over-investment in fixed assets, use of business credit for personal use.

✔ **Market issues:** Strong competition, out-of-control growth.

Many small businesses get into trouble by trying to grow too quickly. My advice is to start small and grow gradually. Fast and immediate growth brings on its own set of problems and can put your business on a downhill slide.

✔ **Product issues:** Lack of patent protection or lack of patent defense.

I'm not trying to scare you, but to prepare you for the rocky path ahead. Underestimating the difficulty of starting a business is one of the biggest obstacles inventors and entrepreneurs face. However, success can be yours if you're patient, willing to work hard, and take all the necessary steps.

Deciding to Go for It

When I think of entrepreneurs, I think of the backbone of our country. Entrepreneurs are the salt of the business world. Large businesses may get most of the attention, but small businesses drive the economy. Small businesses create over 90 percent of new jobs.

A new venture is risky, but exciting. It's true that many reasons exist not to start your own business. But for the right person, the advantages of business ownership far outweigh the risks:

✔ You get to be your own boss.

✔ Your hard work directly benefits you, rather than increasing profits for someone else.

✔ Your earning and growth potential are unlimited.

Running a business provides endless variety, challenges, and opportunities to grow.

In business, just like in life, you don't get guarantees. You simply can't eliminate all the risks associated with starting a small business — but you can improve your chances of success with preparation, insight, and good planning.

After speaking with many inventors and successful entrepreneurs, I've noticed that many of them had influential role models early on in life. Maybe their parents or other close relatives, such as aunts and uncles, were entrepreneurs.

Assessing your skills, education, and experience

Your skills, education, and experience provide you with tools you can use in starting your own business. Recognizing what you have helps you figure out what abilities you need to develop in order to give your business its best shot at success. To get a grasp on the skills you already have, follow these steps:

1. **Sit down with some paper and a pen or pencil.**

   You may need six or seven sheets of paper.

2. **List your personal characteristics.**

   List your ten main strengths and five to seven serious weaknesses. Get someone close to you to do the same thing, and then discuss the similarities and differences.

Give yourself extra points if you list any of the following (which are characteristics successful entrepreneurs share): competitive, creative, demanding, a desire for immediate feedback whether positive or negative, goal-oriented, high energy level, independent, innovative, inquisitive, persistent, risk-taking, self-motivated, self-confident, and a strong drive to achieve.

Write down your talents and discuss situations in which you've used them.

3. **Make a short detailed list, not more than two pages, of what you know about the field or industry you're getting into.**

   If you're well versed, simply outline the general areas. If you're not sure, you should list everything. Concentrate on specific business information.

4. **Identify your entrepreneurial skills.**

   If you start your own business, your innovative abilities don't stop with simply having a new product. If you're a very laid back couch potato who doesn't like to travel, hates to try to sell something to someone else, can't ask for money from family or friends to help you in starting a business, and relies primarily on others to make your decisions, think twice before starting your own business. You may want to consider licensing as an option.

5. **Analyze two decisions you made that did not work well.**

   Figure out why they didn't work and try to identify the point in the process where a different decision could have made a difference.

6. **Write down the particulars of two problems you solved successfully.**

   Analyze the processes and look for ways to incorporate the steps of those good decisions into everyday decision making.

Taking a clear look at your source of motivation and your belief in yourself helps you prepare for the challenges that come with owning your own business.

When I started my business, I sat down and wrote a column that included the things I knew about my business. Then, I sat down and wrote *pages* of things I didn't know about business. I wondered how I was going to succeed without knowing so many crucial things. My solution was to develop a board of advisors — not a board of directors, which is a legal entity whose members may, in fact, have useful advice to offer — but a group of knowledgeable people with a wide variety of interests and expertise. Together, over the years, they have been my right hand in terms of problem solving for my business. The moral of the story is: You can't do it alone. Surround yourself with the best that you possibly can and then take the most important step and *listen to them.*

Planning the steps

Like a chess game, success in small business starts with decisive and correct opening moves. And, although initial mistakes aren't fatal, it takes skill, discipline, and hard work to regain the advantage.

To increase your chance for success, take the time upfront to explore and evaluate your business and personal goals. Then use this information to build a comprehensive and well-thought-out business plan to help you reach these goals.

Follow these steps to get your business off the ground, and consult the chapters in parentheses for more information on each topic:

1. **Apply for a patent or other intellectual property rights.**

   If a patent search shows there is an existing patent on your product (which is highly likely), you may want to nip your business venture in the bud. (See Chapter 3.)

2. **Conduct a market feasibility study.**

   Make sure you have a market for your product before spending a lot of time and money. If feedback on your invention is negative and consumers don't want to purchase the product or if the manufacturing cost is too high for what consumers are willing to pay, drop the idea. Stay home; you'll lose money. (See Chapter 17.)

3. **Write a business plan.**

   The process of developing a business plan helps you think through some important issues that you may not have considered yet. Your plan will become a valuable tool as you set out to raise money for your business. It should also provide milestones you can use to gauge your success. In Chapter 13, I discuss writing a business plan.

4. **Fix funding.**

   I talk about funding sources in Chapter 14.

5. **Nail down the location(s).**

   If your manufacturing plant and your sales shop are in separate locations, you need to figure out distribution channels also. (See the "Finding a home for your business" section later in this chapter.)

6. **Get the manufacturing facility operational.**

   Chapter 16 talks about manufacturing issues.

7. **Sign agreements with suppliers, vendors, and distributors.**

8. **Take out necessary insurance policies.**

   (See the "Buying business insurance" section later in this chapter.)

9. **Design a marketing plan.**

   (See Chapter 18.)

10. **Launch your sales campaign.**

    (See Chapter 18.)

11. **Hire employees.**

    (See Chapter 10.)

12. **Open your doors!**

Along the way, you have many questions to answer and decisions to make. You need to consider what advantage you have over existing firms and whether you can deliver a better quality service, and then create a demand for your business. You also have to consider such mundane matters as what to name your business and how to compensate yourself.

Finding a home for your business

If you're taking on the manufacturing, marketing, and selling of your invention, you need space to accomplish all those tasks. And you need different types of spaces depending on whether you're planning to do everything in one place or in two or more different locations. You also need to think about how you're going to do everything.

Figuring your space needs

On the face of it, it makes sense to do all your manufacturing and selling in the same place, but zoning requirements or the nature of the manufacturing process may make it more desirable to assemble your invention in one place and sell it in another. Of course, if you're selling by mail or Internet and don't need a storefront, you probably can ship directly from the manufacturing plant and not have to worry if the production process is loud or stinky.

You may even have more than one manufacturing location, with a portion of your product tooled in one place and then transferred someplace else for the final sanding and painting.

You have to take all sorts of things into consideration when looking for space. If you're selling your invention from a store, the old real estate maxim *location, location, location* comes into play. Your market research (see Chapter 17) should tell you the best area for your business. You then have to find a place you can afford and that meets your other requirements.

If you don't need a storefront, distribution becomes your main concern. You want to be conveniently located for your preferred distribution method, whether that's land, sea, rail, or air, and keep alternative transportation in mind in case of need.

Don't forget to consider storage for your raw materials and finished product. It may be cheaper to rent a storage space than to rent or lease a space big enough to house both your manufacturing or sales floor and your stored goods.

Leasing or buying

Whether you decide to lease or to buy a facility to operate your business, you're spending a lot of money. But the smart money for a new business is on leasing as the less-expensive option. If you buy, you need to be prepared to pay very high start-up costs for the purchase price, equipment, and renovations, and many other expenses. If you lease, you don't pay for the big-ticket items. Investing in a manufacturing plant moves your break-even point way out into the future — a future that you don't know whether your fledgling company will ever see. If worse comes to worse, you're better off buying out the rest of a relatively short-term lease than owing 30 years for a building and equipment you're not using anymore.

If you decide to lease space to operate your business, here are some questions to ask before signing a lease:

- ✔ Is the tenant's share of expenses based on total square footage of the building or the square footage leased by the landlord? Your share may be lower if it's based on the total square footage.

- ✔ Must the landlord provide a detailed list of expenses, prepared by a CPA, to support rent increases?

- ✔ Does the lease clearly give the tenant the right to audit the landlord's books or records?

- ✔ If use of the building is interrupted, does the lease define the remedies available to the tenant, such as rent abatement or lease cancellation?

- ✔ If the landlord doesn't meet repair responsibilities, can the tenant make the repairs, after notice to the landlord, and deduct the cost from the rent?

- ✔ Is the landlord required to obtain nondisturbance agreements from current and future lenders? A *nondisturbance agreement* says that a tenant can't be forced to move or sign a new lease if the building is sold or goes into a foreclosure. Such agreements prevent a lender from overriding the landlord on leasing agreements and arrangements.

  Such an agreement also protects the landlord from owners demanding that they paint the building, change the electrical wiring, or put on a new roof. The landlord wants to have some control over his property and doesn't want to be disturbed by your lenders or financial investors.

- ✔ Does the lease clearly define how disputes will be settled?

Speaking the language of leases

You need to understand the terms used in your lease. Some of the most common ones are

✔ **Lessor:** Landlord

✔ **Lessee:** Tenant

✔ **Right of first refusal:** Before vacant space is rented to someone else, the landlord must offer it to the current tenant with the same terms that will be offered to the public

✔ **Gross lease:** Tenant pays flat monthly amount; landlord pays all operating costs, including property taxes, insurance, and utilities

✔ **Triple net lease:** Tenant pays base rent, taxes, insurance, repairs, and maintenance

✔ **Percentage lease:** Base rent, operating expenses, common area maintenance, plus percentage of tenant's gross income

✔ **Sublet:** Tenant rents all or part of space to another business; tenant is still responsible for paying all costs to landlord

✔ **Assign lease:** Tenant turns lease over to another business, which assume payments and obligations under the lease

✔ **Anchor tenant:** Major store or supermarket that attracts customers to a shopping center

✔ **Exclusivity provision:** Shopping center can't lease to another who provides the same product or service that existing tenant does

✔ **CAM:** Common area maintenance charges including property taxes, security, parking lot lighting, and maintenance; may not apply to anchor tenants in retail leases

✔ **Nondisturbance clause:** Tenant cannot be forced to move or sign a new lease if building or shopping center is sold or undergoes foreclosure

Buying business insurance

Like home insurance, business insurance protects the contents of your business against fire, theft, and other losses. All businesses should purchase certain basic types of insurance. Some types of coverage are required by law; others simply make good business sense. The types of insurance listed in this section are among the most commonly used and are merely a starting point for evaluating the needs of your business:

✔ **Liability insurance:** Your business may incur various forms of liability, chief among them *product liability,* which protects you should a customer be harmed by your invention. You may have other types of liability related to your specific industry. Liability insurance covers you in the event someone makes a liability claim against your business.

Liability law is constantly changing and complicated enough even when it doesn't change. Getting a competent professional, such as an attorney, to assess your liability insurance needs is vital in determining an adequate and appropriate level of protection for your business.

✔ **Property insurance:** Many different types of property insurance and levels of coverage are available. You need to determine how much of your property you need to insure for the continuation of your business, and the level of insurance you need to replace or rebuild. You must also understand the terms of the insurance — including what it doesn't cover.

✔ **Business interruption insurance:** While property insurance may pay enough to replace damaged or destroyed equipment or buildings, *business interruption* (or *business income*) insurance pays costs such as taxes, utilities, and other continuing expenses due between the time of the damage and the time you're up and running again.

✔ **Key man insurance:** If you (and/or any other individual) are so critical to the operation of your business that it cannot continue in the event of your illness or death, you should consider key man insurance (which can also apply to a woman). Banks or government loan programs frequently require this type of policy. The funds can come in handy during a period of ownership transition caused by the death or incapacitation of a key employee.

✔ **Automobile insurance:** Obviously, a vehicle owned by your business should be insured for both liability and replacement purposes. What is less obvious is that you may need special insurance (called *non-owned automobile coverage*) if you use your personal vehicle on company business. This policy covers the business's liability for any damage that may result for such usage.

✔ **Insurance on a home office:** If you're establishing an office in your home, contact your homeowners' insurance company to update your policy to include coverage for office equipment. This coverage isn't automatically included in a standard homeowner's policy.

These are just a sampling of the more important types of insurance you need to consider. Consult a qualified agent for advice.

Building a Business Structure

When organizing a new business, one of the most important decisions you make is choosing your business structure. This decision has long-term implications, so consult with your business advisors, including your tax consultant and lawyer, to select the form of ownership right for you.

Going solo with a sole proprietorship

A sole proprietorship is the easiest and least costly way of starting a business. A *sole proprietorship* is a business controlled by one individual. Usually, the individual has the day-to-day responsibility of running the business.

As with any business structure, you have to pay fees, obtain licenses, and register to pay taxes, but other than those standard procedures, you can basically find a location and open your door for business as a sole proprietor. What's more, you don't have to pay a lawyer as much as you do to file the more complicated forms required for more complicated businesses.

Being a sole proprietor has several advantages, including the following:

- ✔ You're in complete control, and, within the parameters of the law, you can make decisions as you see fit.

- ✔ The business structure and hierarchy is as simple, or as complicated, as you make it.

- ✔ You receive all the income the business generates and you choose whether to keep it or reinvest it.

- ✔ The business is easy to dissolve. Selling a sole proprietorship can be as simple as selling a house.

With good comes bad, and several disadvantages attach to being a sole proprietor:

- ✔ You have unlimited liability and are legally responsible for all the business' debts. Your business and personal assets are at risk.

- ✔ You may be at a disadvantage in fundraising. Venture capitalists, for example, require a share of the business in return for their investment (see Chapter 14). You may be limited to using your personal savings or taking out personal loans.

- ✔ You may have a hard time attracting high-caliber employees, because small businesses generally pay less and have less room for advancement. You may have to give employees an opportunity to own a part of the business.

- ✔ Some employee benefits, such as medical insurance premiums, aren't directly deductible from business income.

Partnering up

The two most common types of partnerships are general and limited. A *general partnership* is simply an agreement between two or more persons to enter into business together. The agreement can be oral, but I strongly recommend that you have a lawyer draw up a partnership agreement and that all parties sign it. (Legal fees for drawing up a partnership agreement are higher than those for a sole proprietorship, but generally lower than incorporation fees. See "Incorporating" later in this chapter for more.)

You can also set up a *limited partnership,* which allows several investors to create a common business relationship while limiting each investor's personal liability to the amount he or she invested.

A partnership agreement should be very clear about all partners' duties and responsibilities. As well as detailing the type of business, the agreement should cover the following areas:

- ✔ **Control:** Who makes the decisions on a day-to-day basis, the process for making long-term business decisions, provisions for changing the partnership in general or due to death or incapacitation of a partner; processes for settling disputes among partners.

- ✔ **Money:** The amount invested by each partner; how profits (or losses) are distributed among partners, both ongoing and when the partnership is dissolved; provisions limiting expenditures under certain conditions or by certain people.

- ✔ **Time:** Amount of time each partner contributes, how long the partnership is in effect.

Make sure your agreement is specific about terms and conditions for partner buyouts. I know you don't want to think about breaking up when your partnership is so new, but many partnerships split up during times of crisis. Unless you have set up a defined process, you may be in for even greater problems. In a general partnership, an individual partner's share may not be sold or transferred to someone else without all partners agreeing. If a partner dies, the partnership dissolves, so have a contingency plan for that also.

As a partner, you retain significant control of your business and can make the business as big or small as you and your partners like. Partnerships can go along swimmingly for years and make lots of money for all parties involved. However, all partners are responsible for each other's business actions, which may land you in hot water if one of your partners makes a poor decision.

The partnership itself isn't responsible for paying taxes on the income generated by the business. The partnership files a tax return for informational purposes only. Each partner pays taxes on his or her share of the business income. The profits and losses from the partnership flow directly to the individual partners.

Looking at limited liability companies

Limited liability companies (LLCs) are a relatively new hybrid business structure. LLCs provide the limited liability features of a corporation (see the next section, "Incorporating") and the tax efficiencies and operational flexibility of a partnership (discussed in the earlier section, "Partnering up"). An LLC protects each individual partner to an established financial limit, so that if one partner creates a liability above the amount of his or her financial invest-ment, the other partners are liable only for the amount agreed to. Many lawyers and accounting firms have LLCs to try to reduce liabilities.

LLCs must not have more than two of the four characteristics that define corporations:

- ✔ **Limited liability to the extent of assets:** Partner liability is limited to the amount each partner invested. Personal assets aren't at risk.

- ✔ **Continuity of life:** The partnership is in effect for an agreed length of time.

- ✔ **Centralization of management:** Management authority resides in one person.

- ✔ **Free transferability of ownership interests:** The transfer of assets must conform to stated limitations. For example, if I sell my company to another company and this company wants to sell my company to another company, they have to get my permission first.

The *limited* in LLC indicates that the company's length of operation is usually determined when the organization papers are filed. This time limit can be extended by a vote of the members when the original term is over.

Incorporating

A *corporation* is a legal entity in which stockholders are the owners of the corporation. A corporation is considered by law to be a unique entity, separate and apart from those who own it. A corporation, chartered by the state in which it is headquartered, can be taxed; it can be sued; it can enter into contractual agreements. A corporation has a life of its own and doesn't dissolve when ownership changes. The owners/stockholders of a corporation aren't liable for the corporation's debts at any level.

The owners of a corporation are *shareholders* — they hold stock in the company. The shareholders elect a board of directors to oversee the major policies and decisions, which are executed by the corporations' management team. Regular board of directors' meetings and annual stockholders' meetings shape those decisions. Officers of a corporation can be liable to stockholders for improper actions. Liability is generally limited to stock ownership, except where fraud is involved.

The structure of a corporation is usually the most complex and costly to organize. You aren't required to have a lawyer incorporate your business, but you'd be foolish not to make sure that all the details are taken care of. Records of board and shareholders meetings document decisions made by the board of directors. Small, closely held corporations can operate more informally, but record keeping cannot be eliminated entirely.

You may want to incorporate as a C or S Corporation — your tax advisor can help you figure out whether and which. A *C Corporation* is a business structure in which the income or loss the corporation accrues doesn't pass through to the shareholders. The corporation's income is taxed and paid at the corporate level. An *S Corporation* is a small business corporation in which income or loss is determined at the corporate level then passed on to the shareholders. Shareholders pay tax on income and can deduct losses from their tax returns.

Control of a corporation hangs on stock ownership. The person or people with the largest amount of stock control the corporation. Whoever effectively controls 51 percent of the stock is able to make policy decisions, whether that's a group of stockholders acting together or an individual stockowner.

The advantages of forming a corporation are as follows:

✔ As a shareholder, you have limited liability for the corporation's debts or for legal judgments against the corporations.

Generally, shareholders can only be held accountable for their investment in stock of the company. (Note: However, officers can be held personally liable for their actions, such as the failure to withhold and pay employment taxes.)

✔ Some investors are eager to trade their capital for stock in the company, and if the company needs to raise cash, it can generally sell stock quickly and easily.

✔ The corporation can deduct the cost of benefits it provides to officers and employees.

Incorporating and selling stock in your company means sacrificing significant control. You don't make decisions; the board of directors does. The legal and tax ramifications of a corporation are fairly complicated — as is everything else about this most complicated of all business structures.

Adhering to Government Regulations

It may be inconceivable to you that your game factory, electronics plant, or airplane gasket manufacturing company has to comply with the numerous local, state, and federal regulations, but in all likelihood it does.

Avoid the temptation to ignore regulatory details. Doing so may avert some red tape in the short term, but can be an obstacle as your business grows. Taking the time to research the applicable regulations is as important as knowing your market.

This section lists the most common requirements that affect small businesses, but is by no means exhaustive. Bear in mind that regulations vary by industry. If you're in the food service business, for example, you have to deal with the health department. If you use chemical solvents, you have environmental compliance standards to meet. Carefully investigate the regulations that affect your industry. Being out of compliance can leave you unprotected legally, lead to expensive penalties, and jeopardize your business.

For small business regulations applicable in your state, try going to your state government's home page on the Internet and typing a key word or phrase into the search field.

Business licenses

Many types of licenses exist. You need one to operate legally almost everywhere in the U.S. If your business is located within city limits, a license must be obtained from the city. If you're outside the city limits, then obtain one from the county. For more information, contact the county or city in which your business is located or take a look at the state Web sites that offer business license information.

Certificate of Occupancy

If you're planning to occupy a new or used building for a new business, you may have to apply for a Certificate of Occupancy from a city or county zoning department. Qualifying for a Certificate of Occupancy means having enough space and the right kind of space, as determined by local ordinances, to accommodate your workers and your business needs.

Fictitious business name

Businesses that use a name other than the owner's must register the fictitious name with the county as required by the Trade Name Registration Act. This doesn't apply to corporations doing business under their corporate name or to those practicing any profession under a partnership name. For more information, contact your state or local government.

Tax information

Taxes for your employees, taxes for your business earnings — the IRS gets you every which way, and it only makes sense to do your best to meet Uncle Sam's demands.

Business owners are required by law to withhold federal income taxes, state income taxes, and FICA (Social Security) Insurance from employees' paychecks.

You pay income taxes to both federal and state governments. You have to file returns with both entities, and may be required to file estimated tax returns and pay estimated taxes on a quarterly basis.

Everyone must pay Social Security Tax. If you're self-employed, you make your Social Security contribution through the self-employment tax. You need to calculate how best to report earnings and pay your business taxes.

You can go to the IRS's Web site area for business taxes or call 800-829-1040 or your local IRS office to receive a number of publications that are available upon request to small businesses. One of the most helpful is *Your Business Tax Kit,* which includes data and forms for a Federal Employer Identification Number and a tax guide for small businesses that can be ordered by calling Forms and Publications at 800-829-3676 or through a visit to your local IRS office.

The IRS may seem like a complicated maze, but you can find publications, counselors, and workshops to assist you.

Sales tax number

Unless you live in Alaska, Delaware, New Hampshire, Montana, or Oregon, your state has a sales tax that applies to retail purchases on just about every tangible item sold.

You need to get a sales tax number before you open for business, and you have to collect, report, and send in the sales tax you collect on everything you sell. If you're manufacturing your invention and sell it to a retailer, you have a sales exemption certificate. When the retailer sells your invention to the consumer, a tax is collected from the consumer and turned in to the state by the retailer.

Employee protection

All businesses with employees are required to comply with state and federal regulations regarding the protection of employees. For information on state labor laws, work force availability, prevailing wages, unemployment insurance, unionization, benefits packages, and employment services, contact your state government.

Federal information may be obtained by contacting the U.S. Department of Labor.

Unemployment insurance tax

You have to pay unemployment insurance tax to the state if your company has one or more employees for 20 weeks in a calendar year, or pays $1,500 or more in wages.

Immigration Act

The Federal Immigration Reform and Control Act of 1986 requires all employers to verify the employment eligibility of new employees. The law obligates an employer to process *Employment Eligibility Verification Form I-9*. The Immigration and Naturalization Service (INS) Office of Business Liaison offers a selection of information bulletins and live assistance for this process through the Employer Hotline. In addition, INS forms and the *Employer Handbook* can be obtained by calling the Forms Hotline. For forms call 800-870-3676. Contact the Employer Hotline at 800-357-2099.

Health and safety

The Federal Occupational Safety and Health Administration (OSHA) outlines specific health and safety standards employers must provide for the protection of employees. Many states have similar standards.

Workers' compensation

If a business employs three or more people, workers' compensation insurance must be carried to provide protection to those injured in on-the-job accidents. The State Board of Workers' Compensation aids people who need claim assistance.

Minimum wage

Virtually all business entities are subject to the federal minimum wage, overtime, and child labor laws. Information on these laws, and other federal laws, may be obtained from the U.S. Department of Labor, Wage and Hour Division.

Doing Business with the Federal Government

You may find it easy to forget about one of the major purchasers of goods and services: the government. The federal government is the largest buyer of goods and services in the world. While small businesses are often at a disadvantage when trying to win federal contracts, the U.S. Small Business Administration (SBA) can help overcome the barriers. The SBA works closely with other federal agencies and the nation's leading federal contractors to ensure that small businesses obtain a fair share of government contracts and subcontracts. The SBA also seeks fair access to government-owned property and resources that are being sold. In fact, the SBA has many programs to help small firms do business with the federal government. This section lists various programs that I think may be of interest to you.

The Prime Contracts Program

Through the Prime Contracts Program, the SBA helps to increase small businesses' share of government contracts (also call *procurements*).

To expand contracting opportunities for small businesses, the SBA has specially designated *procurement center representatives* (PCRs). PCRs are people who can help review the paperwork that's required in submitting a bid/contract with the government. Sometimes, the paperwork can be difficult, and the PCRs are there to help you answer the questions and concerns you have. They also recommend contracting sources and provide counseling.

There are two types of PCRs: traditional and breakout. Traditional PCRs work to increase the number of government contracts set aside for small businesses. Breakout PCRs work to remove components or spare parts from sole-source to competitive procurement. This effort generates large savings for the federal government.

Subcontracting Assistance Program

The Subcontracting Assistance Program promotes maximum use of small businesses by the nation's large prime contractors. Specially designated SBA *commercial market representatives* (CMRs) visit large businesses to identify and expand subcontracting opportunities for small businesses and counsel small businesses on how to market their products and services to large contractors. For example, if Boeing Aircraft was contracting to build aircraft for the government and airlines, they would outsource many of the major aircraft components to small manufacturers — both national and international. The CMRs help the small manufacturers to get contracts with large manufacturers, such as Boeing.

CMRs also conduct program reviews of large businesses to ensure compliance with subcontracting program requirements.

Certificate of Competency Program

The Certificate of Competency (COC) Program allows a small business to appeal a contracting officer's determination that it's unable to fulfill the requirements of a specific government contract. The reason for denial must be clearly set forth to determine whether it's based upon competency, discrimination, or financial limitations.

When the small business applies for a COC, SBA industrial and financial specialists conduct a detailed review of the firm's capabilities to perform on the contract. If the business demonstrates the ability to perform, the SBA issues a COC to the contracting officer requiring the award of that specific contract to the small business.

Procurement Marketing and Access Network

The SBA's Procurement Marketing and Access Network, or PRO-Net, is a virtual one-stop procurement shop. The Internet Web site at pronet.sba.gov is an electronic search engine for *contracting officers* (specialists who help get government contracts for small businesses), as well as a marketing tool and link to procurement opportunities and other important information. All small firms seeking federal, state, and private contracts can fill out — and update — their own profiles at the site. These profiles are available to federal and state government agencies as well as to prime and other contractors seeking small business contractors, subcontractors, and/or partnership opportunities. Thousands of small firms have their profiles in the database. If your business isn't among them, sign up today.

Making Use of Contacts and Sources of Assistance

You may feel like you're alone. But many sources are available to help you:

✔ **Inventor organizations** offer educational programs and seminars, expertise in new product development, advice on who to do business with and who not to do business with, as well as offering general and specific problem-solving support.

The easiest way to locate the nearest inventor organization is to go to www.uiausa.com, the Web site for the United Inventors Association (UIA). The UIA is a nonprofit international association providing a variety of services to inventors. One of the main services is networking. Their Web site lists inventor organizations in each state, along with a contact name, address, and phone number.

✔ The **Service Corps of Retired Executives (SCORE)** is comprised of retired and working business professionals who volunteer to help new generations of entrepreneurs build and grow their small businesses. SCORE's business counseling and advice services are free, as a community service.

SCORE offers in-depth counseling and training. Its volunteers help prospective and established small business owners and managers identify problems, determine the causes, and find solutions. SCORE counselors can help you weed out bad business ideas, show you how to write a solid business plan, and help you apply for SBA-guaranteed loans.

Local SCORE chapters offer low-cost, prebusiness workshops that address topics such as: assessing entrepreneurial potential, developing a start-up checklist, selecting a legal entity, creating a business plan, and securing funding. To contact your local SCORE office, call 800-634-0245, or find a local office on the SCORE Web site at `www.score.org`.

✔ The **Small Business Administration (SBA)** offers a variety of programs and information. Its Web site at `www.sba.gov` is excellent. If you want to speak with a live person to find out more information about SBA business development programs and services call the SBA Small Business Answer Desk at 800-U-ASK-SBA (827-5722). Two helpful programs are

- **Small Business Development Centers (SBDCs)** are sponsored by the SBA in partnership with state and local governments, the educational community, and the private sector. They provide assistance, counseling, and training to prospective and existing business people. For a listing of the SBDC offices in your state, look on the SBA'S Web site.

- **Small Business Institutes (SBIs)** are organized through the SBA on more than 500 college campuses nationwide. The institutes provide counseling by students and faculty to small business clients.

Chapter 16

Partnering and Manufacturing Arrangements

*U*nless you're an inventor of independent means — and even if you are — you probably aren't prepared to buy a factory to produce your invention. In this chapter, I give you pointers on making arrangements to have your product made either in some kind of partnership or on a contractual basis. You most likely need price estimates for making your product and are deciding if you should make it yourself or locate an existing manufacturing company to make it for you. You may be asking yourself if you should get it made in the U.S. or should have it manufactured offshore. If you're wondering how to get your product manufactured on limited funds and maybe how to partner or co-venture, then read on.

Paying and Partnering Arrangements

You have a variety of options to get your invention produced: You can go it alone and pay a manufacturer to make your product (called *subcontracting*), you can persuade the manufacturer to bear some of the production costs (an arrangement called a *joint venture*), or you can put a whole new spin on the process by arranging a *merger* or an *acquisition*. The following sections explore all these options. If you're a lone inventor and don't have any experience in manufacturing, I suggest that you work with an existing manufacturing company. It will save you time and money in the long run. If you don't have money to pay an existing manufacturer to make the molds for your product and create mass quantities of your invention, consider trying a joint venture with an existing company in order to share some of the costs involved.

Contracting out or joining up

Most production methods involve you, the inventor, paying a manufacturer to produce a specific number of units. To make this arrangement cost-effective, you need to make the order pretty large. And to make producing your invention worthwhile for the manufacturer, you have to pay him upfront.

You know for a certainty that your invention is the wonder of the ages and will sell like hot cakes the minute it hits the market. Unfortunately, every manufacturer has run into a dozen inventors just like you and has been burned by a few of those inventors whose products didn't sell and who ended up not paying their bills. The manufacturer has to answer to shareholders or owners and can't afford to believe in your dream as much as you do. He has to believe in cash upfront.

You can give the manufacturer this upfront payment by way of subcontracting or by entering into a joint venture with the manufacturing company. The following sections, "Subcontracting" and "Going into a joint venture," discuss these two options.

Be cautious when working with manufacturers. Have a patent or strong confidentiality agreement (more on these in Chapter 8). Remember, if a manufacturer can make the product for you, they can make it for themselves. Many times, a manufacturer also has a distribution network. Manufacturers have been known to work around a patent and come out with their own version, so make sure you're thoroughly protected.

Subcontracting

Subcontracting is paying a manufacturer to produce your product. In a dictionary, this process is simply called "contracting," but the manufacturing world calls it subcontracting. So should you. You're going to face enough challenges in bringing your invention to market; you don't want to get hung up on terminology.

If you subcontract, you pay all the production expenses according to the terms you work out with the manufacturer. If your product sells slowly, you don't get more time to pay; if the distributor loses a shipment, you don't get more time to pay; and so on. Basically, it's your baby — you pays your money and you takes your chances.

Going into a joint venture

A *joint venture,* as it's used in this context, is an agreement between two or more interested parties to produce and market a product or a service. Essentially, a joint venture spreads the costs and risks among more than one individual or company.

If a manufacturing company believes that your invention is going to sell like hot cakes, it may be interested in a joint venture, envisioning massive reorders and a lot of profit.

Don't confuse *joint* with *equal*. Generally, you pay the majority of the production costs — you may even have to pay upfront. The manufacturing company may be willing to pay for making the molds you need, or may possibly extend you some credit beyond its normal terms.

Mergers and acquisitions

A *merger* is one company joining with another company to form a new company, which may or may not retain the name of one of the original companies. An *acquisition* is just what you think it is — one company taking over another company.

Generally, your company becomes a candidate for a merger or acquisition because it's doing either really well or really badly. If you're doing well, other companies may want to share the riches; if you're doing badly but have a good product, another company may see the value in bringing your business back to life.

A disagreement among the stockholders of a public company or among the partners in a small business may prompt a merger or acquisition. The merger may involve some maneuvering to determine who holds the controlling interest in the merged company, and divvying up stock is never a smooth process.

The profitability of a mature company or the expected future of a young company often determines the value of an organization. Beyond profit and futures, multiple bidders interested in the products or technologies the company has control over also help determine the value of a merger.

Companies have to undertake product research and development at great expense. For many large companies, purchasing a smaller organization that's successful in a market that the larger company wants a hand in often proves more profitable than the larger company pursuing its own research efforts. If a large company with a diverse marketing plan can acquire a good marketable product that lends itself to the larger company's marketing strengths, the company can expand a product from a million-dollar market into a billion-dollar market by increasing exposure.

If you find yourself in a position to merge with or acquire a production factory that can make your invention, you may have the best of both worlds.

Teaming Up with a Manufacturer

If you don't have the time or know-how to manufacture your product yourself, you need to find someone who does. Whether you license your invention to a company that plans to manufacture, market, and sell it (see Chapters 20 and 21 for more on licensing) or decide to bring your product to market yourself, you still need to speak with manufacturing companies.

Whether you license your product or not, the more information you have regarding the costs for production, the better off you are. Without manufacturing estimates for production, you can't determine profit margins. Inventors wanting to license their invention should speak to manufacturers to get production cost projections in order to bring that info to the table when trying to get a licensing agreement.

Hooking up with a manufacturer is sort of like a marriage. Make sure that you're compatible and can live comfortably together for the long haul.

Locating potential manufacturers

One of the best sources for locating a manufacturer is the *Thomas Register.* This set of books (usually found in the reference section of your library) lists the name, address, and sales numbers for thousands of manufacturers by product line. So if you want to find a manufacturer to make your new sprinkler, then simply look under 'sprinklers.' The reference librarian can also assist you with other directories listing sources of manufacturing companies. Most state chambers of commerce publish a directory of manufacturing companies within their respective state. For example, in Florida, this directory is called the Directory of Florida Industries. You can also search on the Internet.

Always investigate the credit of any company that you're considering doing business with. The beautiful glass structures of their buildings sometimes have a financial disaster within the walls.

When checking references of companies, I suggest that you contact your local credit bureau to run a credit profile for you. They typically charge a minimal fee. Dunn and Bradstreet provides a credit service that businesses can subscribe to in order to investigate the credit worthiness of other businesses that they are doing business with. Also consider speaking with your local banker. Banks also run credit checks before issuing loans. If a bank has a financial interest in your company, they want to do as much as they can to get paid back. Often, they'll run a credit check for you.

Assessing plants

Hiring a manufacturing firm to produce your invention is often the most economical way to get your product to market. You don't have to build a building, find a plant, hire engineers, lease the machines, or do any of the things you'd have to do if you were going to manufacture your own product. Of course, even though you have a whole list of things you don't have to do, you have an even longer list of things you do have to consider. Some of the issues to consider and questions to ask about the facilities as you look for a manufacturer to make your product for you are the following:

- **Number of years in business, reputation, and financial health:** An established company lends you credibility with distributors and retailers. Some retailers want to know who's producing the product before they agree to carry it. To make their money, retailers have to keep their shelves stocked. If they know from experience that a certain manufacturer meets its delivery deadlines, the retailer is more likely to agree to stock a product made by that company.

  You may want to consider running a credit report on a manufacturing company you like, just to make sure that they're in good financial health. (A credit bureau charges a small fee to run a credit report.) The credit report will also tell you how long the company has been in business.

- **Compatibility with your product:** If a manufacturer makes products that are similar to yours, you can have some confidence that it has the ability to make your product. You can also check out the quality of the manufacturer's work. Make sure that it has the proper equipment to make your product. If your invention uses metal molds, does the manufacturer use aluminum or steel? Aluminum is generally cheaper, but steel molds last longer, allowing you to make more parts from one mold. You want to use the method that best suits your needs. If you need metal turning or stamping, does the manufacturer have the experience and equipment to do that?

- **Age and size of facilities:** Does the plant boast the latest, most efficient and cost-effective machinery? Older machinery may break down, causing delays, missed delivery deadlines, broken contracts, and massive headaches for you.

- **Capacity:** Can the plant finish the manufacturing process in-house, or does it have to outsource some steps? If it subcontracts, you need to investigate the subcontracting company, as well.

  Does the plant have enough capacity to produce your invention? If the machines are working 24/7 to meet current needs, when can they make your product?

If your product must be compatible with consumer purchasing habits, such as holiday and seasonal demand, can the plant be sufficiently flexible?

✔ **Standards:** If your product has to meet standards imposed by government agencies, such as the Food and Drug Administration or the Consumer Product Safety Commission, can the plant meet those standards?

How good is the plant's quality-control process? How does the company deal with defective items, and what kind of recompense can it make to you if it ruins a whole production run?

✔ **Timeliness:** What happens when the plant gets backlogged? Become familiar with *penalty clauses,* which set out the remedial action the plant takes in the event it can't meet your deadlines. A penalty clause makes the subcontractor financially responsible and accountable for your loss of sales, as well as the potential loss of your account with retailers that you're selling your product to.

I have seen many clients lose accounts with major retailers because they didn't get their product delivered on time. If you miss a delivery date, you may get a second chance from a retailer, if you're lucky — but don't expect a third. When your product isn't on the retailers' shelves when it's supposed to be, shelf space is empty and that causes the retailer to lose money. The burden is on you, and the fault lies with your manufacturing company.

✔ **Costs and payment policies:** What will be your product's estimated final cost in terms of tooling and production? What quantity discounts does the manufacturing company offer you for manufacturing your product? For example, what's the price per unit to have 1,000; 5,000; 10,000; 50,000; 100,000; 500,000; or 1,000,000 units manufactured?

Does their payment policy leave you any room to maneuver? Suppose that 10,000 units of your product shipped directly to a major retailer. That retailer doesn't pay you for 60 days, but your payment to the manufacturer is due after 30 days. To add to the confusion, the retailer places another order for 50,000 units. Is this manufacturer going to extend you credit?

Product liability insurance is a very expensive necessity. Most of the larger retailers require at least a $3,000,000 product liability policy before they even consider selling your product. You may be able to save yourself some money by having the manufacturer add your product onto its already-existing policy. The manufacturer should have liability coverage already (if it doesn't, you need to find out why), and the cost of adding your product to that policy should be minimal — like adding a third child to a family insurance policy. If your manufacturer can't include you on their insurance, contact your insurance agent. She may not handle product liability, but she can locate a carrier who does.

A match made in heaven

Generally, the manufacturing company just produces your product, but if you're lucky, a company you enter into a joint venture with may market and distribute your product, too. This additional help can be a wonderful benefit if the company has a proven track record; something you don't have, at this point. The marketing manufacturer may produce ads for your product and represent your product at trade shows and media events.

Examining the manufacturer's track record

Look at your manufacturing partner as a potential mate with whom you have a legally binding contract. Look at possible plants with a keen eye and an investigator's background (see the previous section, "Assessing plants," for details on how to find a good manufacturing partner). You need to work with a reputable company. If your product isn't manufactured on time or is made of cheap garbage, you won't receive repeat orders. A shoddy manufacturer can destroy you.

You should speak with several different companies before making a decision. Don't just go to one manufacturing company and think your job is done. Remember, you're going to pay this company to manufacture your product, and they get paid whether your product sells or not.

Your best bet is to check references. Talk to other inventors who use the manufacturing plant to produce their goods. Try to talk with someone in a company that has the kind of continuing relationship you envision your company having with a particular manufacturer.

Watch out for friends of the company posing as customers. Don't be afraid to ask challenging questions about relationships and references.

Compare the results of the questions you asked, listing the pros and cons of the various manufacturing companies and the overall costs associated with the actual manufacturing of your new product. This comparison helps you narrow down your choices and may help you make your final decision.

Negotiating a contract

Making a deal with a potential manufacturer gives you one more opportunity to sell yourself and your product. You want the production people to be as enthusiastic as you are about your invention so that they want to do it right. You may also convince them to invest a little money, too, by becoming a joint partner.

Before you meet with potential manufacturers, put yourself in their shoes and ask yourself what terms and conditions you could live with, as a manufacturer. A good deal — a workable, lasting agreement — is one in which all parties think they've been treated fairly.

You must realize that your manufacturer has to make a profit in order to stay in business, just as you do. The manufacturing environment constantly changes. Governmental regulations can change with the stroke of a pen and cost thousands of dollars in plant improvements; raw materials can double in price in days and triple in months; an act of God — hurricane, flood, power outage — can impact the plant for hours, days, weeks, or months. Your chosen manufacturer certainly has these possibilities in mind as you negotiate the terms of your deal, so you need to be aware of them, also.

If you don't know the difference between bread mold and a manufacturing mold, find a neutral consultant who can evaluate the costs of the molds you need.

Just as you're concerned about the integrity and reliability of the manufacturer, the manufacturer has those same concerns about you. You know, and I know, that you're a completely honest, well-meaning, and well-intentioned individual, but the manufacturer doesn't know that, and in all likelihood has been burned by an irresponsible inventor in the past. Some of the issues a manufacturer may want to address include:

- **Your financial health:** If your product doesn't sell, or doesn't sell as quickly as you anticipate, can you still pay your bill?

- **Your product's prospects:** How good is your product? What have you done to determine whether your product has a market? Do you have retailers on board to sell your product? Does it have good patent protection? If not, the manufacturer is put in a liability situation for possibly infringing on someone else's patent and can be sued.

- **The workability of your prototype:** Does your prototype easily lend itself to duplication and mass production? If not, who's responsible for making a working model or mold?

All too often, an inventor is so much in love with her invention that the practicalities of duplicating it in the real world just don't register. A manufacturing partner can't afford to take the same rose-colored view.

Giving a copy of your business plan to your manufacturer can go a long way in reassuring him or her about your commitment to your invention. (I go through writing a business plan in Chapter 13.)

Partnering Abroad

To go to market, a product must be manufactured at a competitive price. You may want to look at your offshore pricing options and see if it's cheaper to have your invention made offshore, especially if you need several thousand units made: When manufacturing offshore, it's not cost-effective to only have a few made. You will be purchasing by the *container,* meaning train boxcar load.

Matching up with the right foreign partner

The U.S. government recognizes that finding a manufacturing partner is critical to the success of many businesses. To help American businesses connect with foreign manufacturing companies, the Department of Commerce (DoC) offers Matchmaker Trade Delegations. These delegations provide an opportunity for U.S. businesspeople to meet with representatives of foreign manufacturing plants. These meetings take place in the country that the manufacturing company hails from so that you, the U.S. inventor, can actually see the facilities.

The DoC prescreens foreign businesses in an effort to facilitate overseas partner selection, and you can use these delegations as an excellent way to make joint venture and licensee contacts.

If you can't make one of the scheduled Matchmaker Trade Delegations held each year, you may still be able to make use of the DoC's contacts through its Gold Key Service. The Gold Key Service uses the DoC's overseas staff to assist in developing a market strategy, setting up orientation briefings, making introductions to potential joint venture partners, providing interpreters for meetings, and helping with follow-up planning. Fees for these professional services vary from country to country. Here are some of the steps that may be involved in foreign partner selection:

1. **Contact your local DoC office.**

   To find this office, look in the U.S. government section of your local phone book or go to www.commerce.gov and click on the **Commerce Offices and Services Near You** link.

2. **Discuss your target market and what kind of partner you're seeking.**

   The DoC staffer can tell you whether the DoC has a Matchmaker program fitting your needs scheduled. If the DoC doesn't have such a program planned, they can send your request to the appropriate Foreign Commercial Service representative abroad. This representative forwards you a list of potential partners. Contact each one with a letter of introduction. After you get responses from potential candidates, conduct a financial- and business-reference check on the most qualified candidates. If you're unable to do these reference checks in-house, use a credit-reporting firm.

3. **Make a trip to the country where you want your product manufactured.**

   Take this trip either with a Matchmaker Trade Delegation or on your own to meet with potential licensees or joint venture partners.

4. **Choose your partner and negotiate a contract.**

   Pay attention to the issues I raise for considering any manufacturing partner in the preceding "Teaming Up with a Manufacturer" section.

Issues to consider when partnering abroad

Having your invention produced by a foreign company has both advantages and disadvantages. I cover the important issues in this section.

Looking at legal issues

Legal control is most likely your first consideration when you think about manufacturing in a foreign land. U.S. laws don't apply anywhere but in the U.S.

This means that you may not have the same patent protections in other countries and that you're more vulnerable to having your invention copied. It's not unheard of for a manufacturer in the U.S. to copy an invention and produce and market it without the inventor's permission or even his knowledge. If the same copying takes place outside the U.S., you may have a much harder time in the legal arena.

For one thing, you have to find a lawyer qualified to practice in the country in which the plant operates. You also have the added expenses of travel, time away from your business, and so on.

A U.S. patent gives you the right to sue in the U.S. It doesn't mean you have patent protection in other countries. In fact, many times, offshore companies see a product that is selling well in the U.S. and decide to make and sell it in other countries throughout the world. Unless you're a manufacturing giant with a lot of purchasing power so that losing your business doesn't cost you that much, offshore manufacturers can become your greatest competitors. Offshore manufacturers make many highly desirable products and sell these knockoffs for pennies on the dollar compared with the patented product.

If you go the offshore route, you also need to concern yourself with U.S. Customs laws. Basically, you're importing your own invention. You don't have to hire a *customs broker,* a person licensed by U.S. Customs and Border Protection to conduct Customs business on behalf of importers. But many importers opt to do so for the convenience. Customs brokers take the burden of filling out paperwork and obtaining a Customs bond off of the importer's hands. Some import rules, especially regarding a new product, can be particularly complex, so a broker may be the way to go. You're ultimately responsible for meeting Customs regulations, but a Customs broker can save you from making costly mistakes.

Pricing labor costs

Clearly, hiring workers in foreign countries is much cheaper than hiring them in the U.S. China, for example, has an abundance of highly skilled technical workers. Asia, in general, boasts workers with highly developed technological manufacturing skills.

Compared with China, manufacturing labor costs in the U.S. are enormous. For example, a highly skilled mold designer in the U.S. may be paid anywhere from $40 to $70 per hour. The same skill in China may earn the worker $1 to $5 per hour. Not surprising that so many manufactured products have the words *Made in China* stamped on them.

A worker in a third-world country who has little or no technical skills makes under $1 an hour. Such a worker can competently cut and sew garments or work on an assembly line.

The cheap labor costs may be an irresistible lure, but Americans are becoming more socially conscious. If someone accuses your foreign plant of being a sweatshop that exploits the local workers without adequate compensation, your reputation and your bottom line may suffer.

Probing product cost and quality

General production costs in much of the Pacific Rim are about 25 percent less than they are in the U.S. Labor costs play a big part in that, but every other piece of the manufacturing pie is also cheaper overseas — materials, tooling, plant facilities, and so on.

One expense that may not be cheaper and may, in fact, cost you much more than you bargained for is transportation. If you're dealing with time-critical products that have to be shipped by air from the Pacific Rim, you're looking at substantial transportation costs. On the other hand, if your invention can take a slow boat from China, that transportation doesn't add a lot to your manufacturing costs. Just make sure that you account for the transportation when you figure out your production costs.

Be aware that by having your invention made overseas, you basically lock yourself into high-volume orders. If a factory in the next state makes your product, you can start with a smaller production run or have an extra 5,000 units made during your next cycle. Such fine-tuning isn't feasible if the production factory is overseas. Making anything less than 10,000 units generally isn't cost-effective, and speeding up delivery is not an option if you base your pricing on shipping costs — switching to air delivery prices you out of the market.

The greatest risk factors in obtaining quality-for-cost manufacturing in third-world countries are:

- **Honesty of the contracting brokers:** The cost of raw materials can be many times the manufacturing costs. Should these raw materials become misdirected, the costs to you can be enormous.

- **Quality control:** The quality and cleanliness of the finished products can be a problem. If you choose to have your product manufactured offshore, you may want to hire an in-country agent to keep an eye on production for you.

Some trading companies offer full-service packages that provide you with the insight and worldwide relationships you need to make foreign manufacturing work for you. They have insight into the industry's top merchandisers. They source products to be manufactured around the world and help you lower acquisition costs to maximize your profits. These companies can be located through the Department of Commerce, as well as on the Internet. Fees for their professional services vary, so do some price comparisons in addition to checking references.

Chapter 17

Preparing to Take Your Invention to Market

In This Chapter

▶ Finding out what information you need

▶ Researching the market

Being a developer of ideas is like being an explorer; you don't know what you're getting into except that it's new, mysterious, and challenging. In this chapter, I shine some light on marketing basics that you need to know in order to prepare to introduce your product to the market. I give you tips to help you discover whether there's a market for your product and reveal techniques in consumer studies.

If you think getting your patent is tough, let me inform you it's a piece of cake compared to marketing your invention. However, your product won't be successful unless you prepare to market it. It's a hard task, but a necessary one.

Discovering What You Need to Know

Many new inventors who seek my advice assume that everyone is going to love their invention. Unfortunately, that assumption is dead wrong. You may think that because your product is new or because it's patented, people are going to snatch it out of the store. Although a patent will give you an edge, the hard reality is that the "big boys" have them, too. And consumers don't buy something just because it's new unless it's something they need. So, consider finding out what people need and how to give it to them. You have to know who your market is in order to reach it. Basically, you want to know:

✔ Who your customer is

✔ What your customer's needs are

✔ How your invention meets the customer's needs

> ✔ Whether your invention meets the customer's needs better than your competitor's product
>
> ✔ How to package your invention to appeal to the customer
>
> ✔ How much money your customer is willing to pay for your product

Getting the information to address these issues involves gathering facts and opinions in an orderly, objective way to find out what people want to buy. Remember that what you want to sell them and what they want to buy may be two different things.

Marketing is warfare for the sale. The product that the buyer chooses wins. A sale drives revenues for you and the retailer, creates a need to replenish inventory, and exposes the product to others, which hopefully generates more sales and perpetuates the process.

Large corporations pay millions of dollars for research before they ever introduce a new product. You may not have millions, but you can use the same research tools — you may even be able to use some of their research if you can get access to a published marketing study.

Finding out about your customers

The goal of marketing is to establish customers to buy your product. Ultimately, in order to succeed, you must attract and retain a growing base of satisfied customers. To do that, you have to know who your customers are, where they are, and how to get them to buy your product.

You gotta get a profile

I used to work across the hall from a government office called the Southern Technology Applications Center (STAC). Large companies call them to get profiles of potential consumers, which STAC provides for a minimal fee. For example, if a bank wanted to open a new branch office, they ask about three different locations they're considering. The computer analyst can do some research and then give the most profitable site based on Census data, buying, traffic, household income, and other relevant patterns. The Center is also able to provide entrepreneurs who are planning to start a bakery (for example), with the profile of a bakery customer. This is terrific information to know, especially when developing advertising material. Look at it this way; if finding this information is good enough for the big companies, it's good enough for you. I can guarantee that you're going to need profiling info.

Note that *customers* are the focus of every sentence in the preceding paragraph. And for good reason — customers are the be-all and end-all of marketing. Without customers, it doesn't matter how revolutionary, how competitively priced, or how attractively packaged your invention is. Without customers, you may as well not even have an invention. *If you don't know who your customer is, I guarantee that your competitor does.*

So, you need to find out what potential customers like, what they don't like, what they need, how your invention meets those needs, how much they're willing to pay, where they are now, and where they'll go to buy your product. Finding and utilizing that information is what marketing is all about.

Try government resources first when you're looking for profile information — you may as well let your tax dollars work for you. Even if you have to pay for information, the fee is most likely subsidized and therefore quite small. Another source is the *Small Business Sourcebook,* which you can find in the reference section of most public libraries. This sourcebook lists valuable industry contact information. You can also use that valuable research tool, the Internet, to search for profiling information and profiling companies.

Consumers have different purchasing patterns, likes, and dislikes. People of all ages, races, and sexes have different purchasing patterns. Blacks, whites, Hispanics, and Asians all have different purchasing patterns. We all know that men and women think differently, right? Well, we purchase products differently as well. People also display differences in purchasing patterns when it comes to religion. Think of kosher foods. The point is, not everyone is going to purchase your product. You want to focus on the person who *is* going to buy it. The faster you figure out who the consumer is, the more profit you can make. How do you do this? Through market research.

Keeping up with the competition

When trying to place your product, understand that you're in a highly competitive, volatile environment; therefore, you need to know and understand your competition. And don't say you don't have any competition because your patented invention is unique in the marketplace. You're still competing for customers' dollars. Consumers have plenty of other opportunities to spend the same dollar you want from them.

You can gain a lot of insight from your competitors — you're hoping to gain some of their market share, aren't you? Even before that, though, you can take a look at their product and analyze its strengths and weaknesses. Use your analysis to make improvements to *your* product before it gets to market.

You can take advantage of the market research they've done when you decide how to package your invention, what color to make it, where to sell it, and how to price it.

Start a file on your five nearest direct competitors and five close substitutes. Every quarter, or more frequently if warranted, review each file and

- ✔ Evaluate each competitive product's strengths and weaknesses.

- ✔ Estimate whether each competitor's market share is growing, staying steady, or declining.

- ✔ Check pricing strategies and determine whether to adjust your current pricing strategy.

- ✔ Look for ways to adapt your competitors' successful strategies for marketing and advertising to benefit your business.

- ✔ Study each competitor's advertising and promotional materials and their sales strategies.

Visit your competitors' booths at trade shows and look at their booths from a potential customer's point of view. What does their display say about their company? Observing which specific trade shows or industry events competitors attend provides information on their marketing strategy and target market.

Many inventors make the mistake of being interested only in their own products, ignoring even the industry in which their products are sold. Doing so is a good way to make sure the market ignores you all the way to bankruptcy!

Packaging for appeal and profit

Packaging can help sell your invention or it can ensure that your product gathers dust on the store shelf. Remember Pet Rocks? That was nothing but a packing and marketing genius! Even consumers dense as the proverbial box of rocks knew that there were thousands of stones available for the picking, but the "inventor" made a mint through packaging. That packaging, which was designed to look like a pet carrier, enticed people to buy their own Pet Rocks.

Packaging is a key feature in selling your product. It can make or break a sale. Studies show that people look at a product for seven seconds. So you have seven seconds to convince each customer to buy your product. If they can't figure out what your invention is or does in those seven seconds, they most likely put it down and don't think of it again.

You have to find out what type of packaging appeals to consumers and take those qualities into account along with your product's needs for protection or display.

Pricing your product to sell

Everybody understands that price plays a large part in consumers' purchasing decisions. It only makes sense that you spend time figuring out the right balance between the amount customers are willing to pay and the price you need to make a profit.

Pricing your product correctly is crucial for maximizing your revenue. You need to fully understand the market for your product, the channels of distribution, and the competition — *before* you establish prices. You must know all the component costs for manufacturing and carefully analyze them. You should also know the packaging and shipping costs. The consumer market responds rapidly to technological advances, international competition, and the end purchasers.

Pricing isn't as straightforward as you may think. Many entrepreneurs look at the cost of manufacturing, figure in the cost of packaging, transportation, and overhead, and then try to tell the consumer what price he or she is going pay for the product. These entrepreneurs have it exactly backward. You don't tell the consumer what to pay for your product; the consumer tells you. In our free market, you can, of course, price your product whatever you want it to be. However, I suggest pricing it at what a consumer is willing to pay, and then backtracking it all the way down the manufacturing ladder to see if you can have your product produced cost-effectively. If not, stay home. Don't enter the market and lose money.

Consumers know what they want to pay for your product. To find out how much they're willing to pay, do your market research and ask them. Big companies always do market research before introducing their products and you should do the same. Design a sample survey and ask potential consumers whether they're interested in your product *before* you spend a lot of time and money producing your invention.

There are two basic costs in selling a product:

- ✔ **Cost of goods:** The price you pay for manufacturing, packaging, shipping, and handling.
- ✔ **Operating expenses:** These include salaries, advertising, rent, utilities, office supplies, and insurance for both the business and its employees. These costs are not directed to a single item; they're basically calculated into the cost of all the items you sell. The more of your product you sell, the more profit you make, as these costs stay relatively constant.

Generally, the higher a product's price, the fewer items that sell and vice versa. However, you may be able to command a high price by offering personalized service.

It's hard to believe that an inventor's royalty on a product that retails for $20 may be too small to buy a cup of coffee at a convenience store. But remember that a product passes through many stages on its way to a store shelf: It begins as raw materials and then gets packaged so that the consumer knows what it's for and how to use it. It needs a sales representative to sell it to the retailer. It needs advertising so the buying public knows it exists. Many hands get a piece of the action and the inventor is often shocked at his or her share.

Figure 17-1 illustrates where the dollars and cents go. This example follows traditional distribution steps and is merely a guideline.

ROYALTY - 5% OF WHAT?

Retail (or list) price	$20.00
(based on research)	
Discount to retailer	
(40% off list)	- 8.00
Retailer's Cost	12.00
(From Wholesaler)	
Discount to Wholesaler	- 4.20
(40% to 35% off retailer's cost)	
Wholesaler's Cost	7.80
(From Manufacturer)	
Manufacturer's Agent	- .39
(Based on 5% of Mfg.'s selling	
price to Wholesaler as shown	
at $7.80)	
Inventor's Royalty	- .39
Manufacturer's Net Proceeds from sale	$ 7.02

Figure 17-1:
Adding up the costs of pricing.

Out of the $7.02, you have to cover the cost of the goods and your operating expenses, *and* make a profit! If the manufacturer needs a markup of 40 percent, the product cost (including packaging) must be no more than $5.02. If the manufacturer needs a markup of 30 percent, the product cost must be no more than $5.40.

To get a general idea of markup ratios, look at the retail price of a product and divide by 4. For example, if a product sells for $10, the manufacturing, packaging, and shipping costs must be under $2.50. Four is the minimum markup on a product.

Divide the retail price by 4 (minimum) to find out what the maximum manufacturing, packaging, and shipping cost is. The markup on products varies upward from here by industry and product, and also by where the product is sold. Get to know the markups for your industry. Electronic and jewelry-related products are generally marked up by a multiplier of 10. For pharmaceuticals, the multiplier is up to 16. If a product sells on television, the multiplier ranges from 5 to 7 times manufacturing cost with an average of 6 times. If the profit margins aren't there for everyone who handles your product to make money along the way, you're going to lose money in the long run.

If a product is selling on an infomercial for $19.95 (the average infomercial markup is 6 to 1 meaning there is a 600 percent markup from the manufacturer to the retailer), the product's manufacturing, packaging, and shipping should be no greater than about $3.35.

When working with infomercial-related companies, consider negotiating for a percentage of the shipping and handling charge they pass on to consumers. For example, when you purchase a product off of the television, you may pay a $5.95 charge for shipping and handling. However, the real cost to the infomercial company for shipping and handling may be only $2.95; therefore, the profit margin is $3. If this company is going to sell your product, ask them for 50 percent of the shipping and handling charge ($1.50) per unit.

Pricing is one of your more fluid marketing tools. To increase sales and cash flow, you can use any or all of the following tools:

- ✔ Give your regular clients discounts.

- ✔ Give discounts to customers who pay cash.

- ✔ Barter by offering discounts to trade association members, senior citizens, and/or local college, high school, or university students.

- ✔ Offer your customers financing, including installment credit.

- ✔ Partner with a bank to create your own credit card, commonly referred to as *cobranding*.

Doing Market Research

Doing *market research* means gathering and analyzing information about the marketplace or a specific market. Marketing people talk about two basic forms of market research:

- ✔ **Primary research** is asking customers or potential customers about their likes and dislikes, as well as other pertinent statistical information. (I explain the process of doing primary research in the following sections.)

- ✔ **Secondary research** is making use of existing information.

Secondary research information has already been collected (and sometimes analyzed); all you have to do is find it and apply it to your situation. When doing secondary research, you search out published sources like surveys, books, and magazines and then apply or rearrange the information to suit your needs.

The government is a great source for secondary research. Census data, for example, can give you information on the people who live in your area — whether they own or rent, how much money they make, how many people share living space, and what their ethnic background is. If you're shopping for a store location, checking census data for the areas you're interested in is a good first step.

You can also get industry data on purchasing patterns and shopping habits, competitive pricing data, market share, stockholders' reports, and so on in the library or over the Internet.

You can find secondary research material in libraries, colleges, trade and general business publications, the Internet, and national and local newspapers. Some good sources of secondary research include:

- **ASAE Directory of Associations Online:** Your reference librarian can help you find this information.
- **Ask a Librarian:** U.S. Library of Congress at `www.loc.gov`
- **Bureau of Labor Statistics:** `www.dol.gov`
- **Center for Business Women's Research:** `www.dol.gov/wb`
- **Business Research Lab:** Ask your reference librarian to help you locate statistics within the industry of your product.
- **GALES' Directory:** Available at any public library.
- **Population and demographic resources:** `www.census.gov`
- **Public library:** A good reference librarian is an incredible source of information. Ask one for help locating statistics about your industry.
- **Statistics for 100 federal government agencies:** `www.fedstats.gov`
- **Trade associations:** One of the best places to obtain industry data is from the trade associations for related products. The major source for trade association info is the *Encyclopedia of Associations,* which groups trade associations by interest area. For example, if you look under the Toy category, you see associations including Toy Brokers, Toy Manufacturers; Toy Retailers, Toy Wholesalers; and so on. If you call the individual associations, you can obtain all kinds of industry info. This source also lists the number of members of each association so you can get a better picture of how big the industry is.

  You can also find out which trade shows are big in your industry and attend them. (See Chapter 18 for more on attending trade shows.)

If you have a conflict between national statistics and local information, go with the local numbers. Local conditions may buck national trends.

You can also look at customer information you already have. Sales records, complaints, receipts, and other records may show where customers live and work, and how and what they buy. One small business owner found that addresses on cash receipts allowed him to pinpoint customers in his market area. With this kind of information he could cross-reference his customers' addresses and the products they purchased to check the effectiveness of his advertising. Customers' addresses tell much about them. Lifestyles — and buying habits — are often correlated with neighborhoods.

Bear in mind that market research is not an exact science. It deals with people and their constantly changing feelings and behaviors, which are influenced by countless subjective factors.

To do a thorough job of researching customers' likes and dislikes, use the process I outline in the following sections.

Defining the opportunity or problem

Defining the problem or opportunity is an often overlooked but crucial first step of the market research process. You have to figure out what your chance is before you can take it. Is there a hole in the market that your invention can fill? Does your invention perform better than any competitor's, yet cost the same?

Finding the root cause of a problem is harder to identify than its obvious symptoms. For example, a decline in sales is a problem, but in order to correct it, you must find the reasons for the decline and correct them.

To define an opportunity or problem, list every factor that may have influenced it, then eliminate any that can't be measured. Examine this list while conducting research to see if any factors should to be added, but don't let it unduly influence data collection.

Setting objectives, budgets, and timetables

Remember that your market research should be specifically about your product and needs to cover every aspect of your invention. You want to find out who wants to buy your product, how much they're willing pay for it, what they think it should be called, how they want it packaged, what they want it to look like, how they want it to function, and where they want to get it. Most important, find out what they don't like and what they would change about your product if it were theirs.

Your budget for all this depends on who you get to do the research. If you use students, the research should cost about $2,000 or less. You may have to pay them up to $1,500 to get the consumer surveys completed and another $500 to have someone input the data and give you a statistical summary. If you conduct research over the Internet, you're looking at spending about $5,000 for reputable and valuable research and analysis (not like the rip-off invention marketing companies do). Hiring a market research company that asks people questions in a mall may cost up to $8,000 or more.

The amount you must spend varies depending on the nature of your product, as well as how difficult it is to get consumers to answer your questionnaire. If you want to survey parents of 6 to 12 year olds who play soccer, hitting soccer games three nights a week during soccer season and can rack up 500 completed surveys within a month.

I recommend using a company called www.marketreaderpro.com to conduct survey work. They're reputable and I checked them out before I used them.

The timetable for your market research should be about three months — or long enough to get at least 500 completed surveys. Be aware that you most likely need to talk to around 1,500 people to get those 500 responses.

Selecting research types, methods, and techniques

Good research reveals how the customers want your product packaged, customers' preferred colors, and other pertinent consumer information. You can conduct product research in a number of ways:

- **Surveys:** Also known as questionnaires, surveys are a time-honored and effective method of research. You can question people in person, over the phone, or online. An inexpensive questionnaire can give you detailed information on prospective customers, their likes, dislikes and preferences, whether or not they want to buy your product, how much they're willing to pay, and where they would purchase it.

- **Field experiments:** Bringing your actual product to people and letting them sample it is a direct way of getting honest reactions. Think grocery store samples and taste tests. I remember when New Coke came out. I gave my 4-year-old son, Brandon, a sample and *knew* it wasn't going to sell. He said, "Icky, mommy," and handed it back to me. When a 4 year old turns down a soda, you know something's wrong. Hopefully, your product doesn't elicit the same reaction.

✔ **Focus groups:** You get several individuals (up to 15 at a time) together, show them a product and ask them to tell you what they like and don't like about it, what to change about it, and so on. Results from a focus group give you more details than you get from a quick survey; however, it may cost you about the same, if not more, in the long run, because you need to run several different groups.

One of the best ways to get market research is from the industry trade groups. Ask them what they have available, what companies they use to obtain industry information, and so on.

Designing research instruments

Research instruments is a fancy way of saying *questions*. In the following sub-sections, I help you figure out what questions to ask and how to find people to both ask and answer them.

Asking the right questions the right way

In developing a survey form for your product, you want to set things up so that the first answer you get is, "Yes." It is designed this way to be more 'user friendly' and get the survey respondents to continue completing the question-naire. The first question doesn't even have to be about your product. For example, if you're researching a new sporting goods product for hunters, your first question may be, "Do you like to hunt?"

Then you progress to detailed questions about your product to find out how it is perceived. Perception is everything.

You want to know and fulfill the customers' needs. You want to know their color preferences, packaging preferences, whether the size of the product is correct, what price they'd pay, and where they would purchase your product.

You already know what you think, but when it comes to market research, what you think doesn't matter. What matters is what potential customers think.

You also want to know who your customer is, so ask a couple questions at the end about age range, income range, zip code, buying habits, and so on. Always offer ranges for sensitive information such as age and income level. And always, always, thank your participants.

A time-honored and effective way to poll potential customers is to design a survey. What you want a questionnaire to find out is potential consumers' perceptions about your product.

Figure 17-2 shows a sample survey I designed to solicit opinions about a new device (the device in question assists senior citizens when taking their medication). Feel free to use this questionnaire, changing the wording to fit your product.

CONSUMER QUESTIONNAIRE
"AUTOMATIC PILL DISPENSER"

I. Do you take medication on a daily basis?
_____ Yes _____ No

2. If a product were available to remind you when to take your pills, how many you are to take, as well as to dispense your medication, would you purchase the product?
_____ Yes _____ No
If no, why not? _____

3. After seeing a picture of the "Automatic Pill Dispenser," if it were available to purchase, would you purchase the product? _____ Yes _____ No
If no, why not? _____
If yes, would you purchase it for -- _____ Yourself _____ Gift _____ Other
(whom) _____

4. How much would you pay for this automatic pill dispenser?
_____ $ 3.00 - $ 3.50   _____ $ 6.01 - $ 6.50   _____ $ 9.01 - $ 9.50
_____ $ 3.51 - $ 4.00   _____ $ 6.51 - $ 7.00   _____ $ 9.51 - $10.00
_____ $ 4.01 - $ 4.50   _____ $ 7.01 - $ 7.50   _____ $10.01 - $10.50
_____ $ 4.51 - $ 5.00   _____ $ 7.51 - $ 8.00   _____ $10.51 - $11.00
_____ $ 5.01 - $ 5.50   _____ $ 8.01 - $ 8.50   _____ $11.01 - $11.50
_____ $ 5.51 - $ 6.00   _____ $ 8.51 - $ 9.00   _____ $11.51 - $12.00
More than $12.00?_____ If so, what amount? _____

5. Where would you expect to purchase this product?
_____ Wal-Mart _____ Target _____ Eckerds _____ Rite-Aide
_____ Television _____ Grocery Store Pharmacy _____ K-Mart
_____ Medical Supply Store _____ Walgreens
_____ Mail Order Catalogue _____ Magazine Add _____ Newspaper Add _____
_____ Other (please name) _____

6. Would you prefer to purchase in specific colors? _____ Yes _____ No
If yes, what color/s? _____

7. How would you expect to see this product packaged? _____ Box _____ Hang Tab
_____ Bubble Pack _____ Other, please name _____

8. After seeing the "Automatic Pill Dispenser" would you make any changes on the Product? _____ Yes _____ No   If yes, what changes would you make?

9. If this were your product, what would you name this product? _____

10. Personal Information:
Age: _____<20 _____ 21-25 _____ 26-29 _____ 30-34 _____ 35-39
_____ 40-44 _____ 45-49 _____ 50-54 _____ 55-59 _____ 60-64 _____ 65+
Race: ___ White ___ Black ___ Hispanic ___ Indian ___ Asian ___ Other
Sex: _____ Male _____ Female
Income Level: _____ < $15,000 _____ $15,00I - $19,999 _____ $20,000 - $29,999
_____ $30,000 - $39,999 _____ $40,000 - $49,999 _____ $50,000+Additional
Comments:_____
_____

Figure 17-2:
A sample product survey.

The questionnaire should be no longer than three pages, so you have to get the answers you need in a very short time. Give the survey recipients choices to check and a place to add comments if they want to. Don't ask many open-ended questions — you want answers you can code easily. But don't forget one very important open-ended question: "If this product were yours, what would you change about it?" Pay attention to the answer — write it down, see how many survey respondents give that same response.

One of the most important items a survey reveals is what potential consumers don't like about your product. And, that's a good thing. It is just as important to find out what people *don't* like as what they *do* like. I can assure you that finding this out will save you money in the long run: If you find out what changes need to be made and can make them before you launch your product, you're ahead of the game already. For example, if consumers tell you they want your product in red instead of black, you make it in red. If you find out customers prefer a box to shrink wrap, you figure the cost of a box into your profit margins and sell your invention in a box.

It is much less expensive to offer a product consumers already want than to have to spend time convincing consumers they like and want what you have.

The results of your market research may surprise you. You may think a retail store is the best place to sell your invention, but your market research may show that 85 percent of the respondents would buy the product on television. Changing the venue dictates changes in the markup, packaging, and profit margins.

You've heard the expression: A picture paints a thousand words. Make visual arts work for you. It is amazing what a good graphic artist can do with colored sketches or computer drawings of your product. In many cases, you can have artistic renderings of your product completed for a small portion of the cost of a prototype. Show the visuals while people are answering survey questions.

Having the right person ask the right questions

If you're on a tight budget, one of the cheapest ways to conduct primary market research is to hire college students from a nearby college or university. People respond to college students and are often happy to speak with them, whereas professional marketers get the cold shoulder. Think about it: If a professional market researcher approaches you as you're strolling through a mall and asks you to complete a questionnaire, are you more likely to say "Okay," or "No, thanks"? What about when a college student approaches you and says, "I'm a student working on a project, can you help me?" If you're like most people, you'll take a few minutes and answer the questions.

If you don't use college students, you can call your local Job Service and place a free ad looking for day labor work, or you can hire a market research firm and leave everything to them.

The key thing is to check out a market research company before you hire them. Believe nothing unless you take the time to investigate the company and see what kind of research they've conducted in the past. Get the names and phone numbers of references. Take the time to check with the attorney general's office in their home state, the Better Business Bureau, and the Federal Trade Commission to see whether the company has complaints against it. As a starry-eyed inventor who thinks your invention is the greatest thing since sliced bread, you're a prime target for getting ripped off by unscrupulous companies that tell you that your invention is, in fact, the best thing since sliced bread, then charge an arm and a leg to do market research that isn't worthy of the name. Take off your rose-colored glasses when it comes to doing market research.

If you conduct your own research, don't identify yourself as the inventor. You can't afford to have people to be nice to you and tell you what they think you want to hear.

Asking the right people

Send surveyors to public places. You may ask, "What public places?" Well, places where people wait. For example, consider sending surveyors to unisex hair salons, high volume automotive shops where people get oil changes, car washes that detail cars on site, and so on. Shopping malls and airports are great gathering places. Market research companies often rent space in a mall in order to conduct surveys.

Ask permission from the storeowner, mall, airport manager, or whoever's in charge before you start asking questions.

Basically, you want any potential customer to answer your survey, except, and it's a very big *except,* your friends and family. You don't want to be one of those inventors who believes that the deal is sealed because 25 of his closest friends and family members told him his product is going to sell. I tell my clients to ask friends and family who say their invention is going places to invest in getting the invention to market. Give them the opportunity and see what happens. Most don't invest. If you really want to succeed, you want honesty, not kindness. When working with inventors, it is not my job to be nice. It's my job to be professional, direct, and honest. Some dislike me for my candidness, but honesty saves money and heartache in the long run.

In addition to potential customers, survey managers of stores where you think your product might sell. Figure 17-3 is a sample manager survey, which you can adapt to your needs. Finding out this information can be an eye-opening and very valuable experience. Store managers generally rack up several years of retail experience before they become managers. Be aware that when dealing with the large retailers, managers manage people; they have little say about what products the store carries, because national buyers order for all the stores in the chain. That doesn't mean that these managers can't be helpful to you. Just like managers of smaller stores who order their own goods, these managers are aware of products in general, what it takes to sell a product in their store, pricing schemes that help sell goods, the importance of packaging, and other hands-on issues you can benefit from.

STORE MANAGER SURVEY
THE AUTOMATIC PILL DISPENSER

1. What is the policy and procedure for placing products in your store?
   _____
2. Who purchases the products for your store?_____
3. What is the address of your home office? _____
   _____
   _____
4. What kind of packaging would you use to display this product?
   Bubble pack _____ Hang Tab _____ Box _____ Other _____
5. Do you like this product? Yes _____ No _____ If no, why not? _____
   _____
6. If yes, would you consider putting it in your store? Yes _____   No_____
   If no, why not? _____
7. How much would you charge for this automatic pill dispenser
   if it were sold in your store?
   _____ $ 3.00 - $ 3.50   _____ $ 6.01 - $ 6.50   _____ $ 9.01 - $ 9.50
   _____ $ 3.51 - $ 4.00   _____ $ 6.51 - $ 7.00   _____ $ 9.51 - $10.00
   _____ $ 4.01 - $ 4.50   _____ $ 7.01 - $ 7.50   _____ $10.01 - $10.50
   _____ $ 4.51 - $ 5.00   _____ $ 7.51 - $ 8.00   _____ $10.51 - $11.00
   _____ $ 5.01 - $ 5.50   _____ $ 8.01 - $ 8.50   _____ $11.01 - $11.50
   _____ $ 5.51 - $ 6.00   _____ $ 8.51 - $ 9.00   _____ $11.51 - $12.00
   More than $12.00?_____ If so, what amount? _____
8. Who would you talk to within your own company to market a product if you
   had a similar idea? _____
9. What would you name this product? _____
10. If you were in my position, what would you do next to market this product?
   _____
   _____
11. Do you have any additional suggestions that may help me get this product on
   the market? _____
12. Do you have any additional comments? _____
   _____

Figure 17-3:
A sample
manager
survey.

Note that the store manager survey asks very similar questions to the consumer survey. Generally, if you survey store managers and take the average, this figure will most likely be within a 10 percent deviation of the actual selling price. For example, if you survey 15 store managers and they state your product would retail for $4.95, the error rate would place the retail price at a 10 percent differential higher and lower. Your product would most likely retail for $4.50 to about $5.50 with the average of $4.95. So surveying store managers is a great resource.

Try to get a broad sample of managers. For example, if you have a lawn and garden product, talk to managers at garden stores, large home-improvement outlets, and local hardware stores that sell gardening supplies.

You can conduct a manager survey yourself. In this study, you're not asking about your product directly, but about what makes products like yours sell. You can, and should, bring a prototype or drawings, and cheerfully accept any comments or criticism. But your main role is to get the manager to talk about similar products and how they sell. If the manager talks about flaws in products already on the market, you can probe to discover how the product can be improved, and possibly incorporate those improvements into your invention.

Call a store manager to make an appointment, but *don't* identify yourself as an inventor. The mental image most people get when they hear *inventor* is of someone who looks like Albert Einstein and acts like Jerry Lewis in *The Nutty Professor* — someone smart but weird who's going to waste their time. Try *entrepreneur* instead. Say something like, "I'm a start-up entrepreneur with a new product. I am *not* trying to sell you anything; I just want your expert advice. Would you take a few minutes to speak with me?"

There is nothing wrong in asking for help, and many people are very willing to give it. Smart retailers know that entrepreneurs are the backbone of the country, and they're often more than happy to make a contribution to the next great thing.

Organizing and analyzing the data

When it comes time to add up responses, you quickly realize the value of having boxes to check instead of blanks to fill in on your questionnaire. What you want is a tabulation of how many people chose each response to every question and the total percentage of people who chose each answer. For example, if you ask which color people prefer and gave respondents choices of red, yellow, green, and blue, you want to know how many people preferred each color and what percentages those numbers translate to.

If you don't have the expertise yourself to work up a spreadsheet that can calculate numbers and percentages, go to your friendly local college and pay a student $500 to tabulate your responses.

In reality, generating a report of your survey responses is probably the simplest part of the whole process. You just plug in the responses, and out come the numbers. The final report that I get from the person who does tabulation for me is usually not more than ten pages long, including a summary of responses to the open-ended question about recommended changes.

Use the data you gather to build a *customer profile* that tells you who your typical customer is — age, race, sex, income, location, shopping patterns — everything and anything that can help you sell your product.

Chapter 18

Marketing Your Product

· ·

· ·

*L*aunching your invention is a foray into the dog-eat-dog world of the marketplace. Your product competes for the consumer's dollar against similar products (and purchases in general) to find its place in the world. All your work can now be measured in sales revenues as your invention is tested in the court of last resort — the marketplace. The battle is ultimately won or lost here. A purchase is a win; staying on the shelf is a loss. No matter how well developed and one-of-a-kind your product is, if it doesn't sell, it isn't a success.

As an entrepreneur, you face getting turned down by buyers, wholesalers, consumers — everybody, it seems. I've never worked with a successful entrepreneur who didn't go through hard times. Take WD 40, for example. Do you know what WD stands for? *Water Displacement.* Do you know why it's called 40? Because the inventor was turned down by 39 companies before one company accepted the product!

For every dollar you spend on development, you ought to spend ten dollars on marketing. A good product properly marketed wins over a great product poorly marketed.

Everything you do in development, design, protection, branding, positioning, and pricing culminates with marketing your invention and selling it to your customers. In this chapter, I clue you in to what's involved in marketing your product to potential customers.

Developing Your Market Strategy

You wouldn't build a house without a plan, would you? Of course not. Likewise, you need a plan to sell your invention. A sound marketing plan is key to the success of your product.

Marketing is civilized warfare, so get ready for the fight of your invention's life. You're fighting for the same shelf space, magazine space, and TV time as firms with multimillion-dollar advertising budgets. It's not so much that this shelf ain't big enough for the two of you, but that products already on the shelf get squeezed into a smaller space to make room for yours. If that happens at a national chain, break out the bubbly because you have reason to celebrate. On the other hand, getting your product into major stores is rare enough that you don't have to feel like a failure if you don't get your invention placed right away.

A *marketing strategy* identifies customer groups (known as *market segments*) that your business can serve better than your competitors can, and tailors prices, distribution, promotions, and services toward those groups.

Your marketing strategy should accomplish two essential tasks:

✓ **Direct your company's policies and activities toward satisfying your customers' needs.** Every customer has specific needs. Marketing determines these needs, and you develop the product to satisfy them. Market research, focus groups, surveys, and questionnaires are crucial to determining customers' needs.

The most successful products are those that fill *needs* rather than wants or desires. A need is something you absolutely have to purchase; a want is something you'd like to have. For example, if you don't have access to public transportation, you *need* a vehicle. You may *want* that vehicle to be a Porsche, but then that's the difference between needs and wants.

✓ **Price your product for optimum profit.** Realize that making a profit is more important than maximizing sales volume. You may be selling millions of units, but if you aren't making money, you're wasting your time and effort.

You must know your costs and profit margins.

Your marketing plan should include your market research, your location, the customer group you've targeted, your competition and positioning, the product you're selling, pricing, advertising, and promotion. (For more about market research, see Chapter 17.)

From a thousand different approaches and even more methods, marketing programs are all aimed at convincing people to try out or keep using particular products or services. Analyze your products' competitive advantages to develop long- and short-term market strategies. Also, carefully plan your marketing strategies and performance to establish a market presence and keep it strong. You want to establish brand loyalty so that customers come back time after time, bring their friends and family to you, and eagerly purchase any new products you develop.

Staying on top of customers' needs

Use these tips to keep abreast of customers' needs:

✔ Complete at least one marketing activity each day, such as conducting a follow-up call with a customer, attending a business luncheon at the Chamber of Commerce, calling a product rep, or writing a thank-you note to a supplier.

✔ Establish a way of tracking your clients and keep this list updated.

✔ Calculate a percentage of your company's income to spend on marketing functions each year.

✔ Set your marketing goals for the year but review them on a quarterly basis to make sure they're being met.

✔ Keep business cards with you at all times — you'll definitely run into numerous occasions to distribute them.

✔ Create a company pin with your logo to give away to people so they can pin it on their jackets. Custom pin-making companies can easily be found in the back of airline magazines when you're taking a flight.

Mixing it up

Every marketing strategy combines four key components, called the *marketing mix:*

✔ **Products and services:** In your case, your invention.

✔ **Promotion:** Basically, any method you use to get your product into the public's eye and consciousness. Promotion includes advertising, customer relations, direct mail, leaflets, and so on. Chapter 19 has more about advertising.

✔ **Distribution:** The method you use to get your product to your customers. A mail-order business, not surprisingly, distributes through the mail. A retail business, however, may use a combination or a chain of distribution methods — factory to truck to ship to rail to truck to store to clerk to customer, for example.

Distribution includes storage as well. If you have to pay to store your goods, you have to account for those costs.

✔ **Price:** Correct pricing is crucial. You have to determine what customers are willing to pay and figure out how to make a profit for yourself based on that price. See Chapter 17 for more on pricing.

The following marketing tips can help you stay sane in the marketing madhouse:

- ✔ **Use your customers.** Ask them how they found out about you and why they decided to purchase your product. Ask them for marketing ideas — maybe run a contest. Definitely ask customers who return your product why they're returning it.

  Put out a suggestion box and encourage both customers and employees to use it.

- ✔ **Keep up with the industry.** Read trade magazines, subscribe to trade journals, join the trade association. Subscribe to any Internet newsgroups that deal with your industry. Attend educational events and conferences. Join professional organizations.

- ✔ **Keep up with your competition.** Keep and update files on your competitors' ads and marketing materials. You can discover a lot from looking at material about their product features, marketing strategy, pricing information, and packaging material.

- ✔ **Get some free help.** Call the nearest university and see if an intern is available in the College of Business's marketing department who is interested in working with your company in return for a class grade.

- ✔ **Hire a marketing consultant to obtain new marketing ideas and suggestions.** A marketing expert will most likely see your product in a different light and have links, resources, strategies, and comments you may not have thought of.

Targeting your market

If you're like most inventors and start-up entrepreneurs, you have a limited market budget. Concentrating your efforts on one or a few key market segments — target marketing — can save you money and help your business flourish.

In order to target a specific market, you have to identify it — break it out or segment it. You can do this a couple of ways:

- ✔ **Location:** You specialize in serving the needs of customers in a particular geographical area. For example, a pizza parlor may send advertisements only to people living within ten miles of the store.

- ✔ **Customer type:** You identify those people most likely to buy your product or service and target them. Remember, not everyone wants to buy your product. For example, if you have a new baby monitor, you target parents-to-be, new parents, and grandparents, and don't concern yourself with people who don't fit into those segments.

After completing your market research (see Chapter 17), you have a picture of your typical customer. You can hire a company to create a customer profile for you, if you like. Type **customer profile** in the search field of any Internet search engine to find such companies.

Narrowing your market helps you save costs on advertising and helps you serve your customers better. The more precisely you can define your market, the more specifically you can gear your product to meet your customers' exact needs.

Making sales presentations

One of the most effective ways to market your invention is with the personal touch — making sales presentations. If you're good at selling, that's great. If you're not, practice until you are or get someone who's good to do it for you.

When bankrolling new products and technologies, investors bet on you more than on your invention. One of the top downfalls of inventors is that they're so creative they just can't get focused. Most will fail; however, if an inventor has several good ideas to focus on, she can eventually create a winner. I always bet on the inventor — a good inventor will come up with several new products over time — not just one.

You (or someone else, if you can't bear the thought of selling) can sell to the customer in one of two ways:

✔ **Direct selling:** In direct selling, you sell your product directly to the customer through a face-to-face transaction, or via the mail or the Internet. You take home the entire selling price and deduct your costs from that to determine your profit margin. Some direct-sales venues are: craft fairs and festivals, swap meets, your own retail store, direct mail, or your company Web site.

✔ **Indirect selling:** You pay someone else to sell your product. You pass the cost of the salesperson on to the customer. Indirect sales methods include hiring sales representatives (who sell a number of different products and receive a commission on each product sold), placing your product in a retail shop to sell on consignment, or selling your product to a retail shop. The usual markup is between 60 and 100 percent, which is what the retail shop needs in order to cover their operating costs.

You can sell directly to stores, but you may have more success getting an appointment with a sales representative or *vendor* (supplier or seller of goods). Call a store's buyer and don't be offended if you don't get a return phone call. You may have to make five more before a buyer calls you back — buyers are very busy people. When you finally reach a buyer, be friendly.

Don't put her on the spot by asking for a commitment, or even an appointment, then and there. Instead, ask her for the names of the sales representatives she deals with most frequently. The sales reps are the people you really want to sell on your invention.

One of the easiest ways to get your product in the store is to go to a store and search for similar products. Sales representatives are already selling these products in the stores. If a product is already selling in the store, it already has a *preapproved vendor*. Find out who the sales rep and distributors are and then call them and see if they're willing to take on your product. Sales reps are selling on commission and they want to sell new and exciting products. It's easier to sell five products than it is one. That way, customers can choose which one they want to carry.

Different companies have different sales structures, so make sure you're not bypassing a buyer in making a sales pitch to a board of directors. Going through channels makes you more popular and more likely to be listened to.

Sales presentations may feel like the last thing you want to do. But what's the worst that can happen? You may get thrown out, you may not sell your product, you may be insulted. So what? I've probably been asked to leave more companies than most people will ever go into, but I've also placed numerous products. Just remember; the more presentations you make, the higher your probability of getting sales.

When you do make a sales presentation, dress accordingly in business attire.

Attending trade shows

One of the most important things you can do to market your product is to attend trade shows. A *trade show* is an event held in a secure facility, such as a convention center, where manufacturers and marketers can display their products and technologies to potential buyers, retailers, wholesalers, and others in their industry. It is a meeting ground to provide an interchange of new product information between buyers and sellers.

Nearly every industry has a trade show. Sometimes, famous speakers and celebrities are brought in to attract a bigger crowd. Also, there can be educational events with a variety of speakers and topics targeted toward a specific industry.

Trade shows generally take place at a single location — often at the same location each year. They usually last one to three days, and bring together thousands of exhibitors and potential customers. They're a powerful way of selling your product, as well as finding out more about the industry.

Trade shows are designed as an inexpensive way to meet many potential customers face to face in a brief period of time. Be aware that your potential customer at a trade show is a retail chain and not Joe and Jane Consumer. You can use the same marketing techniques; you're just selling on a larger scale.

I consistently encourage the inventors I work with to attend trade shows and I strongly recommend that you do, too. I can sometimes predict on the very first visit that an inventor has the right stuff. The inventor who asks, "Where do I find out about trade shows, how much do they cost, how do I get in, what do I do when I'm there?" has a higher probability of success than an inventor who wants nothing to do with the hustle and bustle of a trade show. In fact, make going to trade shows part of your annual business plan (see Chapter 13 for business plans).

Tracking down trade shows

"How do I find trade shows to attend?" you may ask. The *Encyclopedia of Associations,* I answer. This reference volume lists the names, addresses, activities, and publications of national organizations. You can find the *Encyclopedia* in your public library. Consult it, and then get in touch with the associations that are relevant to your product and ask them to name the biggest trade show in their industry.

For example, if you made a toy, the trade show for you to attend is Toy Fair held each year during February in New York City. Everyone who's anyone in the toy industry is there, and you should be too. Whether you exhibit your product at this point is irrelevant; just be there.

Deciding whether to exhibit

If your budget is down to the bare minimum, regard trade show fees as a necessity *not* to be cut. Trade shows help level the playing field for smaller firms. Booth space is generally inexpensive ($13 per square foot on average, with the typical small booth covering 100 square feet), and even small companies can usually afford attractive displays. With creative marketing and booth design, small businesses can actually appear as substantial as much larger corporations.

If you just want to attend a trade show, often the only cost is for stationery proving that you're in the industry. Some shows are free if you preregister. For example, the Consumer Electronics Show held in January in Las Vegas draws about 200,000 buyers, wholesalers, retailers, and other electronics folks from all over the world. If you're preregistered, it's free. Otherwise, the fee is usually less than $100. Most trade shows charge between $25 and $250 for admittance.

Both exhibiting and attending have their advantages. I go over both in Table 18-1. Just keep in mind that you don't want to exhibit at your very first trade show — no one is prepared for that.

Table 18-1	Exhibiting Versus Attending
Reasons to Exhibit	**Reasons to Just Attend**
Generate sales leads and actual sales.	Meet buyers, wholesalers, distributors, and potential licensees for your product.
Enhance your image and visibility.	Find out how the industry works.
Reach a specific audience.	Check out the big names' big-bucks exhibits and see what you're up against when you decide to exhibit.
Establish a presence in the marketplace.	Become familiar with the language of buyers and sellers. Even the best sales reps practice the lingo in order to become more proficient.
Improve the effectiveness and efficiency of your marketing efforts.	Circulate and see the sights instead of being stuck in your booth for the whole show.
Personally meet your customers, competitors, and suppliers.	
Prospect for new customers.	
Introduce a new product.	
Demonstrate your product.	

If you're an independent inventor, you may not want to spend the money for a trade show booth. Just be there. Anyway, if you have a booth and are by yourself, you can't leave the booth — not even to go to the bathroom. If you're one of my typical clients on a limited budget, you may end up with an 8-foot table with a white skirt around it and homemade posters. This doesn't sound bad until you realize you could spend three days right next to a booth with half-a-million dollar displays!

Planning and preparing to make the most of your time there

The Trade Show Bureau reports that of the firms exhibiting at business-to-business shows, 44 percent have fewer than 50 employees. Sophisticated exhibitors do well at trade shows no matter what their size, while the naive and inexperienced can waste thousands of dollars and countless hours — and maybe do more harm than good.

However, using trade shows effectively takes only a little effort and planning:

✔ **Come equipped, mentally and physically.** Mentally, be prepared to put your best foot forward at all times. You should be friendly and interested and responsive. Physically, be sure to wear comfortable shoes. Plan on a lot of walking on convention center concrete floors. Come prepared with business cards to give to everyone you meet, and you may want to bring a bag to store all the literature and free handouts you'll pick up.

✔ **Plan a course of action.** Note any events you want to attend, and locate any exhibitors whose booths you want to see. Target the people you want to meet and make appointments ahead of time. You can meet buyers, wholesalers, distributors, manufacturers, and potential licensees for your product.

✔ **Take advantage of the unique opportunities a trade show offers.** You can comparison shop among dozens of competing vendors, handle new products and supplies, and test products too large or cumbersome to be brought to the office.

You also get to see new inventions (of course) long before they hit the market. Trade shows really are a showcase for brand-new products, technologies, and trends in an industry. Many inventors hold back a new product so that it can be launched at a trade show.

Making contacts

A trade show is a giant networking opportunity. You can speak to competitors, clients, suppliers, and manufacturers in the space of a couple days. Take advantage of the opportunity to speak with technicians and designers who are directly involved in the forefront of your competition. Don't be shy about introducing yourself and offering to buy a cup of coffee for someone whose brain you want to pick. The cost of that cup of coffee can be a great investment.

You may want your product to sell in one or more of the catalogues, trade journals, or newsletters you sign up for. Bring business cards to get on mailing lists, not only of wholesalers, buyers, distributors, suppliers, but also your competitors. You can also keep on top of your competition —see what they're doing and what new products they're introducing.

Be sure to follow up with contacts you meet. Spend a morning after you get back sending e-mails, making phone calls, and sending any information or samples you promised.

Gathering ideas

Take advantage of the vast amount of knowledge and experience to expand your own understanding of the industry. Your colleagues are fellow trade show participants and their opinions and experiences can help you make decisions about your product and future shows you want to attend.

Find out who the major players are, what they're working on, and where they think the industry is heading.

You can focus on understanding the buyer/seller relationship on the sales show floor, because a lot of wheeling and dealing is going on. You can see what's selling now and get ideas about what may be selling next year.

Keep your eyes and mind open.

Generating sales leads

Because business-to-business shows typically don't allow selling on the show floor, generating sales leads is the most common reason exhibitors participate. (Depending on the venue, you may be able to take orders, but probably won't be allowed to have the products for consumers to take home with them that day.) It is possible during the course of one trade show to personally meet most of your important clients and suppliers, making shows a good way to establish and reinforce relationships.

At trade shows, you get contacts and sales leads and possibly take orders; however, no one has a big inventory in stock — you don't see semi trailers unloading merchandise. Trade shows are generally open only to players in the industry and not to the general public. Wholesalers, distributors, and retailers give out information and price sheets, but don't do much actual selling. Industry buyers who attend often represent hundreds of stores, not just one or two, and it's not cost-effective for them to take small orders from start-up companies who may not be able to deliver what they promised.

The U.S. Department of Commerce estimates that the average total cost of closing a sale in the field is $1,080, while the cost of closing a sale to a qualified trade show prospect is $419. Take advantage of this opportunity to make a larger profit.

Examining the extras

Other trade show extras include special events, promotions, and incentives that encourage attendance and sales on the floor. Free training seminars and workshops are great opportunities to network with colleagues who have similar interests. Vendor-sponsored parties provide an enjoyable social outlet free of selling pressures and full of contacts.

Trade show attendees also have the opportunity to enter a multitude of drawings for a variety of interesting prizes.

Getting your product and customers together

Getting your product into your customers' hands involves the two Ds: distribution and display, both of which I cover in the following subsections.

Distributing widely and well

Distribution is the manner in which you get your product to the customer. You have many factors to consider when it comes to distribution. You need to have a well-thought-out plan. Answering the following questions can help you devise one:

✔ How many products can you store? What is your inventory capacity? Use sales forecasts to decide what your inventory levels *should* be in order to meet customer demands.

✔ What is the turnover rate for your inventory? How does this compare with the standards in your industry?

✔ Do you have cyclical fluctuations or seasonal changes that affect the demand for your product? For example, if you produce lawn furniture, how will you manage peak production and sales periods as well as slow periods?

✔ What's your distribution channel? Describe your distribution channel in detail. Plan on a step-by-step basis for how your products are going to reach your customers.

Every method of distribution has pros and cons. Consider all the advantages and disadvantages of each method of distribution in relation to your situation. Include in your analysis a look at retail stores, craft fairs, selling from home, mail order, sales reps, trade shows, and wholesale. You may want to use one method exclusively or combine several.

Make sure you figure out the cost for each distribution method you're considering and add that into your pricing calculations.

For an item for which you anticipate a relatively small sales volume, such as homemade baskets with antler horns that you intend to sell through a specialty store, the distribution method is such a routine part of the sales contact that it requires only a small amount of thought and description. In this situation, you display your unique baskets in a local store or gallery so consumers can see and purchase them. In other cases, you may want to sell your baskets over the Internet where you ship your product directly to the end purchaser. The whole point is that you just want to get your product in your customer's hands and get paid.

Your method of distribution depends on you and your product. Start with a single system so you can get experience in distributing your product. As your knowledge base grows, you can add additional products to product lines, as well as broaden your customer base.

Whatever you do, deliver your product when you say you're going to. Keep your word. You don't want to promise what you can't deliver. Negative word-of-mouth advertising spreads faster and does more damage than positive advertising can fix. It is very difficult to regain credibility.

Displaying your product to advantage

Getting customers to buy your product often boils down to how it looks in the store. If your packaged invention takes a large amount of display space, stores may be reluctant to stock it. Remember, shelf space is expensive. If your invention doesn't stack, you place it at a disadvantage right off the bat. A large or heavy item requires special handling. You have to keep all this in mind to give your invention its best shot.

Placement is important, too. You don't see name brand products stocked on the bottom shelf of a store. Big companies pay to have their merchandise stocked at eye level. They also pay to sell their product at the end of an aisle. If your product is an impulse-buy item, such as gum or breath mints, you want it placed in a high-traffic, high-visibility area, preferably right by the cash register. Location is less a concern for products that customers are willing to go out of their way to find. If someone needs cold medicine or a special type of tool, that person will look for it and find it.

The recent availability of highly segmented mailing lists and Internet commerce has enabled certain small businesses to operate from any location yet serve national or international markets.

Don't think retailers are going to add store shelf space for your new, unproved product. It's not going to happen. Your product's display and packaging are of utmost importance.

Steering clear of invention promotion companies

I typically see five to seven clients per week who have paid thousands of dollars to fraudulent invention promotion companies. Fraudulent invention promotion schemes have been depriving national economies of thousands of new products and technologies for decades. Unsuspecting inventors have paid hundreds of million of dollars to these con artists and gotten little or nothing in return.

You can find ads for invention marketing companies everywhere — in the back of magazines, in newspapers, on television and radio commercials, and any other media naive enough to take their money. The line these companies use is often something like: Send for your *free* inventor's kit, or submission forms, or whatever is popular at the time. After you get your free kit, you get bombarded by phone calls that let up only when you agree to submit your idea for evaluation (or product overview, or assessment, or whatever).

Unless your idea is illegibly written in crayon, your product is accepted for further development. If you write legibly in crayon, you have a shot, which I proved one time by taking ABC's *20/20* into my children's grade school during invention week. The projects voted most ridiculous were sent in for a market evaluation, and lo and behold, the inventions received high ratings from the rip-off invention marketing companies! Now, children have come up with some fantastic inventions, but the inventions we sent in were chosen for their lack of any quality a reasonable person would find valuable. One of these companies told an inventor that the tea bag he'd ripped the tag off of had the potential to make millions because lots of people drink tea. These people are in it for the money and for no other reason.

Now, enter the marketing directors, assistants to the president, product analysts, marketing staff, or whatever the commissioned sales force calls itself offering to do further research and market testing for you.

You're in the paying-for-a-report phase now. At this point, you're asked to sign a disclaimer, which is often incomprehensible and nearly always misrepresented by the salesperson. I've had hundreds of inventors tell me that the salespeople said something entirely different than what was written. Read the fine print before you sign any legal document.

You get your market evaluation, which I can paraphrase, free of charge. It boils down to:

> Your idea appears to be both patentable and marketable.

The report you receive is not an evaluation of any sort. It is basically worthless information that looks convincing to the uninformed.

Now, the sales force turns on the pressure. They want you, the unsuspecting inventor, to pay them, the unsuccessful promoters, thousands of dollars to promote your idea. They tell you how wonderful your product is. They tell you that your product has multimillion-dollar potential. They tell you this without conducting any real market research. Most use industry data available on the Internet instead of actually talking with potential consumers.

Before you sign up with any marketing company, ask for personal references and check them out. Get the names and phone numbers of inventors whose product the company has successfully marketed. You may get the excuse that the company can't give out this "personal" information. Believe me, my successful clients want to tell their story to as many people as possible. Companies can get permission from their successful clients to release their names for references.

Of course, to patent and fully promote your invention takes money — your money. If you don't have money, and don't want to take out a second or third mortgage on your house or borrow from family and friends, no problem. The promotion agency may have its own financing company. You're now liable for interest on money they scammed you for. When you discover that you've been ripped off and cancel your monthly payment, your account is turned over to a collection agency and your credit rating suffers.

Widening the gulf

It used to be that manufacturing firms were eager to talk to inventors. That's not the case any more. What led to this breakdown? Well, a significant factor is the growth of fraudulent invention promotion schemes. These opportunists flood the system with so many unrefined and undeveloped ideas that many manufacturers don't even open their mail anymore.

I wish that I could say that closing down the fraudulent schemes would let the system mend itself. But other forces are at work. You, the independent inventor, have also contributed significantly to this breakdown.

The majority of independent inventors have ugly babies (inventions). No one likes to hear their baby called ugly, and people are naturally reluctant to hurt your feelings, so far too few inventors get an honest appraisal of their invention. On the other hand, though, the overwhelming majority of inventors tell me that they wish someone had been honest with them very early in the process — before they invested their life savings — and told them that their baby was indeed ugly.

To deal with this, inventors need to establish a mechanism very early in the process that can screen out the truly ugly babies. This mechanism must be affordable, unbiased, and 100 percent ethical. To do this, you have to answer the inventor's chicken-or-the-egg question: evaluation first or patent search first?

Well, I've been telling inventors for years that there are two first steps. Why the conflict? The cost. An evaluation can cost considerably less than a patent search. The good news is: The United Inventor's Association, a nonprofit national inventors association, (www.uiausa.com) is investigating a program that can provide both for the same amount of money. This way, it would become affordable to take both of these first steps for the same price. This program, if implemented, would be available at the local support group level. This program would reduce a grossly overcrowded system.

I believe that the fraudulent invention promoters have the right idea: Provide customers with an evaluation and a patent search very early in the process. They go wrong because their evaluations are generic and their patent searches are self-serving.

And, what do you get for your money? If you're lucky, you get a worthless patent, most likely a design patent that covers only the appearance of your product. If you're really lucky, you get a utility patent with very narrow and limited claims that other companies can easily work around. Plus, you get the disappointment and embarrassment of having been taken in.

As for the promotion part, most of these invention marketing companies simply mail a few brochures to a random list of manufacturers. The major manufacturers are aware of these companies, consider their mailings worthless, and toss them without ever opening them. The marketing company can claim to have done its job by sending the letters. They can't help it if no one is interested in your product.

Your product never gets a fair chance. The promotion firm spends maybe $25 on postage, and maybe sends a press release to your hometown newspaper, but they certainly don't earn the thousands of dollars they demanded from you.

My advice is: Don't utilize the services of or listen to the advice of an invention promotion company, especially one that advertises on national radio or TV. There have been so many indictments, investigations, and poor performance complaints about this industry that you would be well advised to steer clear entirely. Continue to educate yourself and continue to develop your idea; just don't let your enthusiasm for that idea overpower your common sense.

Evaluating Your Ongoing Progress

After implementing a marketing strategy, you must evaluate your product's performance. Every program should have performance standards to compare with actual accountable results. Researching industry norms and past performance helps to develop appropriate standards.

Monitor population shifts, legal developments, and the local economic situation to quickly identify problems and opportunities.

Audit your company's performance on a quarterly basis. The key questions to ask yourself are:

✔ **Is my company doing all it can to be customer oriented?** This reminds me of the young boy who had a lawn service. He called his regular customers after mowing their lawns for a few months and asked them if they're satisfied with their current lawn service. Customers, thinking they were speaking with someone from a different lawn service usually told him that they were very happy with their lawn person. What a great way to see if your customers are satisfied with the service you provide.

✔ **When customers purchase a product, do they want to come back or at least refer business to me or recommend my product to others?**

✔ **Is my product selling at a competitive price?** If your product isn't selling at a competitive price, I guarantee you your competitors' products are. One of the best ways to keep wholesalers, distributors, and retailers selling your product is to be the most competitive you can so others won't even think about entering into the market.

✔ **Who are prospective customers whom I haven't reached yet?** You should always be looking to expand your target customer base. You can use ongoing market research and current market trends to identify potential customers.

You may be doing market research without being aware of it. You look at returned items, ask former customers why they switched products or brands, and check your competitors' prices, don't you? This ongoing research helps you identify areas for improvement and expansion.

Employees may be the best source of information about customer likes and dislikes. They hear customers' minor gripes about the store or service — the ones customers don't think important enough to take to the owner. Employees in your customer service department know what customers want changed or improved about your product. They can often supply good customer profiles from their day-to-day contacts.

Chapter 19

Advertising Your Product

· ·

▶ Looking at what advertising is

▶ Putting advertising to use for you

▶ Expanding advertising's boundaries

▶ Going over some pointers

· ·

*T*his story has been told in different versions through the years:

> A man wakes up in the morning after sleeping on an advertised bed, wearing his advertised pajamas. He bathes in an advertised tub, washes with advertised soap, shaves with an advertised razor, eats a breakfast of advertised juice, cereal, and bread (toasted in an advertised toaster) and glances at his advertised watch. He rides to work in an advertised car, sits at an advertised desk, uses an advertised computer, and writes with an advertised pen.
>
> Yet, this man hesitates to advertise, saying that advertising doesn't pay. Finally, when his business goes under, he advertises it for sale.

The point, in case you missed it, is that most everything is advertised. And advertising is everywhere. You, and every other consumer, respond to advertising whether consciously or unconsciously. You, and every other entrepreneur, need to make use of this powerful tool. In this chapter, I tell you how.

Exploring Advertising Basics

Advertising serves a very basic function — it tells potential customers about your invention. People have to know that this marvelous product exists in order to buy it.

Advertising is the way you communicate with other consumers, companies, and potential purchasers. The buzz term is *marketing communications*. These communications help you to keep in touch with your market and the community. You also get a chance to present your product, your image, and your message the way you want. You have complete control over what's published, broadcast, and displayed, and you determine exactly where, when, and how often your product's message appears, how it looks, and precisely what it says.

Through your ads, you establish a unique identity for your company and product. You set yourself apart from your competition, and you also remind current customers and tell potential customers about the benefits of your product. And you keep on telling them. In order to keep your customers from spending their dollars elsewhere, you must remind potential customers repeatedly about the benefits of buying your product and doing business with you. If you don't, another company does.

Generally, a consumer sees a product seven times before purchasing it!

Design your ad campaign to enhance your reputation and cement your image in the public's mind. To do this, you need to present a consistent image and message repeatedly. People like what they know. The more you can keep your product in the shoppers' minds, the more comfortable they become with the product, and the more they want to buy it.

Your ultimate goal is to establish customer awareness and trust, and, of course, to sell your invention and boost your bottom line.

Although advertising can do many good things for your invention and your business, it's *not* a cure-all. For instance, advertising cannot

- ✔ Create an instant customer base
- ✔ Cause an immediate sharp increase in sales
- ✔ Solve cash flow or profit problems
- ✔ Substitute for poor or indifferent customer service
- ✔ Sell useless or unwanted products or services

You have to start with a solid product and a sound business plan before your advertising can truly be successful.

Designing Your Advertising Campaign

Your advertising campaign must be fluid and adaptable to changes in your product and in the market, but it must also be cohesive and send a consistent message. The specifics can (and should) change, but the basic elements of an effective advertising campaign are

- ✔ Theme
- ✔ Audience

✔ Range of media

✔ Objective with measurable goals

✔ Budget

Say, for example, that you're launching a brand-new product. Your theme incorporates the product's benefits, but the main theme is that the product is new. Your may start out with a target audience focusing on existing customers, though your campaign may expand to include a new target audience. The range of media includes radio spots, a series of newspaper ads, and a direct mailing to your customer list. Your goal is to sell 100 units by the end of your two-week media blitz.

In this section, I explore in more detail each element of an advertising campaign.

Tying into a theme

The first step is to establish a theme that identifies your product in all your advertising materials. The theme of your advertising reflects your business or product's special identity or personality and its particular benefits. For example, cosmetics ads almost always rely on a glamorous and sexy theme. Automobile advertising frequently concentrates on how the car makes you feel when you're driving it.

You want a simple message that customers can easily and quickly understand. Keep in mind that consumers want to know that your product works, not necessarily *how* it works.

A distinctive image, whether it's a logo, trademark, or catch phrase that customers clearly associate with your company, is an invaluable selling tool. Customers recognize your product quickly and easily — in ads, mailings, packaging, or signs — if you use a consistent and distinctive image or tag line. A catch phrase reinforces the single most important reason for buying your product. For example, "Nothing Runs Like a Deere" (John Deere farm vehicles) implies performance and endurance with a play twist on the word "deer." "It's the real thing." (Coca Cola soft drinks) again signifies taste, but also reliability and imagination. "How the Smart Money Gets That Way" (Barron's financial publication) clearly implies money, resources, authority, and intelligence.

Targeting your audience

Your research into the market provides you with knowledge about who your target customer is (see Chapter 17). To form your advertising plan, you need to figure out how you can best reach those people.

Cutting into the competition

One mom and pop barbershop took a very creative advertising route. The kind of barbershop with an old-fashioned barber pole swirling in front of a building was losing its customers to a hair salon in the new mall across the street.

This new styling salon was a part of a national franchise with a significant advertising budget. This salon advertised their $8 haircuts on billboard after billboard leading up to the giant mall. The established mom and pop barbershop had a nearly nonexistent advertising budget. However, they did drum up enough money for one billboard ad. This billboard was placed near all the competition's billboards touting their $8 haircuts and said, simply: "We FIX $8 haircuts!" Simple enough? Effective enough? You bet!

Through advertising, you can encourage existing customers to buy more of what you sell and attract new customers to replace lost ones.

To reach the broadest spectrum of potential customers, use a broad range of advertising methods. Don't put all your money into newspaper ads, radio spots, or any one medium. Psychologist's studies show it takes at least three full exposures to attract a customer to buy a product, which explains why you often see and hear the same advertising campaign for a product on TV, in magazines and newspapers, and on the radio all at the same time. It's known as a *marketing blitz* and it's very effective at getting a product into the public consciousness. You may not be able to afford a full market blitz, but you can give your advertising dollars more impact by spreading them around.

You can target particular areas or people, but you still want to use a variety of ways to reach them. Here are a few hints on how to do that:

✔ Send out media releases by fax to major newspapers, radio, and television contacts.

✔ Write your own stories for the press — make their life easier. People love to read success stories.

✔ Consider writing a letter to the editor of your product's trade magazine.

✔ If you have an article published about your product, make reprints and circulate them to potential customers, wholesalers, buyers, and industry reps.

Choosing the best media for your message

You're a member of the most consumer-driven culture in the history of the world, so you know that your choice of advertising media is varied. Aside from the obvious television, newspapers, and radio, you have a whole host of printed media to make use of.

These days you have to consider the Internet also. You can pay for ads on other people's Web sites and design your own site to advertise and sell your product. You can make use of telemarketing, direct mail, and a variety of magazines, newspapers, and bulletins.

Your target audience helps determine the media you use to reach them. When you're conducting your initial market research, consumers tell you where they anticipate buying your product from. For more on market research, see Chapter 17.

Table 19-1 gives you some suggestions for where to place different types of ads, which, for lack of a better system, I classify as small, medium, and large. Small ads are business card size, and sometimes that's exactly what they are — a reproduction of your business card. Medium ads are the size of a standard piece of paper, and large ads are poster size. Note that ads in newspapers and magazines can be any size, depending on your objective and budget.

Table 19-1	Suggestions for Ad Placement	
Small	*Medium*	*Large*
Church bulletins	Direct mail, or with your invoices	Billboards
Neighborhood association newsletters	Newspaper insert	In buses and subways
Civic and social organization newsletters	Leaflets door-to-door, in parking lots, and on the street	On trash and recycling containers
Alumni publications	Shopping center message boards	On buildings

Don't forget about the Yellow Pages, local business publications, and magazines specific to your geographic or product area.

Advertising in the local free alternative newspaper is much cheaper than in the daily paper. Don't forget to send smaller publications your press releases. They often want filler info.

Setting objectives and measuring results

You have to set an objective for your advertising campaign. If you don't, how can you know when you succeed? Objectives make it easier to design an effective marketing campaign and help keep that campaign on track. Defining your objectives also makes it easier to choose how you want your advertising to reach the customer.

Your objective may be as simple as communicating your message or creating an awareness of your product. To measure those results, though, you generally have to do market testing, which is an added expense. Of course, if you're clever, you can find a way to measure results through the ad itself. If you mail out flyers with a discount coupon that people have to come into your store to redeem, you have a measurement tool right there.

If your objective is to motivate customers to buy your product and increase your sales, you can tell how well you're succeeding by your percentage sales increase.

Coming up with a budget

Big corporations spend millions of dollars on advertising and have separate advertising divisions. They spend even more money hiring advertising agencies to convince consumers to purchase their products. If you're like most of my clients, however, you're on a shoestring budget just trying to raise enough money to get a prototype built (see Chapter 9). Spending money you haven't yet made on an intangible like advertising may not seem like a wise use of the little money you have.

Let me assure you that advertising is key to your success. If you don't let people know that you have a great new product for sale, you're never going to sell it. Getting the word out about your invention is essential. (In fact, if you map out a good business plan, which I go over in Chapter 13, you take advertising expenditures into account from the very beginning.)

You can use a couple different methods to set your ad budget:

- ✔ **Percentage of sales:** Even if you don't have any sales yet, you should have projections for the next year, or three, or five. Allot a percentage of your annual sales; say 10 percent, to your advertising budget. You can adjust up or down as events warrant, but at least you have a number to start with each year when you figure the overall budget.

- ✔ **Cost per customer:** In this method, you use the advertising dollars you spend to determine how much it costs you to sell one product to a customer. For example, if a new product costs $10 and the advertising budget is set at 3 percent of annual sales, then the cost of advertising for this product is basically 30¢.

Tearing out Goliath

A small mom and pop pizza place in Denver found a way to make use of its competitor's big advertising budget.

The small pizza place had a nearly nonexistent advertising budget. Its major competitor was a national pizza chain with franchises throughout the city. The chain spent big bucks to take out full multicolored ads in the phone book listing the phone numbers and locations of all its pizza places.

The mom and pop place couldn't afford phone book ads or even local newspaper ads on a continual basis. But, it could afford radio ads

that aired around the time that new phone books were delivered. The ad promised a free personal-size pizza in exchange for their competitor's full-page ad in the phone book.

People tore out the ads out of phone books at work, at home, in telephone booths, and hotel rooms. It cost the small pizza place numerous little pizzas during the first few weeks, but think about it: For the rest of the year, those pages with the competitor's phone numbers no longer appeared in the local phone books. That's one creative gimmick.

Spending time upfront crafting your message and choosing your markets pays off in the long run. For example, you pay less per ad by signing on to run ads in several issues of a newspaper or magazine rather than paying issue by issue. Likewise, you can save money by having the ad designer prepare a number of ads at once.

If your funds are limited, approach a college or university professor and offer to let their advertising class design an ad for you as a class project. The professor gets a lesson plan, the students get some real-world experience *and* a grade, and you get an ad for far less than you'd have to pay a professional ad designer. You can even make it a contest and give a small cash prize to the winner.

Supplementing Your Regular Advertising

Advertising isn't always obvious and it isn't always expensive. You have many options when it comes to getting the word out about your invention. You can go the low-key route with promotions or the free route with public relations.

Using alternate methods doesn't mean that you don't have to use regular advertising methods. The methods I talk about in the following sections are supplements, not replacements.

Pursuing promotions

Promotion is a form of advertising that takes a more subtle approach. Ads shout, "Come Buy Me!" Promotions are just a quiet image of your business particulars stamped onto a giveaway or eye-catching item. Some obvious and not-so-obvious places to print your contact information and logo (or other graphic image):

- Business cards
- Calendars
- Coffee mugs (especially if you're in food service)
- Delivery vans
- Hats
- Key chains
- Magnets
- Pens
- Postcards — postcards that notify customers that an order is in and postcards that follow up on a sales call or customer service call
- Sales receipts
- Shopping bags
- T-shirts

Some companies — hundreds of them in fact — specialize in nothing but promotional items. These companies are fairly easy to find. They advertise in the back of magazines, especially airline magazines. You may also try conducting a key word search on an Internet search engine under **promotional items**.

Your promotional activities aren't limited to giving things away. Take a look at some other ways to promote your business:

- **Cosponsor events with nonprofit organizations that advertise your participation.** Cosponsoring public safety or awareness activities not only associates your name with a good cause, it also earns you goodwill within the community.

  You can also create a tie-in promotion with another business or nonprofit. A *tie-in promotion* is basically joint advertising with another company. An example is a regional fishing tournament for children in your area. The proceeds from the tournament go to the Boy's Youth Ranch. Your company may cosponsor this event by donating 25 samples of your new product to be used as prizes to the youth attending. In return, your company is listed in all the promotional material as a cosponsor. Thousands see your company and product names. You're promoting goodwill in the community, as well as getting publicity.

✔ **Give an educational seminar.** If you need to educate the public about the benefits of your product or show them how to use it, your costs go up. You can sponsor a free educational seminar open to the public, which sets you back the cost of the hotel conference room you rent, but if you need to educate your customers, you must bear the costs.

✔ **Sponsor an athletic team.** You can sponsor or cosponsor a kids' athletic team and have your name emblazoned on 15 soccer shirts or target an adults' team and have some bowling shirts made.

✔ **Display your product at consumer or business trade shows.** If you can't afford a booth, you can (and should) at least attend the big national shows, just to keep abreast of what's happening at the industry. And as long as you're there, you may as well pass out your card or some promotional item — everyone else is, why shouldn't you? (See Chapter 18 for more on trade shows.)

✔ **Underwrite a contest or sweepstakes to get your product's name in front of consumers.** In order to create a great name for your product, consider hosting a contest at a local elementary school. Ask the teachers to show your product to children and ask them to name your product. Kids think of great names for products — ones that are easy (trademarks) and ones that people can remember. Give the winner or the class that has the winner a prize!

✔ **Develop sales kits with free product samples or application ideas.** Many times the large medical companies give *promos* or free items at local health fairs for senior citizens. You can do the same depending on the nature of your product. If you make a product for sporting goods, give away free samples at the local Monday night hunting club.

The range of promotional tools you can use to deliver your message is limited only by your imagination and budget.

Pushing public relations

In previous years, the public relations department was separate from the marketing department; today, they're one and the same. *Public relations* is an effort to shape people's opinions about a person, company, or product. For instance, politicians launch massive, never-ending public relations campaigns.

Today, corporations pay attention to public awareness, company name recognition, and product/company loyalty by taking an active role to support consumers' interests and concerns.

Public relations is an extremely visual and verbal image of a company's profile. It is not a short-term thing but the creation of a long-term image. It's management's way of verbalizing and visualizing a company's mission, beliefs, and values.

Public relations efforts really come into play when a crisis comes up. For example, if a large oil company creates an oil spill, the company is immediately at the forefront talking about what the oil company does in order to maintain a clean and safe environment. This message can be in the form of paid ads while trying to create good will among potential consumers, or it can be free, such as a press conference or time on the nightly news. It's getting your name out to the public in a variety of forms while establishing a positive image for your brand or company.

Table 19-2 compares paid advertising efforts to free public relations. In paid ads, you control what's being said about your product and when it's said because you provide the advertising material. Unless you're paying for the public relations efforts (like the oil company buying television ad space to create a good image after an oil spill), you have little control of what's said and when the information is given. You are at the discretion of the media.

Table 19-2   Comparing Paid Advertising and Free Public Relations

Paid Advertising	Public Relations Promotions
Must be paid for	Free
You determine the message	Message is interpreted by an editor
You control timing	Timing is at the discretion of the media
One-way communication — using the mass media	Two-way communication — doesn't allow feedback. The company should be listening, as well as talking and the various PR revenues often provide immediate feedback
Message sponsor is identified	Message sponsor is not identified
The intention of most ads is to inform, persuade, or remind about a product — usually with the intention of making a sale	The intention of public relations is often to create goodwill, to keep the company and/or product in front of the public, and improve the company's reputation
Public reception may be negative. People recognize advertising as an attempt to persuade or manipulate them	Public perceives promotional pieces as neutral or believable
Very powerful at creating image	Can create image, but may not be what the subject intends
Writing style is usually persuasive and effective	Writing style relies heavily on creativity, takes a conversational tone, which may inform but not sell

If your company has done its best to be positive and create a good image, you can use your creative marketing talents to "work" with the press and further your company's image for free. Many times, the local media will write success stories on local small businesses. This is free media exposure; you can't control what's being said but you can educate and capture the heart of the writer to be "on your side." The article he or she writes will interest readers who are potential purchasers.

Working up some free publicity

When I called, I sensed something was wrong. My client told me about the rumor that had been going around about his company. I started laughing. He asked in a perturbed voice, "What do you think is so funny?" I said, "It doesn't matter what people are saying about you, whether it's right or wrong, at least they're talking about you. People pay millions simply to be talked about." He realized that simple gossip wasn't a real problem, and said, "You're right, if a problem can be solved by money, it's not a real problem." The point is that you need to get your product's name out there so that people can remember it by any means necessary.

Becoming press friendly

One of the easiest ways to get publicity is to write a press or news release. Newspaper and magazine editors are always looking for copy to fill their pages. If you can offer them an interesting story they can write about or a well-written press release that they can turn into an article without making too many changes, you may receive free press coverage for your product. Try writing a one-page story about your new product, invention, or small business success.

Your headline and story must sell themselves to the individual who receives it at the news desk. Think like a general reader and focus on the most interesting or unusual aspects of your invention or accomplishment. The person you send your release to must be able to quickly understand how your new product or business benefits the public — and most of all how it benefits her publication. If the benefit isn't immediately obvious, your article hits the round file.

Get to know the business editor of your local newspaper. Invite her to do a story on you and your product as a special interest article or feature story.

Write your own press releases or articles in the third person (as if you're talking about someone else) and send them to the major newspapers, local publications, and business journals, as well as magazines, trade journals, and other publications in your field. Be sure to answer all the journalistic questions — who, what, when, where, why, and how — and don't forget to include your name and contact information.

Go to your local library and ask your reference librarian to help you locate books and resource guides that list the names, addresses, phones, faxes, and individual contacts of the major newspapers around the country. Fax the news releases out late Sunday night so that your information is on their desks first thing on Monday morning.

Note some of the most persuasive words used in advertising, whether its paid or free, are the following: free, now, introducing, starting, revolutionary, bargain, hurry, wanted, quick, easy, magic, miracle, announcing, and improvement.

Creating a run on your product

Try this handy trick to spark interest in your product. It works like this: The moment your product hits the stores, you send your family, friends, stockholders, and anyone else you can think of to buy as much of the product as they can. Then, you call the stores and ask if the product is available. Of course it's not available — you just bought it all. If you're really clever, you call the press about the sellout of your new product.

You create a situation and force the stores to reorder your products, so at least the distribution system gets moving. Believe me, I have done this for clients and for products that I have invested monies in. I can assure you I have enough soap, games, and toys stored to last a lifetime!

Looking At a Few Tricks of the Trade

Here are some advertising hints and tips that have worked for others time and time again:

- Choose a phone number that people can remember. For example: 1-800-HILTONS.

- Create Web sites for your product and your company. Link them to each other and keep them up to date. Select an easy URL and e-mail address that consumers can remember and list it on all your product's material.

- Give away freebees, including specialty pens, mouse pads, mugs, and calendars emblazoned with your product or company name, address, phone number, and Web site.

- Join and attend professional trade association meetings within your own industry — specialize and be the best you can be among your own colleagues.

- Create monogrammed shirts with your company's name and logo for your top sales agents and industry reps.

- Send follow-up letters to new people you meet at business luncheons or conferences.

✔ Develop brochures for your new product that use customer testimonials.

✔ Include a postage-paid return mail card with your product or company literature in order to obtain feedback and establish a mailing list.

✔ Publish a newsletter for your customers, buyers, wholesalers, and distributors.

✔ Review nontraditional forms of advertising such as park benches, buses, or sponsoring a youth success team with your company or product's name on the T-shirts.

✔ Code any advertisements and keep track of which ones are the most effective at bringing in new customers. When the a coded coupon is redeemed and processed, you can tell where the customer got it — a newspaper, a magazine, or whether it arrived in the mail.

✔ Promote a contest within a school.

✔ Volunteer to give a speech for career day at a local high school.

✔ Volunteer in your community at charity events, on planning boards, and at community events — get involved and get your product or company name out.

✔ Be a panel presenter at a seminar. Whenever you're a speaker, have your secretary send in a news announcement to the local press for publication.

Chapter 20

Licensing Your Product

· ·

In This Chapter

▶ Looking at licensing and licensees

▶ Renting your patent to one or several companies

▶ Finding potential licensees

▶ Submitting your product

▶ Figuring out what kind of licenses to grant

· ·

*A*fter putting in all the hard work of thinking up your invention and then doing the evaluations and testing, handing your baby over to someone else to produce, market, and sell while you rake in the royalties may sound like a good idea. And licensing is certainly a good option for a number of inventors. However, I must warn you that only a small number of inventors — about 6 percent — succeed in licensing their products.

There's no harm in trying, though, and licensing can be the best way to go if you can hitch your invention to the right licensee. This chapter tells you how to go about it.

Contemplating Licensing

Licensing is a contractual arrangement in which an individual or company grants specific rights to certain intellectual property. They grant another individual or company these rights in return for royalties and/or another form of payment. Basically, licensing means renting your invention to someone else. A *licensee* is a company to whom you give permission to manufacture, market, and distribute your invention.

What are your chances?

No type of invention is more likely than another to be a good licensing candidate. Potential licensees, like investors, are often more interested in the inventor than the invention. If you do your part by investigating the market — choosing potential licensees because they're a good fit for your invention and otherwise doing your homework — you have a much better chance of licensing your invention than someone who is so convinced of their invention's worthiness that they expect the world to beat a path to their door. By putting time, effort, and money into your invention, you can raise the 6 percent rate to approximately 50 percent.

Licensing companies look for proof (as in market studies) that your product can make money and add to the company's overall product line.

In general, companies aren't interested in products that are

- ✔ Harmful to the environment
- ✔ Cause for liability concerns
- ✔ So totally new to the industry that the customer has to be educated about how to use them

Certain industries are more difficult to license in than others, including the soft drink industry and the toy and game market, mostly because just a few companies control these industries.

Weighing the pros and cons

Licensing your invention means sharing both the risks and rewards of getting your invention to market. To produce and market your invention on your own, you must be capable of directing your product from conception to a final salable package ready for the retail store shelf and through all the complicated and costly steps in between. The process costs big bucks, involves lots of risks, and offers no guarantees of success — in fact, you're more likely to lose your shirt than land on easy street. Letting a licensee assume those risks can look mighty appealing.

Of course, the other side of sharing the risks is sharing the rewards, and if you license your invention, you get a small proportion of the profits rather than all of them. All else being equal, the greater the risk factors, the greater the potential for profit.

Advantages of licensing your invention include:

- ✔ Manufacturing and marketing costs are borne by the licensee.

- ✔ You earn royalties immediately rather than waiting for the break-even point for manufacturing.

- ✔ The licensee may already be established in foreign markets and can promote your product there.

- ✔ The licensee's reputation and market position can help sell your invention.

- ✔ Your invention has the support of the licensee's experienced production, marketing, and sales programs. For example, a major corporation may be able to highlight your invention in an ad shown during the Super Bowl — something a small company couldn't dream of.

- ✔ Patent infringement is less likely because potential infringers don't want to take on an established company.

The disadvantages boil down to having no control over the manufacturing and marketing of your invention and generally earning less money than you would if you reaped all the profits. You also run the risk of having the licensee use knowledge gained from your invention to become a competitor. This risk is higher with foreign companies, who may take advantage of patent-law differences. (Consult Chapter 5 for more on protecting your patent.)

Take care to protect your intellectual property by securing the proper patent, copyright, and trademark rights. In the interim before your patent is filed, ask a potential licensee to sign a confidentiality and nondisclosure agreement barring the licensee from manufacturing the product or having it manufactured through third parties. Make sure such agreements conform to the laws of any foreign country either side is subject to.

In the end, the quality of your invention, your personal abilities and limitations, and the state of the economy all play a part in determining whether it makes more sense to license your invention or produce it yourself.

Regarding Licensees

You're thinking about renting your invention, which gives rise to the question of who would want to license your patent and for what reason.

The *who* may be any number of companies — those that deal with similar or complementary products, those that want to branch out into the niche your invention occupies, or those that produce an item that your invention makes more valuable.

Your invention may be a means of extending the use or life of another patent holder's product, in which case it may be referred to as a *wedge* product. A *wedge* also refers to a patent that threatens an existing product or patent's continued success. This may increase the value of that patent or offer a means to replace the existing product. In such a case, the existing patent holder or licensee has a great incentive to license your invention.

The incentive is the one that drives the capitalistic system — money. The profit potential depends upon whether your invention can be developed into something consumers are willing to buy at a price that makes a profit. In order to make a profit, the cost of your product must be considerably less than the selling price. Any potential licensee has to be convinced that your product is marketable in sufficient volume and at a low enough cost to make it worthwhile for the licensee to pay you royalties.

Licensees don't license mere ideas. They buy into patented, or at least patentable, products.

Locating potential licensees

You, better than anyone else, know the intended market for your novel product or unique way of doing things. So you, better than anyone else, know where to start the search for a potential licensee:

- ✔ **The marketplace:** Go where you believe buyers for your invention would look for it. Do your homework and go shopping. Check the labels of similar items or processes to find out who manufactures and distributes them. Collect catalogues from potential competitors and companies who make similar products.

  Note the names, addresses, phone numbers, and Web sites of these companies, and then use that information to find out everything you can about what each company does and how well they do it.

- ✔ **The library:** In the reference section of your library, look for a set of books titled the *Thomas Register*. These books list the name, address, and sales figures of U.S. manufacturers by product line. The complete *Thomas Register* is also available on a CD. Call 800-222-7900 or go to www.thomasregister.com to order the disc.

- ✔ **The Internet:** Conduct a search by type of product on the Internet to find more companies than you could have hoped for. You can also type in the Web addresses of companies you find as you investigate the marketplace and attend trade shows.

- ✔ **Trade shows:** Chapter 18 has information on finding and making use of trade shows to market your invention. Attending trade shows to meet potential licensees is an absolute must.

The vice-presidents of sales and marketing for any or all of the companies you're interested in are almost guaranteed to be at national trade shows. They're not only trying to sell their company's products, but they're also scanning all the new products. If you can interest a VP in your invention, you gain a powerful advocate for your idea.

✔ **The United States Patent and Trademark Office:** Running patent searches on products similar to yours can tell you who the patents are assigned or licensed to.

If you have developed a *wedge* product that either threatens or compliments and enhances another product, the company that manufactures and distributes the primary product can be the ideal licensee.

One of the least productive means of locating potential licensees is approaching the research and development departments of large companies. Their job is to develop new products for their company, and they tend to think that if they didn't invent it, their company doesn't need it.

Considering potential licensees

Your first consideration regarding a potential licensee is the company's financial stability. You want to hitch your invention to a company with a proven track record and a foreseeable future. Make sure that your potential licensee is good at marketing the products or methods it currently holds rights to. You're not looking for a company that produces something that does the same thing as your invention; you want a company that makes items that require the same manufacturing techniques. Many companies can manufacture your invention, but a good licensee also has a distribution system in place.

Put some time into finding out about the companies you're considering. Look at the *operational profiles* of the industry they're in; that is, find out who the major retailers, wholesalers, suppliers, and *jobbers* (like a sales rep in the industry who gets the job done) are in that industry; the average costs of bringing a product to market in the industry; the general market climate and recent history and projected trends for the industry. Find out about each company's sales numbers, their product lines, and how they sell their products. Research any lawsuits or liabilities they're facing. You also want to find out what professionals in the industry think of the long-term prospects of each company you're considering.

Along with the sources you use to find potential licensees (see the previous "Locating potential licensees" section), you can use the Securities and Exchange Commission (SEC) to find out all sorts of things about publicly held companies. Companies with stockholders have to file annual reports with the SEC and you can obtain copies of these annual reports just for the asking. *Form 10-K* is especially useful.

Contact the SEC Office of Investor Education and Assistance at 450 Fifth Street, NW, Washington, DC 20549; phone 202-942-7040; e-mail help@sec.gov, Web site www.sec.gov.

Annual reports contain such valuable information as:

- ✔ When the company was started
- ✔ How much money the company makes and percentages of sales by product
- ✔ The company's marketing techniques — whether they do direct sales, use distributors, independent sales reps, or some combination
- ✔ How much they pay in royalties and when
- ✔ How much they spend in advertising
- ✔ The company's production capabilities
- ✔ Any litigation the company may be involved in
- ✔ Projections of future revenues
- ✔ Product development information — how much they spent on prototypes, molds, packaging, intellectual property, and so on
- ✔ Information on competition, market share, and sales — often presented in a pie chart showing the company's and competitors' slices of the market

With this basic information, you can start to approach both manufacturers and distributors to gauge their interest in licensing your invention.

A couple of potential licensees to be careful of include

- ✔ **One that owns the manufacturing facilities, as well as the end retail sales outlets:** Their profits are derived from different levels of pricing. Many times they control the market and set the prices. If they go out of business or get involved in lawsuits, you can be up a creek.
- ✔ **A retail giant:** If you license to the biggest retailer on the planet, be aware that the company, not you, sets all the terms. They tell you the price they'll pay and it won't be negotiable. It is better to have several smaller accounts than a couple large accounts.

Researching companies before you approach them saves you time, aggravation, and the pain of rejection. You waste time and give yourself a bad name if you approach companies without knowing whether your invention is compatible with the company's outlook.

Assume you find 43 companies that you think would be a good fit for your product. After doing some research, you realize that four of those companies control about 80 percent of the overall market. Your best bet is to approach each of those four companies.

Getting in Touch with Your Potentials

You're ready to start contacting the companies that you determine are best suited to making the most of your invention.

Your basic format must create immediate interest to the potential licensee, in terms of what is required from them before the product or methodology can be packaged and ready for the retail display shelves of the store or catalogue.

Gathering the materials you need

One of the reasons you want to license your invention is because you would rather leave all the market research and selling to someone else. I've got some bad news for you: You have to do both those jobs to sign with a licensee. You must put together a convincing package to market yourself and your product. You need to provide reliable information that includes:

- ✔ **A description:** Tell what your invention is, what it does, and how it does it. Point out your invention's unique characteristics and describe why and how it's better than anything similar that's currently on the market. Tout all its various applications.

- ✔ **Proof that your invention works:** Just because you have a patent doesn't necessarily mean your invention works. Include sketches, samples, and a prototype if you have it, as well as engineering specifications and tooling and manufacturing requirements.

- ✔ **Information on intellectual property:** Let people know where you are in the process of acquiring patents, copyrights, trademarks, and so on.

- ✔ **Market analysis:** Provide documented material and research that shows that there is a market for your product and what a conservative market survey has revealed.

- ✔ **A detailed commercialization plan:** This plan explains the development, markets, sales and distribution, costs, and responsibilities for each on a year-by-year basis. Show break-even points and profit margins. Make five-year detailed projections.

- ✔ **A professional profile of comparative pricing structures:** Show initial tooling costs and production volume estimates.

You also need to be prepared to state what you expect from the company in terms of royalty arrangements and what type of licensing agreement you're looking for. You don't get into the details of the agreement at this point, but you can sketch the broad outlines of what you're thinking. Chapter 21 talks about negotiating an agreement and the "Examining Types of Licensing Agreements" section later in this chapter goes through various kinds of agreements.

Make sure that all the information you provide to potential licensees is accurate and as brief as possible. If you're just setting up a one-on-one appointment to demonstrate your invention in person, you don't need to go into detail about how your invention works; you focus instead on how it fits into the company's product line.

Consider providing a business plan (see Chapter 13 for tips on writing one) to show that you've considered all aspects of producing and marketing your invention.

Making your way to making your pitch

The traditional way of contacting potential licensees is to send a letter to the director of new product development in each company you're interested in. The letter introduces your product and explains how it can fit into the company's product line and increase their market presence and bottom line. Typically, following this approach nets you a rejection letter, if you get any response at all.

If you get an interested response, your next contact is likely to be with someone in the product development department. You are by no means home free. In fact, there's a high probability that your idea will meet with scorn and disdain, because the folks in the research and development area didn't think of it themselves.

The best way to approach potential licensees is to communicate directly with the key decision makers. Even better is enlisting a key decision maker as a champion for your invention. A *champion* is a person who likes your product, understands its value, and is willing to work with you on a mutually beneficial relationship in bringing your product to market. A great licensing agent who knows every contact in the industry can be a champion, as can the vice-president of a manufacturing company who can see the potential moneymaking abilities of your invention for her company.

Joining related trade organizations is a great way to gain an "in" to the industry and is an invaluable resource for networking and gaining inside information on the industry you're trying to break into.

Considering the company's side

Large companies are under constant attack in our increasingly litigious society. Not only are consumers suing them, but so are their employees, other companies, and, most pertinent to this discussion, disgruntled inventors.

Consider this cautionary tale: An inventor approaches the fictional Grill Accessory Company about licensing her new grill gadget and gets turned down. A couple months later, the inventor sees that the Grill Accessory Company is selling a product very similar to hers. The inventor hires a lawyer who slaps a lawsuit on the company and on the retailers carrying the gadget. The Grill Accessory Company's lawyers have to spend time and money defending the company against this lawsuit, and they may have to defend the retailers also. Now, a little common sense would tell the inventor and her lawyer that the similar gadget was in the pipeline long before the inventor approached the company. It takes months and months of marketing studies, production setup and processing, package designing, and shipping and distribution to get a new product to market — nothing goes from concept to market within a couple of months. And still, the Grill Accessory Company has to defend a lawsuit they know they'll win (if, of course, they did things right the first time).

The richer the company, the more lawsuits it attracts. Is it any wonder that many companies aren't eager to talk to inventors?

Most large corporations want you to sign their confidentiality agreement before they review your product, and they often resist signing any confidentiality agreement you provide.

Get sound legal advice to help you deal with such a situation. Signing another company's agreement can give that company free rein to blab your product idea or to keep it secret for just six months or a year. An agreement may prevent you from showing your product to other companies until the first company is ready to turn you down. If you're not careful, you can give your rights to another company to further develop a product based on your idea and go to market with it. I have even seen some agreements that not only take an inventor's current idea in a licensing agreement but also own the rights to all future ideas! You have to depend on your patent rights and hope that your patent is a good one. To make sure you get a good patent, hire a patent attorney who specializes in the area of your product. For more information on patents, see Chapters 2 through 5.

Many inventors think that large corporations are in the business to rip them off. And, though some companies are certainly not on the up and up, in my two-plus decades of working with inventors, I've seen more inventors try to take advantage of large companies than the other way around.

Facing Rejection

Companies reject invention submissions for new products for several reasons. One of the primary reasons is the NIH (not invented here) syndrome. Large companies have in-house research and development personnel including engineers, scientists, and product designers whose job it is to develop new ideas into products. Often, it makes more sense for the company to depend on its employees to develop appropriate products than to risk placing the company in a liability position. A company that relies solely on its own inventors also saves the time and money it takes to review and evaluate new products. To find out information regarding a company's standard policy in working with inventors, contact the company directly and have them send you an information packet.

If you're going to be turned down, make sure it is by a decision maker in the company and not by a receptionist or shipping clerk.

Say you got to make your pitch to the appropriate people in the company (and you really thought they'd go for it), but you got turned down anyway. You may have been rejected for any number of reasons, and very few of them are related to the merits of your invention. Some of the reasons companies don't license inventors' products are

✔ **Product related:**

- The invention doesn't fit into the company's overall market. (You can prevent rejection on these grounds by doing your homework on the company's product line.)

- The product doesn't meet government standards.

- Product life cycle is too short.

✔ **Financial:**

- The company isn't in a position to pursue outside inventions at this time.

- The invention doesn't have a large enough profit margin.

- The invention requires too much long-term investment — in infrastructure or research and development, for example.

- The cost of maintaining *ISO standards* (international standards that are designed to level the playing the field in different countries in regard to quality systems) and environmental and other regulations is prohibitive.

✔ **Market related:**

- The company has tried to market similar products that didn't sell.

- The market for your invention isn't big enough to make producing it worthwhile because the sales aren't going to be enough in the long run.

✔ **Legal:**

- Your product has weak patent protection.

- The company is concerned about liability issues relating to your product, including safety and other concerns.

Licensing to your own company

You've heard of having your cake and eating it, too. Well, this happy situation can be yours if you can license your invention to a company you control.

If you're a serial inventor (not to be confused with a serial killer) who hit it big with an earlier invention that paved the way for forming your own company and retaining controlling interest, you have a ready-made platform for launching subsequent inventions.

Financially, your picture couldn't be rosier. You now have several income sources — a salary as CEO with promotional and travel expense accounts, royalty payments, and potential stock dividends and increasing stock values.

The financial arrangements of licensing to your own company can get a little tricky because you have to keep the company's books and interests balanced. You may need to adjust stock holdings or move to a different corporate and legal structure. Seek sound financial advice from your attorney and accountant or financial planner before striking a licensing agreement with yourself.

One reason your invention may be rejected is one you'll never hear about directly — the inventor is too difficult to work with. If the company thinks dealing with you will cause more headaches than profit, they can, and will, turn you down.

Examining Types of Licensing Agreements

Licensing agreements come in two basic flavors — *exclusive,* which grants one company rights to one or more aspects of making and marketing your invention, and *nonexclusive,* which gives more than one company those rights. I talk about all types of agreements in the following sections.

Being exclusive

An agreement to license your invention can grant the licensee *exclusive rights* to your product and/or method, meaning that one company has total owner-ship worldwide. Technically this one company has permission to manage the entire manufacturing, sales, and distribution process from Kalamazoo (Michigan) to Timbuktu (West Africa).

Granting exclusive licensing rights means that the original licensee may be able to sublicense your invention without your input. If your agreement isn't structured to define sublicensing and the amount of time, resources, and energy you want to contribute, you may lose considerable income.

An exclusive licensing agreement has the advantage of simplifying things — you have one relationship with one business. One company is manufacturing, marketing, and distributing your product.

Always consider federal restraint of trade regulations relative to any marketing agreement concerning the public. *Restraint of trade* is a definition employed by the Department of Justice to prevent one company from controlling the industry and setting prices. Part of abiding by restraint of trade rules is setting a *suggested list price,* which is the price that meets your marketing profiles. That price may be discounted at the option of a distributor, wholesaler, or distributor, but by making it obvious that you have set a fair market price for your product, you help protect yourself from charges that you're abusing fair-trade restrictions.

Licensing agreements are complicated documents. For example, a distribution agreement has to specifically state all the contingencies necessary to distribute the product, including the minimal inventory the distributor has to maintain, the service and repair facilities available, the type and amount of advertising done, the educational programs in detail and what will be provided in these programs (especially if travel is involved), the liabilities involved, and potential technical services rendered.

As with any legal document, seek the advice of a knowledgeable lawyer before signing. You can check out a sample exclusive licensing agreement in Appendix A.

Opening up to nonexclusive agreements

A *nonexclusive agreement* means that you can sell your product to more than one company. You can make a fortune by allowing several different ones the rights to use your new process or product.

If you're going to manufacture your own product, you may want to give the distribution rights to several companies. You can give a huge distributor the U.S. rights and divvy up foreign distribution rights to companies in those countries.

Knowing how these agreements work for you and the licensee

You can sign nonexclusive agreements with several distributors throughout the country or world or sign agreements with companies in different markets or aspects of the business. For example, you can license one company the rights for the mail-order industry, another company the rights for television, and another company the rights to sell retail. This way, you can make money from each specific market instead of concentrating on just one.

Nonexclusive licensing of your invention must consider a number of factors. If it is a commodity with extensive manufacturing costs, potential licensees want to know that if they spend the money on the start-up manufacturing costs, they won't have competition in the same market to sell and distribute your invention. The small, nonexclusive licensee worries that a larger company with more financial resources can develop better tooling to lower manufacturing costs, thus lowering the sale price of the product and/or increasing the large company's profit margins. To deal with these fears, nonexclusive licensing agreements often are restricted by assigned trading areas that give a company exclusive rights within certain geographical areas.

If your invention consists of an add-on to another invention, or a widely used nonpatentable product that a number of companies manufacture, a nonexclusive licensing agreement may be the best deal for all concerned. In the case of the add-on, say you invent a device that increases the efficiency of breathing machines used in hospitals around the world. Nine manufacturers produce the breathing machines, and each one is interested in your invention, because it improves each machine. You can license your invention to each company that makes the breathing machines. Each brand remains competitive and holds onto their existing market, and you sign nine licensing agreements and collect nine royalty payments each quarter. By signing agreements with all the companies you also avoid any restraint of trade troubles.

Looking at ways to use nonexclusive agreements to your advantage

You can license your product for sale in different media. For example, if your product sells on television, you may have one agreement with a shopping channel and another agreement with a firm in the infomercial market. You devise yet a third agreement with a distributor who supplies retail stores, and a fourth with a catalogue company that sells through mail order.

You can also license by geographic location and define the geographical areas however you want. Several years ago, I licensed a client's invention to a company for distribution everywhere in the U.S. except in Florida. The inventor wanted to retain the rights in Florida so that he could continue to sell the invention through the established, family-owned business. I have also used the Mississippi River as a boundary. One company received the right to markets east of the Mississippi and one company had the rights to manufacture, market, and sell west of the Mississippi. Setting out precise areas can remove doubts and settle fears the licensee may have that she will pay you a licensing fee then realize no profit because your product is sold by every third person in the area.

You can license by services rendered. For example, one company has a great distribution system and sells products at a national, as well as international, level, but they don't have a manufacturing plant. You can give marketing rights to one company and manufacturing rights to another company.

Taking Care of Foreign Licensing

Licensing your product to a foreign company requires a carefully crafted licensing agreement. Consulting an attorney is critical because rules on licensing differ from country to country. Remember that your U.S. patent is good only within the U.S. Be careful that the agreement doesn't violate host country antitrust laws. Under the antitrust laws of many countries, the licensor cannot set the price at which the licensee will resell a product.

At times, because of import/export restrictions between trading countries, it is wise to select reliable manufacturing marketers to make and distribute your invention in their trading areas. Coping with the differences in patent law in each country (as well as local customs and regulations) is a challenge even to experienced multinational corporations.

Chapter 21

Negotiating a License

In This Chapter

▶ Valuing your invention

▶ Minimizing your risk

▶ Being guaranteed bucks whether or not your invention sells

▶ Licensing your product to your own company

*T*he construction of the licensing agreement is the key to a profitable mutual relationship. A licensing arrangement can be a long-term commitment, so you want to take time before you sign on the dotted line to be sure that you want to be associated with this company and these people for the long haul. And any company worth having such a relationship with has similar questions about you.

In this chapter, I go through the various stages of the negotiations and offer tips for achieving a successful and equitable contract.

Employing the Art of Negotiation

The fine art of negotiation is very closely related to the fine art of compromise. A negotiation starts when one party makes a bid to obtain something from another party. In the back and forth of negotiation, each side makes concessions in an effort to seal the deal. Almost all agreements end up as a compromise between the negotiators.

In all likelihood, your negotiation session with a potential licensee will feel as if you're David taking on Goliath. Try not to feel intimidated by the prospective licensee's team of lawyers, engineers, scientists, and marketing analysts who confront you — all focused on obtaining the best bargain for their employer. Meanwhile, your focal point is bartering a deal that supports your interests. Somehow, together, you must forge an agreement that serves both parties' goals.

A successful negotiation ends with both you and the licensee feeling that you have a good deal. Everyone's best interests are served by getting along after the deal is done. You can be a great asset to the company from a consulting standpoint, and the company may want to have first right of refusal on additional products you invent. Also, wars between the two of you only benefit your attorneys.

In the following sections, I discuss key points in the negotiation process and show you how to make them work for you.

Submitting to an evaluation

If you don't get a *ding* letter (also known as a rejection) right away, consider yourself lucky. At least 75 percent of all patents are rejected within a short period. But even if you're fortunate enough to be one of the lucky 25 percent picked for further review, don't start counting your royalties yet. Any company considering licensing your invention wants an opportunity to look at your product from every angle in order to determine whether they're interested in pursuing talks with you.

The company investigates your product and examines its own resources to discover:

- ✔ Whether your invention truly has a market and how big the market is
- ✔ Whether they have the equipment and staff to manufacture and market it effectively
- ✔ What the estimated costs are for manufacturing, marketing, and distribution
- ✔ What the competitions' reaction may be to your invention
- ✔ How much time and effort is needed to introduce your product to market
- ✔ Whether the risk is worth the reward — simply put, whether your invention can make enough money

During the examination, the company may also explore potential marketing strategies and determine whether they have the facilities to service your invention.

Make sure you get a signed confidentiality agreement before you turn over you invention for evaluation. See Chapter 8 for more on confidentiality agreements.

While all this scrutinizing is going on, the potential licensee may not want you to show your invention to anyone else. That can mean weeks of losing opportunities to present the invention to other prospective licensees. For this you deserve to be compensated. Before you turn over your invention for testing, ask the company for a *letter of intent* that details the specifics about the evaluation period — how long it is, what tests they may and may not conduct during the evaluation, and how much you are to be compensated. Figuring out what to ask for in compensation is tricky. Basically, you try to determine what it's worth to the evaluating company to not have you show your invention to anyone else. If the level of interest is high, you can ask for more than you can if your invention would make a nice addition to their product line but isn't expected to be a big moneymaker.

It is generally in your best interests to allow this evaluation. After all, would you really want a licensing agreement with a company that didn't do its homework? Worse yet, would you want to find out, after the agreement is signed, that the company couldn't get the product to market? The latter is particularly bad if your royalties are based on a percentage of profits generated by sales.

Nonetheless, permitting the evaluation involves acceptance of certain risks. For example, by scrutinizing your invention, the examiners may discover how to make a better product. They can then choose not to license your invention, go to market with their own product, and never pay you a cent beyond the evaluation compensation. Horror stories about such happenings circulate throughout the invention community. Some inventors become so distrustful of companies — so fearful of their inventions being stolen — that they never show their inventions to anyone. Obviously, such overprotection doesn't benefit the inventor. Instead, let common sense prevail in determining who sees your invention and when. Until someone who can produce the device sees it, your brainchild has no chance of its potential being realized.

Whether or not a company decides to license your product after evaluating it, you should seize the opportunity to find out what the company likes about your invention and what they don't like. Especially if they end up not licensing your product or process, knowing what put them off can help you fine-tune your invention for the next suitor.

Prepping for the meeting

Having your paperwork in order and your presentation polished is key to getting what you want at the negotiating table. Remember, this is a potential multimillion-dollar deal. It makes sense to show that you consider your invention worthy of significant consideration by being prepared to negotiate. This is crucial.

Gather up-to-date prototype, drawings, schematics, and engineering notes. Likewise, be able to back up your sales projections with numbers from your market research, and be ready to produce credible production-cost estimates.

Be ready to answer the following questions:

- ✔ What type of consumer does your invention appeal to?
- ✔ How many of these buyers are there?
- ✔ How much will they pay for the product?
- ✔ How much will your invention cost to produce?
- ✔ What are the projected sales figures for the first year?
- ✔ What does the competition offer and how can that be beaten?
- ✔ What are at least three significant differences between your product and that of your competition?

Be prepared to back up your answers with credible data. If you can get statements of intent to buy from potential customers to back up your sales projections, do so. Documentation supporting your projections of your invention's market value can be very helpful to your cause — particularly if it was done by a professional marketing firm or comes from a recognized authority in the field. However, expect the company to conduct its own market survey.

Having such factual information shows the licensee that you aren't in the dark about the potential worth of your product and helps establish the reasonableness of your payment demands.

Do your best to anticipate the questions or issues that may be brought up by the company in the meeting, and devise a strategy for dealing with them. Walk through your worst-case scenario and come up with ways to diffuse a negative situation and keep the discussion on a positive path.

In the same vein, try to anticipate concessions for both sides. Run a reality check on the feasibility of the requests you plan to make of the company, and try to figure whether there's something you want that would cost the potential licensee little to give up. Recognize that the company you're negotiating with spent time contemplating what your requirements might be and what trade-outs they may make to conclude the negotiation in their favor.

Thinking ahead pays off during the actual negotiating situations. Such in-depth planning for the meeting has several benefits:

- ✔ Your confidence in your ability to make this sale increases.
- ✔ You may avoid making hasty decisions you may regret later.
- ✔ Well-thought-out offers and counteroffers enhance your image and credibility at the negotiating table.

TIP

TIP

Tabling stress

Stress gums up your mental processes and hinders clear thought. Stress at the bargaining table may prompt you to give away too much.

You can relieve a lot of stress by preparing well and anticipating issues and answers. You can also help reduce stress in the moment by making use of a couple of techniques before a meeting, during a break, or even during a negotiating session:

✔ Take three or four slow, deep breaths. Hold each breath in at the top for a few seconds before slowly exhaling all the way.

✔ Mentally and physically relax your muscles. It may help to clench everything for a few seconds, and then let go all at once. Or, you can work your way up your body, mentally telling each part of your body to relax.

Periodically tell yourself that you're doing fine, that everything is okay, and that the process is going forward just as it should.

In addition, talking through what's important to you with your lawyer ahead of time clues you both in to what considerations are important to you.

And you need to be emotionally prepared. Before going into the meeting, get psyched up. Mentally review all the reasons the company should license your product — and why you're the person to convince them to do it.

Laying out the agenda

Reaching the negotiating table means that a lot has gone right for you, but things are definitely becoming more challenging also. You must effectively handle the rigors and pressures of bargaining in order to walk away from it as a winner.

If your patent hasn't been granted yet, you and the prospective licensee should sign a formal document that specifically identifies the intellectual property you intend to discuss — before the real negotiations start. This agreement provides some protection for your invention for a stated period of time. However, recognize that preventing nonsigners with access privileges from leaking information may be difficult.

Make certain that the licensee agrees not to challenge or contest your patent rights or employ any other means of voiding and trying to work around your contract during the duration of your licensing agreement.

Every deal is different but the overall goal is the same: You want to obtain a fair price from the right company to produce your product. The important issues you need to address to get there are:

✔ **Negotiating how much money you get upfront:** See "Getting reimbursed upfront" later in this chapter.

✔ **Determining the royalty rate and how it is computed:** The upcoming section, "Researching royalty rates," has more on this.

✔ **Setting a minimum annual royalty guarantee:** The "Getting bucks no matter what" section covers this.

✔ **Arranging the commencement date and dates of royalty payments:** Typically royalties are paid quarterly.

Make sure that you and/or your accountant have the right to review the books of the company you're licensing to.

✔ **Limiting the length of your licensing agreement:** State how long the agreement is good for.

✔ **Laying out the terms of the default clause:** See the "Getting bucks no matter what" section.

✔ **Examining the terms and obligations you're bound to by the agreement:** Chapter 20 goes through the different types of licensing agreements.

The potential licensee wants to know what you're thinking in relation to royalties and a licensing agreement, to make sure that you're both in the same ballpark and negotiating is worthwhile. From a negotiation standpoint, it's better to have the licensee make an offer to you after you've sold them on your product. That way, you can see what they're thinking and counter-negotiate. When a potential licensee asks what terms I'm looking for, my response is, "My terms are negotiable. What I want to do is to create a win-win situation for the both of us. What do you think is going to work best for you, given your past record?"

Be very careful if the licensee wants to renegotiate your agreement. The company is most likely trying to get more favorable terms for itself, and any modification of the existing agreement may automatically and legally cancel all or part of the original agreement.

Big lesson: Negotiate when you're poor, because when you have money, people want a piece of you.

Regarding your bargaining position

Your bartering power with a potential licensee depends upon how badly they want access to your invention.

Your greatest strength comes if you have a *wedge* patent, one that adds value to — or threatens — an existing product. You next-best position is having an invention that complements the primary product line of a manufacturer or marketer.

Aside from these two situations, your negotiating position is dictated by how well you can present your invention to a manufacturer or marketer in terms of earning power. In order to make a convincing case, you have to provide the market data to support your claims.

Negotiating like a pro

The art of professional, hard-nosed negotiation is one of careful determination. Each side wants to see how much the other side will concede without terminating discussions. Each side must be aware of the other's position and attempt to bring the sides together with acceptable compromises.

Keep the following in mind as you negotiate:

- ✔ **Be ready to walk out if you must.** Set your minimum requirements ahead of time and be prepared to end the talks if it becomes clear that the company isn't willing to meet those minimums.

  Don't reveal your bottom line too early in the negotiations. You may be offered more than you anticipated.

- ✔ **Don't walk out too quickly.** Don't use any little excuse to stop the negotiations. After all, you want to license your invention, and you got to this point with this company, so give the process a chance.

- ✔ **Don't enter the strategic maneuvering arena alone.** Take along someone who can help level the playing field, such as an attorney experienced in negotiating licenses. Legal issues abound in any licensing agreement and unless you've done this before, you're a babe in the woods and you'll be lost in no time.

- ✔ **Don't take the negotiations personally.** Don't interpret questions about your invention as criticisms, and don't take criticism of your invention as a slur upon your character. Remember that this is business.

- ✔ **Keep your emotions in check.** Don't get mad, don't be defensive, don't give attitude from the get-go. Negotiating calls for calm, cool, and collected behavior. If this isn't you, have someone else represent your interests at the negotiations.

  Likewise, rein in your glee. You may have to put that high you're feeling in check until . . . well, until you cash your first royalty check.

- ✔ **Give reasons for your responses.** If you say no to a proposal, explain why. If you disagree strongly, say so — nicely — and propose a compromise if you can.

A serious and realistic inventor accepts failure as part of the inventing process. Treat rejection during the licensing process as just another problem to solve. Analyze why you couldn't get together with your target licensee; perhaps you two were a mismatch from the beginning. Often what hurts the most is having reached a point in the transaction where all that is required is finishing up a few minor details, when suddenly a major obstacle comes out of left field and kills the deal. Even then, your motto should be: Try, try again. Tomorrow is another day.

If the deal seems too good to be true, it's probably just the opposite. Get good sound legal advice before signing any licensing agreement.

Estimating Your Invention's Value

In order to negotiate a licensing agreement, you and the licensee have to establish a mutual value for your invention. This is the first issue in a series of negotiations.

All inventions have value — at least to the inventor. However, the question isn't how much value you place on your invention, but how much value other people perceive it to have. Value, like beauty, is in the eye of the beholder.

Face it; nothing you can invent today is absolutely essential to anyone's survival. A new medical invention may save lives, but in most cases, no one's going to die if they can't have your new invention. As the inventor, you're naturally inclined to assign a high worth to the product of your inspiration and perspiration. However, if you want to license your product, you need to live in the real world where your invention is worth only as much as the profit it can make. So, keep your ego and your grandiose dreams in check while you're at the bargaining table.

Back in the real world again, perceived value is a little hard to measure, which is why you need to go to the negotiating table with some real facts and figures at your fingertips. You want to show potential licensees estimated production costs and the results of studies that indicate how much customers are prepared to pay. For more on figuring out how much customers are prepared to pay, take a look at Chapters 17 and 18.

At this point, all anyone can do is *guesstimate* (a not-too-technical combination of *guess* and *estimate* that sounds more reliable than plain old *guess*) about costs and sales, but the better the numbers are to begin with, the better the chance both sides will be happy down the road when guesstimated numbers come close to actual figures.

Be aware that guesstimating is an imprecise science. The only thing you can do is analyze the industry, look at the sales and market share of a similar product selling within the industry, and project growth rates based on industry averages. You use existing information as a base for your projections, and then make guesses based on those guesses. Certainly an experienced manufacturer can make educated guesses as to materials and production costs, but even these are affected by sales volume and may turn out to be more or less off the mark.

Perhaps the most valuable asset you have going into negotiations is an experienced and skilled negotiator. Someone who knows the industry and knows how to represent your invention to its best advantage can get you a deal worth much more than you would have gotten on your own.

Many agreements use guesstimated numbers with provisions for altering the terms in line with actual figures. Keep in mind that getting people to buy a new product necessitates change in their behavior. As a species, humans resist change, and overcoming this resistance to get people to buy your invention costs time and money. The licensee has to bear the expense of educating consumers about your invention and how to use it.

Contemplating Compensation

Getting paid for your work is what licensing is all about. From your perspective, you've already done the hard part; now it's time to kick back and rake in the royalty checks. Of course, few of us inventor-types can name a price and have companies begging to meet it, so you have to get your head out of the clouds long enough to figure out how to negotiate realistic and fair compensation. Inventions are valued in a variety of ways. In most situations, the major items reviewed to come up with the estimated value of your invention are based upon sales of similar products, the profit margins, estimated market share your invention will maintain in a competitive environment, who the competitors are, the product's overall patentability, how strong the claims on your patent are, and the long-term projected growth rates. Again, an important factor here is how well you or your designated negotiator can negotiate.

Be creative about how you are compensated. Consider including stock options, or receiving a certain amount of money per item sold or per use, or whatever other creative scheme you and the licensee can come up with. Most important, remember that everyone involved needs to profit, or no one wants to sign an agreement.

Don't get greedy. I've seen more deals ruined by greed than any other factor.

Getting reimbursed upfront

In addition to the actual royalties, many licensing agreements include the licensee (the company) reimbursing the licensor (you) for money already spent or in compensation for time.

For example, if your invention requires a long development and manufacturing period, you can include a provision that provides you with some income during the introduction period.

In addition, a typical license agreement includes an *upfront fee,* which is a payment the licensee makes to help you recoup some of the costs you put forth in doing research and development, conducting market studies, and obtaining intellectual property law protection.

Many inventors assume that this fee adds up to big bucks — maybe even millions. Sorry to burst your bubble, but upfront fee amounts vary by product and industry. For example, though it can take millions of dollars in research and development costs and FDA (Food and Drug Administration) approval for a new type of medical device or drug, the same costs for a new screwdriver are minimal.

For a consumer oriented, mass-merchandise product, the licensee typically pays between $10,000 and $250,000 in upfront fees. It all depends on the product, the industry, how far advanced you are in your product's life cycle, how much you had to spend to get your product to that point, and how well you can negotiate.

Getting bucks no matter what

No matter what the rest of the agreement ends up looking like, make sure that you get a guaranteed minimum payment that isn't dependent on sales or production numbers and that you have a nonpayment clause that specifies what happens if the licensee doesn't pay up.

Especially if your invention threatens your licensee's product, you run the risk of licensing your product or process to a company that has no intention of ever marketing it. For example, say you invent run-proof hosiery. You know that you have a surefire winner, because every woman who has to wear pantyhose to work will happily pay a premium if she can be assured that she won't have to buy a new pair of hose every time she snags her stockings on her desk. You negotiate with a company that currently has the largest portion of the hosiery market. The exclusive, lifetime agreement offers you a 10 percent royalty on every pair of your run-proof stockings the company sells. You jump at the offer because you know the industry standard is closer to 5 percent, and your stockings will sell for a bit more because they last longer than regular stockings. You go home and wait for the grand announcement of the new boon to womankind. And you wait . . . and wait . . . and wait . . . until finally it dawns on you that the announcement is never coming.

See, the top hosiery company has no interest in (and no intention of) replacing their product that women buy weekly with your product that women would buy monthly or even less frequently — it just doesn't make financial sense. And not only is all the time and effort you put into inventing and testing the hosiery down the drain, the exclusive, lifetime agreement you signed means that your invention is, to all intents and purposes, dead. If the hosiery is never offered for sale, no one ever buys it, and 10 percent of nothing is nothing. Without a minimum performance guarantee clause, the licensee can sit on your invention while you starve to death. Don't make this mistake!

Insisting on a default clause

The way to avoid this pitfall is to make sure you get a payment upfront and a *default clause* that forces the company to actually produce your invention. Essentially it says, "Look, manufacturing company, you say you can manufacture, market, and distribute my product for me and I trust you to do so; now, if you go back on your word, it's not my problem — it's yours. After all, I gave you — and not anyone else — the rights to make and sell it and that costs me money; therefore, you guarantee that you will sell x number of units per year or pay me x amount of money regardless. It's not my fault that you can't sell." Including a default clause is a must.

Also, think twice or even three times about granting a company lifetime, exclusive licensing right to your invention. Your goal as an inventor is not to have the licensee pay you a minimum guarantee to keep your product or methodology out of the marketplace in order to prevent competition with another of their products. Nor do you want them to be satisfied with a minimal licensing return because of a limited distribution system.

Steering clear of balloon payments

Don't enter into agreements with *balloon payments,* which means getting all your money at the end of the agreement term. The company may not be able to pay you by the time your money is due. They may make money selling your invention, but lose money through bad management or any other reason, and you never get a penny if they run out. I recommend asking for quarterly payments, but other kinds are negotiable.

Including a nonpayment clause

A *nonpayment clause* states that if the licensee doesn't pay royalties to the inventor for a specified length of time (usually a quarter), the agreement can be cancelled. This clause should stipulate that the licensee pay a cancellation fee equal to three to five times the annual minimal payment, stop marketing the invention, and give any unsold product to you. Insist on a nonpayment clause as well.

Researching royalty rates

A *royalty* is a share of the proceeds paid to the owner of intellectual property in compensation for using the property. The royalty can be a lump sum payment, a set amount per year, a percentage of sales, or it can be calculated as a fixed amount per item sold.

One common industry rule states that one-quarter to one-third of the net profits of an invention goes to the licensor — that's you. A problem with this rule is that royalties are almost never stated as a percentage of profits; they're typically stated as a percentage of the overall manufacturing cost. Another problem is that even if they were, profits are easy to hide and to manipulate, and as the outside inventor, you're at a severe disadvantage in trying to spot or stop such shenanigans.

Watch the wording of your agreement for everything, but especially when it comes to the royalty schedule. You may be hoodwinked by terms such as

- ✔ **Net:** The highest price the manufacturer receives for the product from the distributors and wholesalers they sell it to.

  This is a very touchy subject and has been judged numerous ways in courts as there are surcharges on net price.
- ✔ **After discount:** Suggested selling price less the percentage discount to the wholesaler or distributor.
- ✔ **Wholesale:** The price at which the manufacturing company sells a product to a wholesaler or distributor.
- ✔ **Suggested retail price:** The price the manufacturer considers to be a fair market price for the consumer to pay.
- ✔ **Retail:** Price the product actually sells for.
- ✔ **Sales promotion discount exceptions:** The additional discounting of a product to wholesalers and distributors used exclusively for sales promotions.
- ✔ **Lot quantity:** A discount on a volume basis. The higher the volume, the bigger the discount.

Always require that royalties be expressed in U.S. dollars the year the contract was negotiated and/or as a percentage of the price negotiated, to accommodate for annual inflation.

The typical royalty rate is generally between 2 and 10 percent. The most commonly cited number is 5 percent, which means that you get 5 percent of the money received by the manufacturing company when they sell the product embodying your invention. Although 5 percent is commonly stated in the inventors' community, I've seen royalty rates vary from .01 percent to 20 percent; it all depends on the product, the industry, the strength of the patent, and how well you can negotiate. Table 21-1 lists commonly accepted royalty percentage ranges for various industries.

Table 21-1	Typical Royalty Percentages	
Industry	*High*	*Low*
Auto/Aftermarket	8.76	4.73
Electric/Consumer	9.03	6.26
Hardware/Housewares	9.47	4.67
Machining	7.68	4.97
Packaging and Plastics	9.18	5.30
Plumbing/Heating	13.50	6.32
Retail-Consumer	12.29	5.65
Sporting Goods	13.00	6.55

Inventor's Handbook

The more developed the technology, the higher the royalty rate the inventor receives. The average royalty may be around 5 to 7 percent, but this varies greatly from field to field. Technologies requiring lengthy and expensive regulatory approval may pay lower royalties than less complicated inventions. Yet royalties on some high margin products, such as farm machinery, can range up to 20 percent and royalties on software can range up to 35 percent.

Your best bet is to base your royalties on a percentage of the sales price and make sure that you receive them according to a schedule, though the specifics of the payment schedule can vary widely. The fee amount may be based on the suggested list price or on the price the licensee charges the retailer, which is significantly lower. Some schedules include a flat fee per unit sold. Some schedules call for sliding fees, which are demonstrated in Table 21-2.

Table 21-2	Sliding Royalty Schedule
Number of Units Sold	*Royalty Percentage*
1,000	10
1,001 – 10,000	8
10,001 – 100,000	5
100,001 and over	2.5

Don't allow the licensee to insert that royalties aren't paid until the licensee is paid by its customers. The licensee's credit arrangements are its business, not yours.

Ideally, royalties should be paid *quarterly,* that is, four annual payments (every three months); however, if you're dealing with a big-time retailer, they may have other ideas about when you get paid.

Don't expect to be paid royalties on items that were returned to the manufacturer. Your royalty payments are based on items sold, not items shipped. Customers may return a product to the store or the product may have to be recalled for some reason, and your royalty payment is reduced because of these losses.

If your invention is part of a sales promotion and is sold at a discounted price to wholesalers and distributors, your price-based royalty payment is reduced to reflect the discounted price.

Part V
The Part of Tens

In this part . . .

In this part, you can find some helpful lists that include notable inventions, inspirational inventors of our time, and contact information that every inventor should have.

Chapter 22

Ten Key Contacts

This chapter lists a range of helpful services and resources that every inventor should know about.

Evaluation Services for Your Invention

You may want to have your idea evaluated, in order to judge whether it has a chance to succeed — *before* you spend a whole lot of time and money on it. The three organizations in this section can help you do just that. (The first one is my own company.)

Innovative Product Technologies, Inc.

Innovative Product Technologies, Inc. (IPT) is the company I founded and that I run to this day. IPT helps inventors just like you evaluate your idea before you commit significant time and money to a full-scale marketing effort. We offer individual consultations and give personal assistance as well as group training, education, and information. The company assists you with its national network of federal and state agencies, universities, funding organizations, inventor's associations, high technology companies, and manufacturers.

We do an evaluation of each product performed by a group of product commercialization experts, using the PIES format, which I talk about in Chapter 11. In addition to your PIES Evaluation Report, which examines the commercial strengths and weaknesses of your invention or idea, you also receive a copy of the PIES evaluation manual, *Assessing the Commercial Potential of Ideas, Inventions and Innovations: A Balanced Approach.* This book is designed to help inventors better understand the innovation process and to explain the PIES evaluation format and implications for the evaluators' findings on each of the evaluation criteria.

Innovative Product Technologies, Inc., 4131 N.W. 13th Street, Suite 220, Gainesville, FL 32609; phone 352-373-1007, fax 352-337-0750; Web site www. inventionevaluation.com and www.independentinventor.com, e-mail pam@independentinventor.com. Also: P.O. Box 817, Sandpoint, ID 83864; phone 208-265-5938, fax 208-265-4482.

Wisconsin Innovation Service Center

The Wisconsin Innovation Service Center (WISC) is a nonprofit program sponsored by the University of Wisconsin-Whitewater, the University of Wisconsin-Extension Small Business Development Centers, and the U. S. Small Business Administration (SBA). WISC specializes in new product and invention assessments and in evaluating market expansion opportunities for manufacturers, technology businesses, and independent inventors. Since 1980, WISC has researched the viability of over 6,000 projects.

Wisconsin Innovation Service Center, 402 McCutchan Hall, University of Wisconsin-Whitewater, Whitewater, WI 53190; phone 262-472-1365, fax 262-472-1600; e-mail www.malwicd@uww.edu, Web site academics.uww.edu/busines/innovate/innovate.htm.

The Innovation Institute and the WIN Evaluation Center

The WIN Innovation Center provides inventors, entrepreneurs, and product marketing/manufacturing enterprises with an honest and objective third-party analysis concerning the risks and potential of their ideas, inventions, and new products. WIN is a program sponsored by the Innovation Institute located in the Center for Business and Economic Development of the College of Business Administration at Southwest Missouri State University.

Center For Business Research and Development, Dr. Gerald G. Udell, Executive Director, S.W. Missouri State University, Springfield, MO 65802-0089; phone 417-836-5751, fax 417-836-7666; Web site www.wini2.com.

The Federal Trade Commission

The Federal Trade Commission (FTC) works to prevent fraudulent, deceptive, and unfair business practices in the marketplace. Inventors (who want to be told that their brainchild is beautiful) are vulnerable to unscrupulous firms who seek out information on new patents and then contact inventors telling them that they have companies interested in buying their patent rights. The inventor then invests money and energy but gets nothing in return. The FTC has full-time investigators assigned to some of these companies. It also provides information to help consumers spot, stop, and avoid less-than-reputable businesses and business practices.

The FTC enters Internet, telemarketing, identity theft, and other fraud-related complaints into Consumer Sentinel, which is a secure, online database available to hundreds of civil and criminal law enforcement agencies in the U.S. and abroad.

The Federal Trade Commission, 600 Pennsylvania Avenue, N.W., Washington, DC 20580; phone 1-877-FTC-HELP (1-877-382-4357), TTY 866-653-4261; Web site www.ftc.gov.

Inventors' Digest Magazine

This magazine is *the* magazine for inventors. It has special interest articles and success stories geared toward inventors. It lists information on upcoming tradeshows, does educational features, informs readers about companies seeking new products for distribution and licensing, suggests funding contacts, and keeps readers informed about scams. All this is in addition to passing along a variety of inventor contacts and providing basic, need-to-know information that every inventor can benefit from.

Inventors' Digest Magazine, Ms. Joanne M. Hayes-Rines, Publisher, JMH Publishing Company, 30-31 Union Wharf, Boston, MA 02109; phone 617-367-4540, fax 617-723-6988; e-mail InventorsD@aol.com, Web site www.inventorsdigest.com.

The Library of Congress Copyright Office

The Copyright Office promotes protection for authors and other creators. Its Web site, at www.loc.gov, offers copyright registration forms (many in fill-in format), informational circulars, general copyright information, and links to related resources. The Web site also provides a means of searching copyright registrations and recorded documents from 1978 forward.

Library of Congress, Copyright Office, 101 Independence Avenue, S.E.; Washington, DC 20559-6000; Public Information Office 202-707-3000; Web site www.copyright.gov.

National Aeronautics and Space Administration (NASA)

NASA offers a variety of programs to small businesses, including procurement opportunities and grant money for the development of new technologies. The Office of Small and Disadvantaged Business Utilization (OSDBU) at NASA Headquarters manages NASA programs that assist small, disadvantaged, and women-owned businesses.

When reviewing NASA's Web site, you may also to look at the Technology Research and Development Authority Program at Kennedy Space Center in Florida. This program offers special assistance to innovators with new technologies and technology-related problems.

National Aeronautics and Space Administration, 300 E Street, SW, Washington, DC 20546; phone 202-358-2088, fax 202-358-3261; Web site www.nasa.gov.

Small Business Development Center Program

The Small Business Development Center (SBDC) program, run by the Small Business Association, helps small businesses by offering up-to-date counseling, training, and technical assistance in all aspects of small business management. Whether you've already started a business or are just thinking about it, you can go to the SBDC for help with financial, marketing, production, organization, engineering, or technical problems and for feasibility studies. Special SBDC programs are located in most major cities and are designed to assist you with free one-on-one counseling as well as a variety of seminar topics.

Association of Small Business Development Centers (SBDCs), 8990 Burke Lake Road, Burke, VA 22015; phone 703-764-9850, fax 703-764-1234; e-mail info@asbdc-us.org. Web site www.asbdc-us.org.

Toy Industries Association

The Toy Industry Association (TIA) provides valuable free information and contacts to anyone involved in the toy and game industry. TIA publishes numerous must-have guides if you have a new toy product. Some of the TIA publications include:

- ✔ *Toy Inventor/Designer Guide:* This brochure describes ways to sell your invention, product, or design. To get a copy, write to Toy Inventor/ Designer Guide at the address below.

- ✔ *Fun Play, Safe Play:* This booklet on toy safety can be yours by sending a postcard with your name and address to the address below.

- ✔ *Let's Play: A Guide to Toys for Children with Special Needs:* For a copy of this publication, listing the toys appropriate for blind and visually impaired children, please send your name and address to the address below.

Toy Industry Association, 1115 Broadway, New York, NY 10010; phone 212-675-1141; Web site www.toy-tia.org.

United Inventors Association

The United Inventors Association (UIA) is a not-for-profit corporation formed solely for educational purposes. A membership organization, the UIA's mission is to provide leadership, support, and services to inventor support groups and independent inventors. The UIA works to improve the national image of independent inventors and the inventor community in general. UIA shares information with the media and law enforcement about invention marketing scams, thereby saving many inventors from being preyed on by fraudulent companies.

Go to the UIA website in order to locate a local inventors' organization. It lists the associations by state and gives you the name, address, and phone contact of the president of your local organization.

United Inventors Association, P.O. Box 23447, Rochester, NY 14692; phone 585-359-9310; e-mail UIAUSA@aol.com, Web site www.uiausa.com.

The United States Patent and Trademark Office

For more than 200 years, the basic role of the United States Patent and Trademark Office (USPTO) has remained the same: To promote the progress of science and the useful arts by securing for inventors the exclusive right to their discoveries for a limited time. A bureau of the Department of Commerce, the USPTO examines and issues patents and trademarks. It administers patent and trademark law and is the government advisory arm on intellectual property issues. It is also a veritable font of information where you can go to find out how to apply for a patent, do a patent search on the Web site, get information on trademarks, domain names, and copyrights, and much more. You can also find out about the National Inventors Hall of Fame.

U.S. Patent and Trademark Office, USPTO Contact Center (UCC), Crystal Plaza 3, Room 2C02, P.O. Box 1450, Alexandria, VA 22313-1450; phone 800-786-9199 (In U.S. or Canada) or 703-308-4357, TTY 703-305-7785; Web site www.uspto.gov.

Small Business Administration

The Small Business Administration (SBA) is a government program designed to offer support and assistance to small businesses in the U.S. If you're a small businessperson, the SBA can help with financial matters (even offering loans to disaster victims), assist you in applying for a federal contract, offer management advice, and help you explore international trade possibilities. The SBA has specialized outreach to women, minorities, and armed forces veterans.

Small Business Administration, 6302 Fairview Road, Suite 300, Charlotte, NC 28210; phone 1-800-U-ASK-SBA (1-800-827-5722), TTY 704-344-6640; e-mail answerdesk@sba.gov, Web site www.sba.gov.

Chapter 23

Ten Inventions (and Inventors) That Changed the World

In This Chapter

▶ Looking at the inventors whose dreams became reality

▶ Discovering how inventions enhance the quality of our lives

*W*hen people talk about inventors who changed the world with their inventions, they're talking about people just like you and me. Looking at the inventions here, you can clearly see that technology has no beginning and no end. From the caveman's flint tools to the engineer's computer, there has been progressive innovation throughout history. When one looks at the technological advances of the past hundred years, one can't even envision what man will come up with during the next century.

Cottoning On to Eli Whitney

Eli Whitney is a prime example of both the benefits and hazards of inventing. Whitney is best known for inventing the cotton gin, a machine that took the seeds out of a bale of cotton in minutes in contrast with the days it took workers — most often slaves — to handpick the seeds. Whitney received a U.S. patent on his cotton gin in 1794.

Whitney is remembered for the cotton gin, but perhaps a more lasting credit is that his inventions used interchangeable parts, which paved the way for the mass production of items from guns to food grinders. Whitney's innovations in mass production contributed to the American industrial revolution.

The cautionary part of Whitney's tale comes from the fact that unscrupulous infringers copied the cotton gin and were able to undercut him in price without paying a royalty. This led to Whitney's cotton gin manufacturing company closing its doors in 1797, just three years after the U.S. patent was issued. Whitney's patent on the cotton gin expired in 1807, some 13 years after it was issued, and Congress refused to issue new patents on the improvements Whitney had made because the gin was so valuable economically.

Meeting Metal Man Henry Bessemer

Englishman Henry Bessemer accumulated some 110 diverse patents during his lifetime, from diamond polishing wheels to telescopes to graphite pencil leads to solar furnaces. Bessemer was a shrewd businessman and innovator who became a millionaire from manufacturing and sales of his various innovations.

Bessemer saw the need for better-quality steel during the Crimean War when the low-quality steel cannon barrels regularly fractured. Impurities in steel weaken it, making it more brittle and more prone to crack or break. So, Bessemer Converter produced high-quality steel from impure pig iron. Essentially, the Converter consisted of an egg-shaped vat that held molten iron with all its impurities. Cold air was forced up through the vat through many small hoses. Then it floated all the bad materials (impurities) to the top to be skimmed off, leaving pure iron below.

Steel played a major role in the western industrial revolution, and Bessemer's Converter was an important catalyst. The process was used until the mid-1900s.

Reaping with Cyrus Hall McCormick

Cyrus Hall McCormick is a study for all inventors, for not only did he conceive, design, and patent many farm machines; he also manufactured them. In 1834, McCormick patented a reaping machine that drastically reduced grain loss. Farmers using the reaper could more than double the acreage they planted because harvesting was so much more efficient.

McCormick was also very good at marketing. He licensed his invention to other manufacturers and increased sales that way. He sold his reaper door-to-door, offering farmers written guarantees on his equipment. Another sales innovation was delivering his farm equipment in self-assembly kits, complete with spare parts. In 1874, McCormick established one of the premier farm equipment manufacturing facilities in Chicago, which became a model industrial plant for the nation. McCormick also invested wisely in his later years, putting money into railroads and mining interests.

Sterilizing and Louis Pasteur

During his academic years in his French homeland, Louis Pasteur became interested in fermentation and the role of yeast in that process. Hired by an industrialist to investigate bad batches of wine, Pasteur postulated that microorganisms other than yeast were cultured during the fermentation process. He called them *germs*.

Pasteur believed he could trace food and beverage spoilage to these microorganisms and studied how they got into the food chain. This led him to the belief that destroying or containing the microorganisms that were already present could prevent the spoilage of perishable food products. He also realized that food had to be protected against reinfection.

Pasteur advanced the theory that heating a food or beverage to 160 degrees Fahrenheit for a period of time destroyed the microorganisms — the process known today as *Pasteurization*. Pasteurization still remains an important sterilization technique in hospitals. And even today, with all our means to keep our foods clean and sterile, many people become ill or die from food poisoning.

Calling Alexander Graham Bell

The telephone provides a mass means of communication to many homes and businesses throughout the world. The man behind the basic telephone invention is Alexander Graham Bell.

Bell didn't rest upon his accomplishments with the telephone. A few of his other areas of interest were:

- The photophone, which transmitted sound on a beam of light and was a predecessor of fiber optics (invented by Donald B. Keck in the 1960s)
- Developing techniques to teach speech to the deaf
- Medical electronics, which led to methods of examining the heart electronically
- Aerial vehicles and hydroplanes, which he investigated with Glenn Curtis

Cooling Off with Willis Haviland Carrier

Within a year or two of his graduation from Cornell University in 1901, Willis Haviland Carrier had created a working prototype "apparatus for treating air" in a printing plant in Brooklyn, New York. Carrier's air conditioner removed water from the air as the air was cooled, which lowered the temperature and dehumidified the air. The hot air and water were dumped outside the building.

Carrier's invention provided the first safe, low-pressure centrifugal refrigeration machine using nontoxic, nonflammable refrigerants. He later received a patent on new improved refrigerants. Carrier's invention changed the living and working environments for thousands of people in hot and humid climates. With the advent of air conditioning, workers could function efficiently year-round.

Flying High with the Wright Brothers

The airplane can get you from Boston to L.A. in a few hours. You can thank two brothers for foreshadowing the quick airplane ride in 1903.

Wilbur and Orville Wright were mechanically inclined and interested in flight right from the start. By 1903, they had moved to Kitty Hawk, on North Carolina's outer banks where the wind rarely stopped blowing. On the morning of December 17, their heavier-than-air airplane, powered by a motor the brothers had created, left the ground under its own power and ushered in the Age of Aviation. While the first flight was measured in seconds, by 1904 the Wright brothers' planes stayed in the air for five minutes or longer. By 1905, they'd accomplished a sustained flight of 24 miles. By 1908, they completed an agreement to build a Wright Airplane for the U.S. Army.

Assembling Henry Ford

A gifted engineer, Henry Ford constructed his first steam engine at the age of 15. He went on to build an internal combustion engine, a single cylinder gasoline model leading to his first motorcar in 1896. He founded the Ford Motor Company in 1903 to produce Model T cars. Just as important as the components of the cars was the way they were put together. Ford designed an *assembly-line* process in which an unskilled worker was taught one task in the production process and then did that one task on every car. The ability to hire unskilled (and therefore low-wage) workers enabled Ford to sell his cars at a price the average working man could afford. Henry Ford became an American legend by providing a reliable automobile at an affordable price.

Animating Walt Disney

Walt Disney was born in Chicago on December 5, 1901, and spent much of his childhood in Missouri. He drove an ambulance in France during World War I; when he came back from the war he became a commercial artist. Interested in animation, Disney turned the multiplane camera upside down to film through several layers of drawings to create more realistic motion. Perfecting his innovative animation processes and using Disney's multiplane camera, Disney animation studios released *Snow White and the Seven Dwarfs* as its first full-length movie. The rest is history.

Disney rapidly adopted new entertainment venues, such as television, where his *Wonderful World of Disney* television show delighted children and families for years. He also branched out into amusement parks, opening Disneyland in Anaheim, California, in 1955. Before his death, Disney completed plans for another entertainment park near Orlando, Florida.

Plugging In to Steve Wozniak

Like so many inventors, Steve Wozniak started turning his dreams into reality in his garage (near what later became California's Silicon Valley). The Apple computer, recognized as the world's first personal computer, came into being in 1977.

At the time, computers existed to serve many specific personal uses, but they lacked flexibility. Wozniak's computer had more memory, a keyboard for data entry, a disk drive on which to save programs and documents, and marvelous color graphics. Wozniak cofounded the Apple Computer Company in 1976 with Steven Jobs. The Apple II computer, complete with a floppy disk drive, sold for $1,300 and in just six years, the Apple Computer Company grew to a $500-million-a-year computer company. Wozniak and Jobs started a billion dollar industry. Though both founders have since moved on, and despite business and marketing errors, the Apple/Macintosh Computer Company still exists today.

Chapter 24

Ten Inventors to Emulate

When writing this book and looking back over 20-plus years of working with inventors, I realized how honored I am to have known and occasionally worked with some of the very best inventors of our time. I know nine of the ten inventors listed here and the tenth was a close friend of my husband. I chose these folks for this chapter because I know that in addition to being renowned for their inventions, they're also contributors to society in humanitarian ways.

Each of these innovators and creators has numerous patents, and each is a dedicated, persistent creator who doesn't take no for an answer. As well, each inventor in this chapter is people oriented and a civic leader. They give of their time and talents. They are the ones who take time with the young and old, with beginners, and with their peers. These inventors, and others like them, changed the world. When I attended the 200th Birthday Celebration of the United States Patent and Trademark Office during 2002, I looked at the inventors who had been inducted into the National Inventors Hall of Fame and realized how just one person can start an industry and change the world. Many of you have the same talents. Use them wisely.

Dr. Forrest M. Bird

Inducted into the National Inventors Hall of Fame in 1995.

Quote: "Physiology is God's engineering — in the body."

Inventions: Fluid Control Device; Respirator; Pediatric Ventilator; Respirator/ Ventilator

Forrest Bird, my husband, truly knows the meaning of sweat equity: He built his company, Bird Corporation, with no stockholders and no investors. In today's world, this is unheard of. Bird Corporation manufactured his many medical respirator designs. He then merged his debt-free corporation into the 3M Corporation.

Bird's respirators help patients in about every hospital in the world. He developed the first mass-produced small Bird Mark 7 Respirator in the 1950s, which eliminated the iron lung (a huge tank slightly larger than the patient that the patient actually lived inside). He tested the device by traveling in his own airplanes to medical schools and asking doctors for their most ill patients. In each case, known therapies had failed and the patient was expected to die of cardiopulmonary failure. Of course, the respirator didn't save every patient, but even the failures pointed the way for further improvements in the device. In 1969, he developed the first effective respirator for very small premature babies: the Babybird. Before this invention, over 70 percent of premature babies with major heart and lung problems died. The Babybird reduced this death rate to below 10 percent in two years.

James L. Fergason

Inducted into the National Inventors Hall of Fame in 1998.

Quote: "Bringing a new invention to market is a full-contact sport."

Invention: Display Devices Utilizing Liquid Crystal Light Modulation, commonly known as Liquid Crystal Display or LCD

James Fergason holds a series of patents that form the foundation of the multibillion-dollar LCD industry, which has been rapidly growing since Fergason demonstrated the first operating LCDs in 1971. Prior to the invention of LCDs, a light-emitting diode (LED) was in use. The LED, however, used a large amount of power, provided a limited life, and had poor visual contrast. LCD technology, including that in quartz watches and calculators, has completely redefined many industries, such as computer displays, medical devices, industrial devices, and the vast array of consumer electronics.

Fergason currently works as an independent inventor. He donates hours and hours of time to assisting other innovators, educating young inventors, and working with community organizations.

Helen M. Free

Inducted into the National Inventors Hall of Fame in 2000.

Quotes: "Don't ever let anyone tell you you can't do something because you're a girl." "Chemistry is everywhere."

Invention: Glucose detection device for diabetics

Free is a small-town girl who enrolled in a small Presbyterian college intending to train to teach Latin and English. Instead she obtained a BA degree in chemistry (with minors in math and physics) in three years. She and her husband, Alfred, were both chemists working at a biochemistry research lab group at Miles Laboratory. They were two of the world's leading experts on urinalysis. Their contributions include the development of dry reagents that have become the standard in laboratory urinalysis and the patient-friendly dip and read tests that first enabled diabetics to easily and accurately read their blood glucose levels on their own.

After having six kids and continuing full-time job promotions, as well as preaching how great science is to young people for 55 years, Free found herself being inducted into the National Inventors Hall of Fame in the year 2000. She often tells young people, especially girls, that they can do the same thing if they want to badly enough.

Dr. James Hillier

Inducted into the National Inventors Hall of Fame in 1980.

Quote: "Inventors must recognize that bringing a new product to market can be a very chancy, double-risk process, often requiring one or more completely new manufacturing processes and then an original marketing approach."

Inventions: Electron Lens Correction Device; Electron Microscope

Hillier was a pioneer in developing useful applications for the electron microscope in various scientific disciplines, including medical and biological sciences. His work on the electron microscope began in college. While graduate students in 1938, he and Albert Prebus designed and built the first successful high-resolution electron microscope in the western hemisphere. The electron microscope allows researchers to see the microscopic world we live in by allowing us to see things so small that they can't be viewed the human eye, such as bacteria and cellular structures. Hillier retired as the executive vice president and senior scientist of RCA Labs. He reaches out to other inventors and works to assist them. He is an inventors' advocate.

Dr. Marcian E. (Ted) Hoff

Inducted into the National Inventors Hall of Fame in 1996.

Quote: "A famous quotation stated that if you build a better mousetrap, the world will beat a path to your door. That is not true, unless you are a good salesman as well as a good inventor."

Invention: Memory System for a Multi-Chip Digital Computer

In 1969, the Japanese calculator manufacturer Busicom asked Intel to complete the design and manufacture of a new set of chips. Ted Hoff, working for Intel, was assigned to work with Busicom's engineers. Hoff realized that the Busicom's 12-chip design, which used separate chips for keyboard scanning, display control, printer control, and other functions, could not meet the cost objectives for the project. He proposed an alternate architecture in which a single-chip computer central processor (CPU) would be programmed to perform most of the calculator functions. Busicom accepted the Intel proposal. This single chip, the size of a thumbnail, had as much computing power as the first electronic computer, which filled a room.

The microprocessor is one of the most important developments of the twentieth century. It is found in virtually every automobile, medical device, and computer in the modern world. From its inception in 1969, the microprocessing industry has grown to hundreds of millions of units per year. Hoff was named the first Intel Fellow, the highest technical position in the company. He spent a brief time as VP for Technology with Atari in the early 1980s and is currently VP and Chief Technical Officer with Teklicon, Inc. Other honors include the Stuart Ballantine Medal from the Franklin Institute.

William P. Lear

Inducted into the National Inventors Hall of Fame in 1993, 25 years after his death.

Quote: "Do your homework, then take a big bite."

Inventions: Radio Apparatus; Car Radio

Bill Lear created the first automobile radio, which he named the Motorola. He also made the first real portable all-band aviation radio, the Learavia. Later, he conceived the first four-track small stereo for use in the car, boat, airplane, or home.

At heart, Bill was an airplane buff; he was not only a proficient pilot, but also a pure genius in terms of conceiving, designing, and building airplanes and their accessories. Bill designed the first real mass-produced sophisticated autopilot for aircraft, capable of automatically flying the aircraft. Later, against all political and financial odds, Bill designed the first real business jet, called the Learjet, which offered military performance for use by private aviation. To do so, he redesigned WW II Aircraft by making them considerably faster with greater fuel range and safety for business aviation.

Edward Lowe

Quote: "My life has been a testimony to the credo of the entrepreneur. People like me who have lived the dream should share their knowledge with others because if private-sector business doesn't help, then the American entrepreneur won't survive."

Invention: Kitty Litter

Trying to help a neighbor in 1947, Edward Lowe brought cats indoors by creating cat litter from clay he was using as an industrial absorbent. By doing so, he created an entirely new category of consumer product that changed the lives — and lifestyles — of millions of cats and cat lovers: Kitty Litter. Lowe had a hunch that other cat owners would also love his new cat-box filler, so he filled ten brown bags with clay, wrote "Kitty Litter" on them, and called on the local pet store. With sand available for next to nothing, the shop owner doubted anyone would pay 65¢ for a five-pound bag of Kitty Litter and suggested Lowe give it away — advice he followed. Soon customers were asking for more — and now they were willing to pay for it.

Edward Lowe Industries Inc. was the nation's largest producer of cat-box filler, with retail sales of more than $210 million annually. Kitty Litter Brand, which was 99 percent dust free, was sanitized with Healthguard and provided a better environment for cats and their owners by controlling the growth of odor-causing bacteria. Ralston Purina eventually purchased the company in the early 1990s. Lowe moved from being an innovator to an entrepreneur.

After spawning a billion-dollar industry that established the cat as the nation's most popular pet, Lowe set his creative sights on another goal — fostering and nurturing the American entrepreneur. Lowe and his wife, Darlene (also a successful entrepreneur), established the Edward Lowe Foundation. Its mission is to champion the entrepreneurial spirit by supporting networks and organizations that encourage entrepreneurs to listen to, learn from, and innovate with each other.

Dr. Jay Morton

Quote: "Faster than a Speeding Bullet, More Powerful than a Locomotive, Able to Leap Tall Buildings with a Single Bound, The Man of Steel, Superman, Defending Truth, Justice and the American Way."

Invention: Scriptwriter who brought Superman to life

Jay Morton wrote Superman stories. He was also a publisher, a banker, an artist, and an inventor. Maybe he wasn't a man of steel, but Morton led an extraordinary life that comes close to rivaling Superman's. Morton began his varied career as a child actor in the pre-Depression era *Our Gang* comedies. A graduate of New York's Pratt Institute, with a Masters from *L'Institut de Montparnasse* in Paris, he biked across Europe before he turned 18. Upon returning to America, Morton introduced and wrote the Superman cartoon for Fleicher Studios of Miami, Florida, under assignment for Paramount Studios.

In 1997, he unveiled a creation of an 8-foot bronze statue of Admiral Richard E. Byrd (the Navy Explorer of the South Pole) that currently graces the entrance to the Joint Judicial Center in Winchester, Virginia, birthplace of the famous explorer. When I was in his house one day, he had a prototype Admiral Byrd's statue in his house. I asked Jay why he chose to do the statue of Admiral Byrd. He replied, "Because he pinned my Eagle Scout badge on me, that's why."

Until his death in 2003 at the age of 92, Morton sat on the Board for my company. Morton spoke six languages fluently. He continued to work with young children, teaching them various languages and taking time to listen to them and truly care.

Dr. Robert H. Rines

Inducted into the National Inventors Hall of Fame in 1994.

Quote: "Inventors rarely want for the talent to create new ideas; but they often want for the good sense to share such ideas with others possessing the vital talent for successful commercialization."

Inventions: Electric System; Microwave Scanning System; Sound Ranging System; High Resolution Radar and Sonar

Robert H. Rines learned the value of education, critical thinking, and commitment at a very early age from the people he trusted most in the world: his parents. With such influential role models, young Bobby Rines was an excellent student, but, more important, he was encouraged by his parents to be inquisitive.

When his academic success gained him entrance to MIT, he was well prepared for the rigors of its challenging curriculum even at the tender age of 15. But even gifted teenagers are still teenagers. Attending MIT had been his father's dream and not his — so, as any self-respecting teenager would do, he rebelled and managed to flunk out of school. Nonetheless, he returned to MIT, was a stellar student and, after December 7, 1941, graduated early to join the Army as a second lieutenant in the Signal Corps. He was loaned to the British to help with their radar defenses of England against German aircraft. On the island of Saipan, in a desperate attempt to detect low-flying enemy aircraft, he and his men created and then installed a prototype of the first imaging radar unit. Later that day, as the low-level Japanese bombers approached the island, the U.S. Army squadron was ready and waiting for them.

In peacetime, his inventions formed the basis for the high-definition sonar scanning systems used in locating the *Titanic* and the *Bismarck*. They are also used in new medical instrumentation allowing noninvasive ultrasound imaging of internal organs. His patents underlie nearly all the high-definition image-scanning radar used to provide early warning, weapons fire control, and some of the artillery and missile detection radars used during the war in the Persian Gulf.

James E. West

Inducted into the National Inventors Hall of Fame in 1999.

Quote: "Good ideas are fun to think about, but really hard to reduce to practice."

Inventions: Electroacoustic Transducer; Electret Microphone

Dr. West co-invented the microphone while working at Bell Laboratories. It was patented in 1962. West's microphone became widely used because of its high performance, accuracy, and reliability, in addition to its low cost, small size, and lightweight. Ninety percent of today's microphones are electret microphones, and they are used in everyday items such as telephones, camcorders, and tape recorders.

These days, West is also the leader of a Bell Labs science program that mentors minority high school students. Being a minority in this country deprived West of many opportunities normally afforded to others. West feels that this deprivation stimulated him to do better then his competition in every possible way. However, he feels that this is paradoxical, because most minorities never recover from a deprived state. Therefore, he devotes as much time as possible to working with underrepresented minorities by bringing them the message that they, too, may overcome adversity with lots of hard work. He wants to share the competitive spirit that helped him to make significant contributions to the advancement of science.

Part VI
Appendixes

1853 INVENTORS CONFERENCE
INVENTOR OF THE YEAR
CLAYTON HAIR
INVENTOR OF THE HAIR TRIGGER

"I'd also like to thank my assistant, Tom, who's been loyal, courageous, and amazingly resilient all these years."

In this part . . .

Somewhat dry, but very useful, forms and agreements
make up the appendixes, along with a listing of helpful online resources.

Appendix A

Sample Agreements

Following are the sample agreements mentioned in Chapters 8, 10, and 20.

Sample: CONFIDENTIALITY AND NON-USE AGREEMENT

COMPANY: _____
RECIPIENT: _____
_____
_____

Effective Date _____

Recipient has requested that Company disclose Information owned by Company relating to in order to allow Recipient to _____ ("Purpose"). In consideration for disclosure of Information by Company to Recipient, Recipient agrees as follows:

1. Recipient will not disclose the Information to any third party, nor use Information other than for Purpose for a period of _____ (_____) years after the later occurrence of the effective date hereof, or after completion of the Purpose of this disclosure, unless specifically authorized by Company in writing.

2. Recipient will limit access to Information solely to those employees necessary to perform the Purpose of this Agreement and to supervise the performance of same. Recipient will inform each such person given access to the Information of the confidential nature of the Information and of the existence and importance of the provisions of this Agreement.

3. The foregoing obligations of non-use and non-disclosure shall not apply to Information which Recipient can show (a) by writing in the possession of Recipient, was known to Recipient prior to the disclosure thereof, (b) is in the public domain or becomes part of the public domain through no fault of Recipient, or (c) was disclosed to Recipient by a third party as a matter of right having no obligation to Company. It is understood that all Information is, and shall remain the property of Company and no copies of the Information shall be made by Recipient.

4. After completion of Purpose, Recipient agrees to return to Company all Information, and copies thereof, if any, disclosed to it by Company and that prepared by Recipient based on Information in accomplishing Purpose. Recipient further agrees that it shall continue to maintain Information in confidence and to make no further use of such Information.

5. Should any invention related to Information be conceived or made by Recipient while accomplishing Purpose under this Agreement, or any subsequent Agreement, Recipient agrees that Company shall own such invention, and insofar as deemed necessary by Company, Recipient will assist Company to file and prosecute any patent applications on same. No license under any patent owned, or licensed, by Company is granted to Recipient by this Agreement.

The Parties hereto both agreeing to be bound and to faithfully perform the foregoing obligations do hereby enter into this Agreement effective as of the date first above written.

_____

By: _____ Title:_____
By:_____ Title:_____

SAMPLE CONFIDENTIALITY AGREEMENT

AGREEMENT and acknowledgment between _____ (Owner) and
_____ (Recipient).

Whereas, the Owner agrees to furnish the Recipient with certain confidential information relating to his or her business affairs for purposes of:

Reviewing, Analyzing and Evaluating for possible purchase and/or license the rights to and/or for manufacturing and/or commercial development of the Owner's
_____;

Whereas the Recipient agrees to review, examine, inspect or obtain such information only for the purpose described above, and to otherwise hold such information confidential pursuant to the terms of this Agreement,

BE IT KNOWN, that the Owner has or shall furnish to the Recipient certain confidential information (including, but not limited to the items on the attached list), and may further allow the Recipient the right to interview the Owner, all on the following conditions:

1. The Recipient agrees to hold all confidential or proprietary information or trade secrets ("information") in trust and confidence and agrees that the information shall be used only for the contemplated purpose, shall not be used for any other purpose or disclosed to any third party.

2. At the conclusion of our discussions, or upon earlier demand by the Owner, all information, including written notes, photographs, memoranda, photocopies of the confidential material or notes taken by you, the Recipient, shall be returned to the Owner.

3. This information shall not be disclosed to any employee or consultant unless they agree to execute and be bound by the terms of this Agreement.

4. It is understood that the Recipient shall have no obligation with respect to any information known by the Recipient prior to the date of this Agreement (other than information disclosed to Recipient by Owner) or generally known within the industry prior to the date of this Agreement, or which becomes common knowledge within the industry thereafter through means other than by default of this Agreement by Recipient, or after ten (10) years from the date of this agreement.

5. This Agreement may be modified only by a writing, signed by both parties.

(Owner)

Dated: _____   By _____

(Recipient)

Dated: _____   _____

Signed By_____

Title _____
For _____

SAMPLE CONSULTANT OR EMPLOYMENT AGREEMENT:
INNOVATION AND PROPRIETARY INFORMATION

In consideration of my engagement as an independent consultant or and employee by _____ (the Company), I agree to:

1. Disclose and assign to the Company, as its exclusive property, all inventions, technical or business innovations developed or conceived by me solely or jointly with others during the period of my engagement, (a) that are along the lines of the businesses, work or investigations of the Company or its affiliates to which my engagement relates or as a result of which I may receive information due to my engagement, or (b) that result from or are suggested by any work which I do for the Company, or (c) that are otherwise made through the use of Company time, facilities or materials;

2. Make and maintain for the Company adequate and current written records of all such inventions or innovations;

3. Execute all necessary papers and otherwise provide proper assistance (at the Company's expense) during and subsequent to my engagement, to enable the Company to obtain for itself or its nominees or agents, any patents, copyrights or other legal protection for such inventions or innovations in the United States and abroad; and

4. When my engagement terminates, to promptly deliver to the Company all written and other materials which are of a secret or confidential nature relating to the business of the Company or its affiliates. The terms "secret" and "confidential" are used in the ordinary sense and include materials, information and data such as drawings, manuals, notebooks, reports, models, inventions, formulas, processes, machines, compositions, computer programs, accounting methods, business plans and information systems;

5. Not to use, publish or otherwise disclose (except as required by the Company), either during or subsequent to my engagement, any secret or confidential information or data of the Company or any information or data of others which the Company is obligated to maintain in confidence; and

6. Not to disclose or utilize in my work with the Company any secret or confidential information of others (including any prior employers), or any inventions or innovations of my own which are not included within the scope of this Agreement.

7. The obligation not to disclose secret or confidential information shall remain in effect for ten (10) years after my engagement terminates or when the information becomes generally known in the industry.

8. This Agreement supersedes and replaces any existing agreement between the Company and me relating generally to the same subject matter. It may not be modified or terminated, in whole or part, except in writing signed by an authorized representative of the Company. Discharge of my responsibilities in this Agreement is an obligation of my executors, administrators, or other legal representatives or assigns.

_____(Signed/Dated)_____(Signed/Dated)
C.E.O. or Representative of   Consultant or Employee
Corporation

_____   _____

Witness   Date   Witness   Date

ASSIGNMENT
AND WORK FOR HIRE AGREEMENT

WRITER: _____

_____
(List full name and address of writer).

EMPLOYERS: Reading Friends XXXXX Company, L.P., 5228 Pershing Road, Fort Worth, TX 76107.

      WHEREAS Employers desire to hire and employ the above referenced Writer to write, draft and/or edit instructional text and materials (including any accompanying illustrations, designs, diagrams or other graphic representations); and

      WHEREAS Writer desires to perform services, it is hereby agreed by and among the parties hereto as follows:

1. DESCRIPTION OF WORK: Employers hereby retain the services of Writer to perform services as an author, writer and/or editor for the creation of instructional text and materials (including any accompanying illustrations, designs, diagrams or other graphic representations), whether in printed or electronic form, to be used in connection with Employers' school and instructional curriculum.

2. ASSIGNMENT OF COPYRIGHT: Writer acknowledges and agrees that his/her services are prepared within the scope of this Agreement as a "Work Made For Hire," as such terms are used in the United States Copyright Act. Writer further acknowledges that Employers are the exclusive owners of all copyrights with respect to the instructional materials (including any accompanying illustrations, designs, diagrams or other graphic representations) actually used by Employers and all preliminary drafts leading to the final draft actually used. Employers have the right to exercise all rights of the copyright proprietor with respect thereto, including, but not limited to, all exclusive rights specified in 17 U.S.C. fl106 and the exclusive right to secure registration of the instructional materials with the United States Copyright Office in the name of Employers. In the event that Writer is ever deemed to be the copyright owner in the instructional materials subject to this Agreement, Writer hereby assigns, transfers, sets over and conveys to Employers and their successors and assigns that portion of all right, title and interest set forth above in and to the printed instructional materials including the copyrights and proprietary rights therein and in any and all versions or derivatives regardless of the media used whether physical or electronic and now known or hereinafter developed, and any renewals and extensions thereof (whether presently available or subsequently available as the result of intervening legislation) in the United States of America and elsewhere throughout the world, and further including any and all causes of action for infringement of the same, past, present and future, and all proceeds from the foregoing accrued and unpaid and hereafter accruing. Writer agrees to sign any and all other papers which may be required to effectuate the purpose and intent of this Assignment, and hereby irrevocably authorizes and appoints Employers as Writer's true and lawful attorney-in-fact to take such actions and make, sign, execute, acknowledge and deliver all such documents as may from time to time be necessary to convey to Employers or their successors and assigns, all rights granted herein.

3. FURTHER WORKS: Writer further agrees that if Employers should ask him/her to draft new, revised, updated or additional instructional materials, and if Writer agrees to do so, any and all such materials will also be deemed to be a "works made for hire," and that in the event a determination is ever made that such materials do not constitute "works made for hire," the transaction will be deemed to include and provide for the transfer to Employers all copyright, Writer's rights and other intellectual property rights in and to such new, revised, updated or additional instructional materials, as set forth in paragraph 2 above.

4. COLLABORATION: Writer will not use assistants or other writers in collaboration with creating the instructional materials subject to this Agreement without express approval from Employers and any such person or persons, if approved of by Employers, must expressly agree in writing to be bound by the terms of this Agreement.

5. ENTIRE AGREEMENT: This Assignment/Work for Hire Agreement sets forth the entire agreement between the parties with respect to the subject matter hereof, and no modification, amendment, waiver, termination or discharge of this Agreement, or any provisions hereof, shall be binding upon any party unless confirmed by written instrument signed by all parties.

6. NON-WAIVER: No waiver of any provisions or default under this Agreement shall affect the right of any party thereafter to enforce such provision or to exercise any right or remedy in the event of any other default, whether or not similar.

7. SEVERABILITY: If any part of this Agreement is determined to be void, invalid, inoperative or unenforceable by a court of competent jurisdiction or by any other legally constituted body having jurisdiction to make such determination, such decision shall not affect any other provisions hereof, and the remainder of this Agreement shall be effective as though such void, invalid, inoperative or unenforceable provision had not been contained herein.

8. GOVERNING LAW: The validity, construction and effect of this Agreement and any and all extensions and/or modifications thereof shall be governed by the laws of the State of Texas and federal Copyright law. In any legal action between the parties, the prevailing party shall be entitled to recover damages, injunctive or other equitable remedies, its court costs and reasonable attorney's fees. This Agreement shall be binding upon the parties hereto, their heirs, personal representatives, successors and assigns but shall not take effect until executed by Writer and Employer.

IN WITNESS WHEREOF, the undersigned have executed the foregoing Assignment/Work For Hire Agreement as of this _____ day of _____, 20__.

WRITER:

_____

EMPLOYER: READING FRIENDS,

By:_____

SAMPLE CONTRACT
MANUFACTURING LETTER AGREEMENT

(Your Letterhead)

(Date)

TO:

Subject: Contract Manufacturing Agreement

Dear Mr._____ :

We are pleased to submit this proposal for (The Manufacturer's Name) , hereinafter called the "Manufacturer," to perform contract manufacturing services to (Your Company's Name) , hereinafter called the "Company," for our (Your Product), hereinafter called the "Product."

The Parties herein agree that:

The Company shall purchase from Manufacturer and Manufacturer shall exclusively supply to the Company items and products listed in Exhibit 1 attached. The parties further agree that only Company's orders shall be valid and binding when written on Company's purchase orders and transmitted from the Company to the Manufacturer.

The Company may, at its option, cancel this Agreement before the stated termination date upon the occurrence of:

1. Presentation of a true and verified proposal from a competitive manufacturer of a unit price of 5% or greater, LESS THAN THE PRICE stipulated in this Agreement. However, the Manufacturer has an option to modify the cost by reducing the unit cost to within 3% of the verified competitive proposal and thereby render this Agreement NOT subject to cancellation under this provision.

2. Delays of 30 days or more in production from the date of the Company's postmarked purchase order to the Manufacturer's shipment date unless waived in writing from the Company.

3. Manufacturer's declaration of bankruptcy or insolvency.

4. Acquisition of Manufacturer by another company or entity.

5. Majority of stock issued by Manufacturer being purchased or acquired by another firm or person.

Payment terms are two percent (2%) ten days, net thirty (30) days. The Manufacturer is not required to continue shipping if the Company does not meet its payment terms.

The Parties hereto further agree that all products, drawings and samples, whether complete or in progress, are the property of the Company. The Manufacturer agrees to assign all patents and products improvements to the Company. In the event of termination of this Agreement, if the Company changes its source of supply as above listed, the Manufacturer agrees not to manufacture Products listed in Exhibit 1 for any other firm or person, for a period of no less than (5) years beginning from the termination date.

The Manufacturer agrees that the Company owns all molds, dies and fixtures used in the manufacture of the Company's Products, except for those that the Company has not paid or has been invoiced. In the event the Company elects to change its source of supply, as stated above, the Manufacturer either will immediately deliver (delivery carrier to be specified by the company) to the Company all such tools, dies, molds and fixtures or will sell all said tools, dies, molds and fixtures at their current book values as calculated by generally accepted accounting standards, at the Company's option. (The proceeds of said sale will also immediately be delivered to said Company). The Company shall be entitled to seek immediate injunctive relief to obtain possession of these items.

The Manufacturer also agrees that no employee will use knowledge of any of the Products gained during their employment with the Manufacturer to manufacture or market the Company's Products or similar products either directly or indirectly or to advise, counsel or in any way assist any third party to compete with the Company. Furthermore the Manufacturer agrees not to use any information provided by the Company, directly or indirectly, for the Manufacture's own benefit or for the benefit of any other person, firm or corporation.

The Manufacturer agrees to use its best efforts to insure high quality products and workmanship. The Manufacturer warrants all products sold to the Company under this Agreement will be free from defects due to poor workmanship or material for a period of thirteen (13) months. If Products are defective the Manufacturer will be responsible to replace the defective Products without charge, credit the Company's account, or issue the Company a refund, at the Company's option. The warranty shall supersede all previous warranties of any kind whether written or implied.

The Company agrees to keep the Manufacturer apprised of product sales; and the Company further agrees to use its best efforts to sell the Products.

The Company agrees to hold the Manufacturer harmless from any patent infringement.

Either Party may terminate this Agreement by giving ninety (90) days written notice sent via Certified U.S. Mail, Return Receipt Requested. If this Agreement is terminated, the Company has the sole option to purchase the Manufacturer's inventory of said Products over a six (6) months period. If the Company elects not to purchase the Manufacturer's inventory of Products, the Manufacturer may dispose of such finished goods inventory in any method it chooses.

The terms of this Agreement shall survive in the event of termination.

This Agreement is not assignable by either Party except by written agreement by both Parties. If this agreement is assigned, the assignee shall be bound by the terms and conditions of this Agreement.

Correspondence shall be addressed to the individuals on Page 1 of this Agreement.

Exhibit 1 - Products

Product(s) to be manufactured or supplied by the Manufacturer:
1.
2.
3.

Agreed By:

_____   _____
(Manufacturer)   (Company)

_____   _____
(Signature of officer)   (Signature of officer)

_____   _____
(Print name and title)   (Print name and title)

_____   _____
(Date)   (Date)

SAMPLE EXCLUSIVE LICENSE AGREEMENT

AGREEMENT, made this _____ day of _____, 2____, by and between _____ a_____ corporation with its principal place of business at _____, (hereinafter called "_____"), and _____, a corporation with its principal place of business at _____ (hereinafter called "_____").

WITNESSETH:

WHEREAS, _____ represents and warrants that it has developed and is the owner of all right, title, and interest in and to _____ (hereinafter "_____"); and

WHEREAS,_____ represents and warrants that it is the owner of all right, title, and interest in and to U.S. Patent Nos. _____ for _____ (hereinafter called "Patents"); and

WHEREAS, _____ desires to secure an exclusive, worldwide license to make, have made, and sell the Products and to practice the invention disclosed in the Patents to produce Products for _____(field of use limitation)_____ (hereinafter "Field"), including the right to sublicense thereunder in Field, and MCCOY is willing to grant the same upon the terms and conditions herein set forth;

Now THEREFORE, in consideration of the mutual covenants and undertakings of the parties, it is hereby agreed as follows:

(1) _____ hereby grants to _____, its subsidiaries and affiliates, the sole and exclusive, worldwide right and license (including the right to sublicense) in Field to make, have made, and sell Products and to practice the invention covered by the claims of the Patents.

(2) _____ shall pay to _____ the sum of $50,000 upon execution of this Agreement and a running royalty of two percent (2%) of Gross Sales (Invoice Amounts), less returns, by _____, its subsidiaries and affiliates, of the Products until Patents expire. A sale will accrue for royalty purposes when an invoice is sent to purchaser of Products.

(3) Payments hereunder shall be made quarterly by _____ within thirty (30) days after the end of each calendar quarter. Payment shall be accompanied by a report of the Gross Sales (and returns, if any) of the Products and the computation thereof during the preceding calendar quarter.

(4) All royalties payable hereunder on Gross Sales effected in countries other than the United States shall accrue in U.S. dollars at the exchange rate of the currency of the country in which the sales are made on the date of such sale as set forth in Paragraph (2) above. _____ shall secure U.S. dollar transfers in respect of royalty amounts and shall make payments to _____ as if such sale is made in the United States regardless if collection of such amount is made by _____ or not. Every payment of royalty based upon Sales in foreign country shall be a net amount undiminished by imposition of any tax of the country where sale is made. Foreign sales shall be reported separately by country on such quarterly reports filed under Paragraph 3.

(5) _____ shall keep accurate records of Gross Sales and returns for a period not to exceed two (2) years, unless in dispute, in which event they shall be kept until said dispute is settled, and such records shall be open during reasonable business hours at the place where such records are customarily kept, for examination by an independent certified public accountant selected by _____ and acceptable to _____, for the propose of verifying the accuracy of such Sales reported to_____ and royalty payments due thereon. Said accountant shall not disclose any information that he may thereby obtain other than that necessary for the purpose of enabling _____ to determine the accuracy of such reports and payments made in connection therewith.

(6) In the event_____ fails to make timely payments to _____,_____ may terminate the exclusivity of this License effective 30 (thirty) days after written notice to _____, unless paid in that time and offer other non-exclusive licenses to Field as _____ sees fit. All other terms of the Agreement shall remain unchanged.

(7) _____ shall have the right to cancel this Agreement any time on three (3) months notice in writing to_____. Upon such termination, _____ shall pay to _____ all royalties accrued as of such termination date and _____ shall no longer make, have made, or sell Products.

(8) _____ hereby indemnifies and holds _____, its subsidiaries, affiliates, and sublicensees, harmless against any and all actions, suits, claims, or demands whatsoever, including the costs and expenses connected therewith, which any of them may incur or become liable to pay by reason of any claim, suit, or demand of infringement of a patent because of the manufacture or sale of the Product, provided _____ shall be promptly notified of any such action, suit, claim, or demand.

(9) In the event that infringement of Patents, or either of them is reasonably believed to be occurring, _____ shall proceed to bring an infringement action against such party at its sole expense. No provision of this Agreement shall be abated because of such action and _____ shall retain all amounts recovered through judgment.

(10) The term of this Agreement shall be for the life of the last to expire of the Patents identified above, and any modification, extension, or reissue thereof.

(11) This Agreement shall be binding and shall inure to the benefit of the parties and to their heirs, successor, and assigns.

(12) Neither party shall have the right to assign this Agreement, in whole or in part, without prior approval of the other, provided, however, that _____ shall have the right to assign this Agreement, in whole or in part, at any time to the purchaser of the entire business to which this license applies; provided, such assignee shall agree in writing with _____ to assume all other obligations thereof. _____ shall have the right, upon written notice to _____, to assign the collection of royalties hereunder, but in no event shall _____ be obligated to deal with more than one (1) party in the payment of said royalties.

(13) All matters affecting the interpretation, form, validity, and performance of this Agreement shall be decided under the laws of the State of _____

(14) No amendment shall be made to this Agreement except in writing and signed by both Parties.

THIS AGREEMENT IS EXECUTED by designated Officers of Parties authorized to execute such documents and is effective from the date of the last signature on it.

SIGNED:

Title:_____   Title:_____

Appendix B

Online Resources

• •

*H*ere I list a variety of sources that can help you walk the walk in bringing your product to market.

USPTO and Related International Links

In this section, I list intellectual property law contacts for you on an international basis. These are great contacts for you to further investigate your product's patentability and trademarks in various parts of the world.

- ✔ Australia Patent Database since 1979: www.ipaustralia.gov.au
- ✔ Canadian Patent Database: patents1.ic.gc.ca/intro-e.html
- ✔ CFR: www.access.gpo.gov/nara/cfr/cfr-table-search.html
- ✔ Community Trademark Information (Europe): oami.eu.int
- ✔ Database Boolean Search: 164.195.100.11/netahtml/search-bool.html
- ✔ Delphion Intellectual Property Network: www.delphion.com
- ✔ European Patent Office: www.european-patent-office.org
- ✔ Fedlaw: www.fedlaw.gsa.gov
- ✔ Foreign Patent Searching: patent.search-in.net
- ✔ Government Printing Office: www.acccess.gpo.gov/#info
- ✔ Ignatz — Patent & Intellectual Property (Patent Info Sites & Foreign Patent Offices): www.ignatz.net/patents.htm
- ✔ Intellectual Property Mall: www.ipmall.fplc.edu
- ✔ Internet Patent News Service: www.bustpatents.com
- ✔ International Trademark Association: www.inta.org
- ✔ Legal Information Institute: www.lii.law.cornell.edu
- ✔ LexPat: www.lexdis-nexis.com
- ✔ Japanese Patent Office: www.jpo-miti.go.jp

- New Zealand (patent & trademark attorneys): `www.piperpat.com.nz/resource/patoff.html`
- TMEP Second Edition: `www.uspto.gov/web/offices/tac/tmep`
- Trademarks: `www.uspto.gov`
- QPAT: `www.qpat.com`
- U.K. Patent Office: `www.patent.gov.uk`
- U.K. Search UK Patents: `www.gb.espacenet.com`
- U.S. Code `www.uscode.house.gov/usc.htm`
- U.S. Patent and Trademark Office (USPTO): `www.uspto.gov`
- USPTO Patent Searching on line: `www.uspto.gov/patft/index.html`
- USPTO Database: `www.uspto.gov/tmdb/index.hml`
- USPTO FORMS: `www.uspto.gov/web/forms/index.html`
- USPTO Independent Inventor Resources: `www.uspto.gov/web/offices/com/iip/index.htm`
- USPTO Kid's Pages: `www.uspto.gov/go/kids`
- USPTO Search U.S. Patent Office Database: `www.uspto.gov/patft/index.html`
- U.S. Patent Law by Cornell University: `law.cornell.edu/topics/patent.html`
- Yahoo Intellectual Property Directory: `www.yahoo.com/government/law/intellectual_Property`

Important Links for Copyrights

Check out these sites for copyright info.

- Circulars: `lcweb.loc.gov/copyright/circs`
- Library of Congress (LOC): `www.loc.gov`
- U.S. Copyright Office: `lcweb.loc.gov/copyright`
- U.S. Copyright Office Search Records: `lcweb.loc.gov/copyright/rb.html`

Domain Name–Related Links

These links are handy if you want to register an online domain name.

- Internet Corporation For Assigned Names and Numbers (ICANN): www.icann.org
- Hasbro Games: www.hasbro.com
- Hasbro Toy Group: www.hasbro.com
- Inventors Digest Magazine: www.inventorsdigest.com
- Mattel, Inc. www.mattel
- Network Solutions Inc. (search & reserve domain names): www.networksolutions.com
- Register.com (search & reserve domain names): www.register.com
- Worldwide Domain Name Search: www.allwhois.com

Law–Related Links

Check out these links if you need legal advice related to your invention.

- American Bar Association: www.abanet.org
- American Bar Association's Section of Intellectual Property Law: www.abanet.org/intelprop/home.html
- American Intellectual Property Association: www.aipla.org
- CFR Titles: www.access.gpo.gov/nara/cfr/cfr-table-search.html
- Copyright Clearance Center: www.copyright.com
- Cornell Law Library: www.law.cornell.edu/library
- Federal Legislative Information: thomas.loc.gov
- FindLaw: Forms: www.findlaw.com/16forms/index.html
- Internet Legal Resources: www.findlaw.com
- Intellectual Property Center: www.ipcenter.com
- Legal Information Institute: www.law.cornell.edu
- Multimedia Law-Resource to New Media: www.batnet.com/oikoumene/index.html
- Online Law Library Internet Edition: www.fplc.edu/ollie.html
- Software Publishers Association: www.spa.org
- U.S. Code: uscode.house.gov/usc.htm
- U.S. Court of Appeals for the Federal Circuit: www.fedcir.gov and www.law.emory.edu/fedcircuit

✔ U.S. Federal Courts: `www.uscourts.gov`

✔ U.S. House of Representatives: `www.house.gov`

✔ U.S. Patent Law: `www.law.cornell.edu/topics/patent.html`

✔ U.S. Senate: `www.senate.gov`

Other Important Legal, International, and Organizational Links

Here I list links that tell the story of how our culture is formed by human creativity and invention, provide complete background info on some of the inventors who've completely changed how we live our daily lives, and list contacts for licensing agents to help you sell your intellectual property rights in the U.S. and throughout the world.

✔ American Society of Composers, Authors, and Publishers: `www.ascap.com`

✔ DaVinci Design Resource: `www.uspatentinfo.com`

✔ Engines of our Ingenuity: `www.uh.edu/admin/engines/engines.htm`

✔ Federation of Inventions: `www.invention-ifia.ch/ifianyouth.htm`

✔ FPLC The Intellectual Property Mall Annotated Guide: `www.fplc.edu/ipmall/ipdirect.htm`

✔ History of Invention: `www.cbc4kids.ca/general/the-lab/history-of-invention/default.html`

✔ Hoover's Online The Ultimate Source For Company Info: `www.hoovers.com`

✔ Invention Dimension: `www.mit.edu/invent`

✔ IBM Patent Server Home Page: `patent.womplex.ibm.com`

✔ Inventors Online Museum: `www.inventorsmuseau.com`

✔ Intellectual Property Network: `www.patents.ibm.com`

✔ Intellectual Property Owners (IPS): `www.ipo.org`

✔ International Trademark Association: `www.inta.org`

✔ Internet Society: `www.inventionconvention.com`

✔ InventNet Forum: `www.inventnet.com`

✔ Inventor's Bookstore: `www.inventorhelp.com`

✔ Inventor's Digest Online: `www.inventorsdigest.com`

✔ Inventure Place: `www.invent.org`

✔ Innovative Product Technologies: `www.inventionevaluation.com`

✔ Lawyer Search: `lawyers.martindale.com/aba` and `www.martindale.com/locator/home.html`

✔ Lexis (general legal materials): `www.lexis.com`

✔ Licensing Executive Society: `www.usa-canada.les.org`

✔ Links to International Treaties: `www.bsos.umd.edu/icons/treaties.htm`

✔ Minnesota Inventors Congress: `www.invent1.org`

✔ National Inventors Hall of Fame: `www.invent.org`

✔ National Technology Transfer Center (NTTC): `www.nttc.edu`

✔ Patent Café: `www.patentcafe.com`

✔ Patent It Yourself: `www.patentityourself.com`

✔ Ronald J. Riley's Inventor Resources: `www.inventored.org`

✔ Software Patent Institute: `www.spi.org`

News, Search, Manufacturers, and Law Associations–Related Links

Here I list links for searching industry contacts and funny patents, as well as other links that can assist you in commercializing your invention.

✔ American Electronics Association: `www.aeanet.org`

✔ EDGAR Database: `www.sec.gov/edaux/searches.htm`

✔ The Harry Fox Agency, Inc.: `www.nmpa.org`

✔ Patent Law Links `www.patentlawlinks.com`

✔ PCT USPTO Receiving Office: `www.uspto.gov/web/offices/pac/dapps/pct`

✔ Silicon Valley News Mercury Center: `www.mercurycenter.com/svtech/reports/gmsv`

✔ Songwriters Guild of America: `songwriters.org`

✔ Thomas Register (locating manufacturing companies): `www.thomasregistser.com`

✔ United Inventors Association: `uiausa.com`

✔ Wacky Patent of the Month: `www.colitz.com/site/wacky/htm`

✔ World Intellectual Property Association (WIPO): `www.wipo.org/eng/index.htm`

✔ World Intellectual Property Organization PCT Gazette: `http://pctgazette.wipo.int`

Additional Government Resources

I list government resources at your fingertips here in this section. The contacts listed here can provide you with detailed info on anything from the consumer product safety rules that are required for your product to how to incorporate your business.

- Index to Government Web Sites: usgovinfo.about.com/newsissues/usgovinfo/blindex.htm
- NASA: www.nasa.gov
- U.S. Consumer Information Center: www.pueblo.gsa.gov
- U.S. Consumer Product Safety Commission: www.cpsc.gov
- U.S. Department of Agriculture: www.usda/gov
- U.S. Department of Commerce: www.doc.gov
- U.S. Department of Education: www.edu.gov
- U.S. Department of Energy: www.energy.gov
- U.S. Department of Health and Human Services: www.os.dhhs.gov
- U.S. Department of Homeland Security: www.dhs.gov
- U.S. Department of Labor: www.dol.gov
- U.S. Department of Transportation: www.dot.gov
- U.S. Department of Veterans Affairs: www.va.gov
- U.S. Economic Analysis: www.bea.doc.gov
- U.S. Environmental Protection Agency: www.epa.gov
- U.S. Federal Trade Commission: www.ftc.gov
- U.S. FedStats: www.fedstats.gov
- U.S. FedWorld Information Network: www.fedworld.gov
- U.S. FirstGov: www.firstgov.org
- U.S. Food and Drug Administration: www.fda.gov
- U.S. Health Statistics: www.cdc.gov
- US Securities and Exchange Commission: www.sec.gov
- U.S. Small Business Administration (SBA): www.sba.gov

Index

• Q •

• R •

FOR DUMMIES®

A world of resources to help you grow

FOR DUMMIES®

Plain-English solutions for everyday challenges

COMPUTER BASICS

0-7645-0838-5

0-7645-1663-9

0-7645-1548-9

Also available:

PCs All-in-One Desk Reference For Dummies (0-7645-0791-5)

Pocket PC For Dummies (0-7645-1640-X)

Treo and Visor For Dummies (0-7645-1673-6)

Troubleshooting Your PC For Dummies (0-7645-1669-8)

Upgrading & Fixing PCs For Dummies (0-7645-1665-5)

Windows XP For Dummies (0-7645-0893-8)

Windows XP For Dummies Quick Reference (0-7645-0897-0)

BUSINESS SOFTWARE

0-7645-0822-9

0-7645-0839-3

0-7645-0819-9

Also available:

Excel Data Analysis For Dummies (0-7645-1661-2)

Excel 2002 All-in-One Desk Reference For Dummies (0-7645-1794-5)

Excel 2002 For Dummies Quick Reference (0-7645-0829-6)

GoldMine "X" For Dummies (0-7645-0845-8)

Microsoft CRM For Dummies (0-7645-1698-1)

Microsoft Project 2002 For Dummies (0-7645-1628-0)

Office XP For Dummies (0-7645-0830-X)

Outlook 2002 For Dummies (0-7645-0828-8)

Get smart! Visit www.dummies.com

- **Find listings of even more *For Dummies* titles**
- **Browse online articles**
- **Sign up for Dummies eTips™**
- **Check out *For Dummies* fitness videos and other products**
- **Order from our online bookstore**

Available wherever books are sold. Go to www.dummies.com or call 1-877-762-2974 to order direct.

FOR DUMMIES®

Helping you expand your horizons and realize your potential

INTERNET

The Internet For Dummies
0-7645-0894-6

The Internet All-in-One Desk Reference For Dummies
0-7645-1659-0

eBay For Dummies
0-7645-1642-6

DIGITAL MEDIA

Digital Photography For Dummies
0-7645-1664-7

Photoshop Elements 2 For Dummies
0-7645-1675-2

Digital Video For Dummies
0-7645-0806-7

GRAPHICS

PowerPoint 2002 For Dummies
0-7645-0817-2

Photoshop 7 For Dummies
0-7645-1651-5

Macromedia Flash MX For Dummies
0-7645-0895-4

Available wherever books are sold. Go to www.dummies.com or call 1-877-762-2974 to order direct.